Big Bear

D0769263

Big Bear
The End of Freedom

Hugh A. Dempsey

University of Nebraska Press
Lincoln and London

Douglas & McIntyre
Vancouver/Toronto

Copyright © 1984 by Hugh A. Dempsey

All rights reserved. No part of this book may be reproduced or transmitted in any form by any means without permission in writing from the publisher, except by a reviewer, who may quote brief passages in a review.

Douglas & McIntyre Ltd.
1615 Venables Street
Vancouver, British Columbia V5L 2H1

Canadian Cataloguing in Publication Data

Dempsey, Hugh A., 1929–
  Big Bear

Bibliography: p.
Includes index.
ISBN 0–88894–449–7

1. Big Bear, Cree Chief, d. 1888. 2. Cree Indians —
Biography. 3. Indians of North America — Prairie
Provinces — Biography. I. Title.
E99.C88B5 1984   971.2'00497   C84–091389–3

Published simultaneously in the United States of America by the University of Nebraska Press, Lincoln, NE 68588–0520

Library of Congress Cataloging in Publication Data

Dempsey, Hugh Aylmer, 1929–
  Big Bear : the man and his people.

  Bibliography: p.
  Includes index.
  1. Big Bear (Cree Chief). 2. Cree Indians — Biography.
3. Cree Indians — History. 4. Indians of North America —
Great Plains — History. I. Title.
E99.C88B543 1984   970.004'97 [B]   84–13105
ISBN 0–8032–1668–8

Design by Barbara Hodgson
Maps by Amely Jurgenliemk
Typeset by Evergreen Press
Printed and bound in Canada by D. W. Friesen & Sons Ltd.

Contents

Preface

IN 1974, WHILE TEACHING a summer course at the Rocky Boy Reservation in Montana, I met Four Souls, grandson of Big Bear and for many years chairman of the local tribal council. During an evening visit to his home, he commented that he and my wife were related. After some discussion, we determined that he was right; my wife's uncle had married Four Souls's aunt's daughter. In Indian circles, that meant my wife and Four Souls were sort of cousins.

Over the next couple of days, Four Souls told many stories about Big Bear and his family and of the terrible struggle the Cree had gone through to gain a reservation in Montana after the Riel Rebellion. It was during this visit that the seeds of an idea were sown for writing a book on Big Bear. All that existed were two articles, one by William B. Fraser in *Alberta Historical Review* and another by R. S. Allen in *Saskatchewan History,* as well as Rudy Wiebe's work of fiction, *The Temptations of Big Bear.*

Four Souls and I worked closely together on this project, and though he had read and approved the manuscript, I was saddened by his death just two months before the scheduled publication date. Many other people also assisted me in bringing this book to fruition. Stories and information came from the Rev. Stanley Cuthand, Little Pine Reserve; Alphonse Little Poplar, historian on Sweetgrass Reserve and grandson of Little Poplar; Jimmy Chief, Onion Lake Reserve, grandson of Cut Arm and Little Bear, both of whom died as a result of the 1885 rebellion; Joe Buller, North Battleford, son of Four Sky Thunder; John Sokwapance, Little Pine Reserve; Joe Kennedy, Little Pine Reserve and John Samson, Samson Reserve.

Acknowledgement should also be given to the Library and Archives of the Glenbow Museum, Calgary; Public Archives of Canada, Ottawa; Saskatchewan Archives Board, Regina and Saskatoon; Provincial Archives of Alberta, Edmonton; Provincial Archives of Manitoba,

Winnipeg; Montana Historical Society, Helena; National Museums of Canada, Ottawa, and the Library of the University of Calgary. My particular thanks to Mrs. Shirlee Smith, Hudson's Bay Company archivist, Winnipeg, for making "Big Bear" McLean's reminiscences available to me, and to the Hudson's Bay Company for permission to quote passages from journals and other holdings in its archives. For guidance and general advice, I also thank John C. Ewers, Ethnologist Emeritus at the Smithsonian Institution, Washington, D. C., and Ted Brasser, anthropologist at the National Museum of Man, Ottawa.

But the greatest thanks must be to my wife, Pauline, and my children, James, Louise, John, Leah and Lois, for putting up with the strange peregrinations of a writer in the family; and to Duncan S. Cameron, Director of the Glenbow Museum, as well as to its Board of Governors, for giving me the time and encouragement to write this book.

Hugh A. Dempsey

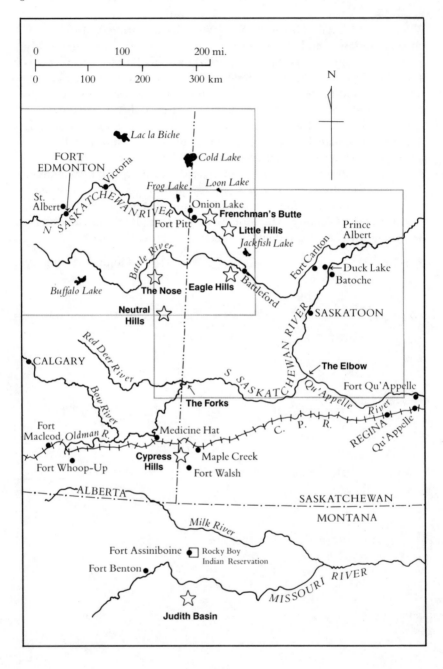

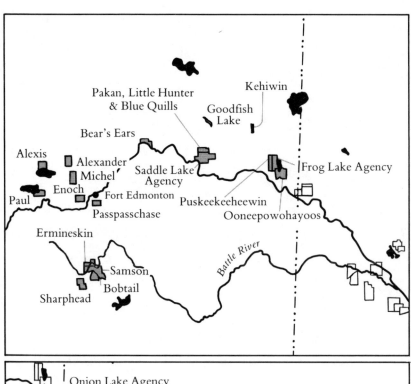

Pakan, Little Hunter
& Blue Quills

Kehiwin

Goodfish
Lake

Bear's Ears

Alexis

Alexander

Michel

Saddle Lake
Agency

Frog Lake Agency

Enoch

Fort Edmonton

Puskeekeeheewin

Paul

Passpasschase

Ooneepowohayoos

Ermineskin

Samson

Battle River

Sharphead

Bobtail

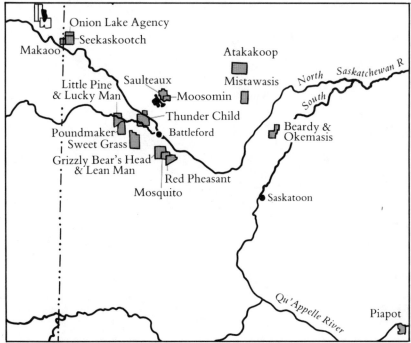

Onion Lake Agency

Seekaskootch

Makaoo

Atakakoop

North Saskatchewan R

Saulteaux

Mistawasis

Little Pine
& Lucky Man

South

Moosomin

Thunder Child

Poundmaker

Battleford

Beardy &
Okemasis

Sweet Grass

Grizzly Bear's Head
& Lean Man

Red Pheasant

Mosquito

Saskatoon

Qu'Appelle River

Piapot

Beginnings

N THE FALL of 1824 marauding Crees fell upon a large camp of Blackfoot who were wintering near Fort Edmonton; when the battle was
over, the Crees had slaughtered more than four hundred of the enemy
and taken twenty women captive. So began another round in the age-
old conflict between the two tribes, a war marked on one hand by
bravery and daring, on the other by fear and doubt.

As the hostilities carried over into 1825, many Crees fled retribution
by crossing the North Saskatchewan River to the safety of the woods.
There, on the shores of Jackfish Lake and away from the cauldron of
blood and terror on the plains, a baby boy was born. The child was
given the Cree name of Big Bear, *Mistihai'muskwa,* even though he was
the son of an Ojibwa chief named Black Powder, or *Mukatai.*[1] His
mother, whose name has been forgotten in the mistiness of the past, was
either Cree or Ojibwa — no one is quite sure which. Yet she was the
mother of a child who was destined to become a famous figure in
Canadian history.

The boy's father, Black Powder, was the leader of a small mixed band
of Cree and Ojibwa who normally camped near Jackfish Lake, ranging
onto the edge of the plains for buffalo in the summer and into the woods
to trap and hunt in winter. The man was a wanderer; one day he might
turn up at Edmonton House, and two months later he could be in his
skin lodge in the Eagle Hills. Spring might find him in his bark canoe,
bringing furs from his winter catch, but in the autumn he could be
astride his best buffalo runner, acting as though he had spent his whole
life on the plains.

★ ★ ★

The plains were not unknown to the Cree and Assiniboine prior to the
arrival of British fur traders, but most bands preferred the security of the

woodlands, where they lived by hunting small game and fishing the many lakes. The Cree migration onto the plains started in earnest in the early 1700s, when, armed with guns and tools from the traders on Hudson Bay, they had become middlemen in the great European fur hunt. Taking the trade goods inland, the Cree had exchanged them with their brothers in the woods for furs and had even boldly penetrated the plains to trade with the Blackfoot, Gros Ventre and others who lived off the buffalo. Another woodland people, the Assiniboine, an offshoot of the Sioux nation, also were a part of this middleman trade; they were uneasy allies of the Cree and brought in rich yields of beaver.

As the Cree moved westward, their main route was the mighty Saskatchewan River, which in many regions was flanked by the open plains. This offered an ideal situation for them to cast off their woodland life and to adopt a prairie culture. At first, they were canoe users who owned few horses; they went to the plains only when the buffalo were close and their enemies far away. Then, as they gained more confidence and more horses, they made extended journeys out to the sea of grass, adopting the customs and habits of those who were there before them. Some found the prairie life so exciting and rewarding that they gave up all thoughts of woodland culture. Instead of retreating to the protection of the forests to fish and trap during the winter, they chose a prairie stream that offered enough wood and shelter for the winter. From there, they hunted the buffalo as they had in summer, and gloried in a life that was untrammelled and free. No longer did they need to stay in tiny family groups as they stalked a lone deer or moose; now they could gather in large bands to pass the winter months by visiting, feasting and participating in the religious activities of the tribe.

Others chose to be transitional people. Summer found them far out on the plains, but as soon as the snow clouds began to gather in the late fall, they had their final hunt of the season and returned to the woods, laden with dried meat and pemmican. There, secluded from the sweeping prairie winds and enemy ambush, they fished and hunted for the furs that the traders coveted.

The Cree had already reached the Jackfish Lake region when a few Ojibwa families drifted in from the east. Another woodland people, the new arrivals mingled with their Cree relatives and slipped easily into the transitional life. The Ojibwa spoke a language that was similar to that of their allies, though Cree became the *lingua franca* of the region. Generally stockier and more heavyset than the Cree, the Ojibwa were good fighters, but were better known for their mysticism and healing powers.

★   ★   ★

In 1825, the year of Big Bear's birth, the Ojibwa were relatively new to the Jackfish Lake area and their numbers were few. The major tribes were the Cree and Assiniboine, and among them were people who never ventured from the bush — the traders called them Thickwood Indians. Then there were the transitional people, called the Strongwood Indians, and finally, there were those who lived entirely upon the plains. At that time none of the Plains Cree or Plains Assiniboine traded as far upriver as Edmonton House; they all went to Carlton. This included thirty lodges of Beaver Hills Cree, seventy lodges of Middle Cree, who usually camped in the Eagle Hills area, and three hundred lodges of Plains Assiniboine. Other plains tribes in the south went to trade at Qu'Appelle or Fort Ellice, while to Edmonton House came almost two thousand lodges from the Blackfoot confederacy: this included the Blood, Peigan, Blackfoot, Sarcee and Gros Ventre. About thirty lodges of Thickwood Crees from the bush also ventured to that fort. According to the Hudson's Bay Company census for the period, only sixty lodges of mixed Ojibwa and Cree traded in the entire upper Saskatchewan region. Black Powder was the leader of one of these bands, with probably no more than about twelve lodges, while Bad Meat and Flat Head also had small followings.

For the first two years of Big Bear's life, the war between the Indian nations continued unabated; the Cree joined with the Assiniboine and the more southerly Crow Indians to attack the Blackfoot. In the summer of 1826, a Blackfoot war party discovered a camp of Cree near Moose Woods, forty miles (64 km) south of Carlton House. Sweeping down on their unsuspecting prey, they killed nine people, wounded twenty-one others and destroyed every lodge in the camp. In retaliation, a mixed party of Cree and Assiniboine raided a Blackfoot village near Edmonton House and, though no one was killed, captured the entire Blackfoot horse herd. And so it went. The tribes spent more time at war and less time hunting and trapping. Starvation in winter became frequent, as Cree hesitated to travel to the plains; at the same time the Blackfoot lacked sufficient horses for their usual hunts.

Early in 1827, a trader at Edmonton House noted that the Plains Indians were "as miserable as poverty could make them."[2] That spring, the Blackfoot tribes, beset by enemies on all sides, decided to sue for peace. Old Swan, whose band had been decimated by the 1824 slaughter, represented the Blackfoot tribe, Bull Back Fat came from the Bloods, and Cut Nose from the Sarcees. Travelling first to Edmonton House, they smoked with a few Crees and "left Tobacco and a little weed and a piece of Buffalo back fat tied together to be sent to the Stone [Assiniboine] Indians and Crees of Carlton."[3]

On both sides, most of the chiefs were tired of war, so the Cree passed along the message that they would be prepared to discuss peace terms.

Accordingly, an advance party of Blackfoot set out for Carlton House, where they planned to trade and to use the good offices of the fort to effect a settlement. When the Blackfoot peace party reached the Eagle Hills, no one in their ranks would risk going on to the fort, so they sent out a scouting party, which captured two Cree women. The oldest of these was given a buffalo robe, moccasins, paint and tobacco as a peace offering to her tribe, and she agreed to escort them to her village. However, when the peace mission reached the Saskatchewan River, it was seen by Black Powder, who was on his way to the fort. Swiftly, he guided his canoe to a small island, where he watched from hiding as the Blackfoot took their horses down to the water to drink. Just as they reached the shore, he opened fire, killing a warrior and his horse. The others abandoned the Cree woman and fled.

Gleefully, Black Powder collected the freed captive and paddled to Carlton House, where he strutted about, proclaiming his successful attack. The traders were less than enthusiastic, particularly when the old woman said that the Blackfoot "were well loaded with provisions and its [sic] evident that they were coming to the house on a Trade & at the same time to make peace with the Crees."[4]

For a couple of weeks the traders were afraid that the warfare would continue unabated, all because of Black Powder's precipitous action. But when the Blackfoot got back to their territory, wiser heads determined that the shooting had been an unfortunate incident, not a rejection of peace. Therefore, Bull Back Fat, Old Swan and Cut Nose assembled a massive party of four hundred men — too large for a frontal attack — and the Cree, Ojibwa and Assiniboine gave them a wide berth when they went to Carlton House to trade and to talk peace. The expedition was not entirely successful, as most of the Cree and Assiniboine failed to put in an appearance, but the seeds of unity had been sown. In the following summer a solid peace pact was made, with only a few dissenters from downriver and the Qu'Appelle regions.

Peace had come at last to the prairies. As symbols of friendship, Blackfoot and Cree began to camp together, and in some instances they even went to war together. The Blackfoot, freed from attack on their northern and eastern flanks, began to concentrate on other enemies: the Crow from south of the Missouri River, and the Kootenay and Nez Percé across the mountains. In spite of a few local skirmishes, the treaty remained virtually intact for the next five years. Peace also meant that the Cree could now camp and hunt around such prairie places as Sounding Lake, Manito Lake, The Nose and Red Deer Forks without fear of attack. Many transitional Cree moved onto the prairies, gradually taking on more aspects of a plains buffalo-hunting culture.

Black Powder and his Cree-Ojibwa followers were among those who became more and more plains-oriented. The horse supplanted the canoe as their primary means of travel, and though the Jackfish Lake region remained his winter quarters, Black Powder might be found anywhere south of the Saskatchewan River to the Red Deer Forks.

This was a pleasant time for Big Bear's childhood. While he was a toddler, he was under the supervision of women. In the summer they travelled to the Little Hills between Jackfish Lake and the Saskatchewan River when they went to pick strawberries, cranberries or chokecherries. The children played while their mothers dug into the black loam for wild onions, wild turnips and various roots that were used for food and medicine.

At about the age of seven, Big Bear was taken in hand by the men. Because his father was a chief, people went out of their way to teach him and to tell him stories. One elder in particular became his regular teacher, showing him how to ride, hunt, and use a bow and arrow. He also taught the boy about warfare, travelling on the prairie and watching for signs of the enemy.

With equal ease, the young boy learned the secrets of hunting moose and deer in the woods and stalking the buffalo on the open prairies. He learned how to fish, how to catch ducks in the reeds before they had learned to fly and how to dig a beaver out of its den. He was as familiar with the sight of the sun rising over a lake, its rays flickering while undulating over the broken waters, as he was with the sun setting on the vast prairie, where only a horizontal line divided the sea of grass from the billowing clouds overhead.

Although Big Bear's father was an Ojibwa, the boy probably considered himself to be a Cree. He learned Cree as his first language, though he could also speak Ojibwa. Like the others in the band, his life was divided between the plains and the woodlands.

When they went to the plains, Black Powder and his family switched to a diet of buffalo meat. While they were among the herds, meat was usually boiling in a kettle, so that people could help themselves anytime during the day. In the meantime, the women in the household were busy tanning hides and drying meat for the winter.

Yet life was not an endless round of feasting and hunting. When Big Bear was eight, a terrible famine caused great hardship. The winter of 1832–33 had been an open one with little snow on the ground, and Black Powder and his hunters could not find buffalo within ten days' march of Jackfish Lake. In the spring, when the situation might have been expected to improve, heavy snows made it impossible for them to travel, so they lived on the verge of starvation until summer. In May 1833, a puzzled fur trader at Carlton House noted the absence of buffalo:

"It is now 9 months since they left this neighbourhood and what has been the cause of our being so much distressed for Provisions, as also the Indians belonging this Post, and the cause of them not being able to hunt Fur bearing animals."[5]

One result of this calamity was that the Cree and Assiniboine had to go farther afield in search of game, thus running the risk of upsetting the peace with the Blackfoot. Finally, over the following winter, the peace treaty was torn to shreds when Cree attacked the Blackfoot out on the plains, and Blackfoot war parties raided Cree camps. The confict might have escalated to the destructive point it had reached a decade earlier, but a greater threat soon wiped out all thoughts of war.

In the spring of 1837 the dreaded disease of smallpox was taken aboard the American Fur Company's boat, the *St. Peter's,* as it steamed up the tortuous Missouri River, carrying goods and supplies to the upriver posts. En route, the disease infected the Mandan Indians, almost wiping out the entire tribe, and then found its way to Fort Union, where some Cree and Assiniboine had gone to trade. At first, the Americans shut the gates and were successful in keeping the scourge inside, but the Indians would not be denied their trade goods and demanded entry to the fort in spite of warnings. The contagion quickly spread; of the thousand Assiniboine who went to the post, only a hundred and fifty survived. In fear, the remainder fled the spectre of death and unknowingly carried the disease to relatives farther afield. The sickness "has made some large blanks in their different Camps," commented a trader, "but what is worse, some of those fellows who were badly with it took the disease to our Establishment of Carlton," and before the onset of winter "the small pox was at that time raging with alarming appearance at the Establishment."[6]

The traders vaccinated the Indians near the trading posts with cowpox, but at Carlton the vaccine was ineffective and failed to halt the epidemic. Black Powder's camp was struck down like the rest, and rumour spread that even the chief had succumbed to the disease. Big Bear, who was then twelve years old, did come down with smallpox. He survived, but was left with disfiguring marks on his face.

Each time a person became ill, the terror spread. They all knew the symptoms: "The Sickness . . . begins with a dreadful pain in head, back, neck and bleeding at the Nose, which they say carries them off in two or three days at most."[7] If someone contracted the disease and survived, he became immune to further ravages of the pox and could care for the sick and dying. More often, however, people simply fled in fear.

"Just across the river [from Fort Pitt], on the bench lands," wrote a journalist in 1885, "are several large mounds which mark the spot where lie the bones of hundreds of victims of smallpox. Half a century ago that dread disease rushed over this country like a prairie fire. It swept all before it. Whole camps were carried off and the prairie was dotted here and there with the swollen and decomposed corpses of the victims. Neither man, woman nor child was safe; it was a very carnival of death."[8]

After the smallpox epidemic, the Cree found it even easier to move onto the prairies, for the Blackfoot had lost two-thirds of their people to the disease. The Hudson's Bay Company post of Fort Pitt, which had been opened in 1834 to serve the Blackfoot, now became a centre for Cree who were spending part of their time on the plains. Fort Pitt was considered to be the buffalo provisioning post of the HBC, as the herds were usually just across the river and out on the plains.

Black Powder and his following found Fort Pitt to be a useful jumping off point to the plains. Travelling upstream from Jackfish Lake in the spring, they passed the Little Hills and Frenchman's Butte until they came to Fort Pitt, which they called the "little fort," because it was a smaller version of Carlton. From there they could go south to The Nose and out to wherever the buffalo happened to be. By now Black Powder was considered to be one of the leading chiefs of the Jackfish Lake region and was described by a traveller as "a great warrior and horse thief, the two most important qualifications for a chief."[9]

Big Bear, the son of a chief, was in a favoured position as he grew up. People recognized in him the quality of leadership, though he was less flamboyant than his father. He had a ready wit, was highly intelligent and made friends easily. "When he was a boy," said a Cree elder, "people noticed him because he was smart right away. Even then they knew he would be a leader because he got to know so many things when he was still young. He was wise even then."[10]

Having an Ojibwa father also made him different from the Cree boys in camp. The two tribes were closely allied, yet the Ojibwa were recognized for certain differences. Most important of these was their relationship with the supernatural. The Ojibwa were the ones who most often went away to seek visions. They were the ones who made powerful medicines, which could strike down an enemy or help a friend. They made the hunting amulets so prized by the Cree hunters and could foretell the success or failure of a war party. Of course, the Cree had medicine men, too, but their reputations paled in comparison to the power of the Ojibwa.

Immediately after the smallpox epidemic, Big Bear had a vision. It was the first of several visions he was to experience during his lifetime, but it was one with far-reaching implications. In this vision he saw "the coming of the white man, his purchase of the land, the bounteous presents from the Great Mother," and as it was sarcastically described in later years, "the generosity of the new-coming race to his."[11]

The Cree knew that the smallpox had come from the white men, so when Big Bear caught the disfiguring disease, it was his first real "gift" from them. The dream was a warning that sickness would not be the only tragedy, because all the omens of the vision were bad. In 1838 no one could imagine the white man's presence consisting of any more than a few forts along the rivers and a large settlement at Red River. True, they were responsible for the growing half-breed population,[12] but there was no reason to think that the white man would ever be anything more than a small, necessary evil in their lives. Certainly, no Cree had even thought of selling his hunting grounds to the white man. Who in his right mind would give up the millions of buffalo on the plains, the lakes teeming with fish, and the forest with its game and fur animals? Besides, what would the white man ever do with the land? And what would he do with the Indians?

Yet Big Bear's vision was there, to be recalled and retold whenever significant events occurred in the years to come.

Shortly after this mystic experience, Big Bear went to war. It was customary at that time for a young man to choose a comrade, someone from his own camp, whom he called *niwitcewahakan,* "he with whom I go about."[13] They travelled together, watched out for each other's safety in battle and made sure they got away safely from the scene of the conflict. During times of peace, young horse raiders had to sneak away from camp, or else the camp police would not let them go. But when the Cree were at war, a seasoned warrior would go through the camp, publicly announcing his intention of going on a raid and singing his own war song. When he had selected twenty or thirty young men to travel with him, they gathered for a ritual known as the Sioux Dance before leaving the camp.

Most of Big Bear's war experiences have now been forgotten. So great was his role as a political leader that his activities as a youth were seldom retold and less frequently remembered. One elderly woman recalled that "as children she and her brother would be sent to so-and-so's lodge on winter evenings when the nights were long to listen to some elder tell stories. Each night the story telling would be held in a different lodge. During the story telling, all the children had to be very quiet and pay attention. The stories told on these nights were varied and many stories of Big Bear were told; how he raided Blackfoot camps, how he stole horses from Blackfoot camps; they told of the supernatural powers he possessed . . . but I have forgotten all of them."[14]

Even when he was young, Big Bear was not a good-looking person, and the smallpox scars made him even homelier. But if he was sensitive about his looks, he did not show it; rather, he used to poke fun at his own appearance, perhaps realizing that his charisma and intelligence far outweighed any setback caused by his looks. An example of his ability to mock his own appearance occurred while he was still a teenager. At the onset of spring, Big Bear set out with friends to raid enemy camps in the south and was gone for most of the summer. With bravado and daring, he succeeded in capturing numerous Blackfoot horses, but each time he completed a raid he refused to go home. Instead, he had other members of the party who were going back to Cree country deliver the horses to his father. Then, with a wave and a good-natured grin, he was off to find another raiding party to join. When he arrived home in the fall, he was welcomed back as a hero. As people crowded around him, singing their honouring songs and praising him, he gave away all the horses he had captured and shouted happily, "Now I feel very handsome!"[15]

Big Bear seldom kept any of the horses he captured on his raids. Some he gave to his father and close relatives, and others to the needy in camp. On one hand, this was a sign of generosity that was important for a budding chief, but in Big Bear's case it was also the fulfilment of another vision. In this dream, a spirit man approached him and said, "Come with me and I'll give you a chance to have all the horses you'll ever want." The spirit led him to the mouth of a big cave, and inside, Big Bear could see all kinds of horses — mares, stallions, all colours and all sizes. "Go to the centre of the herd," the spirit figure instructed, "and take the horse that you find there. Don't take any other horse, just that one." He said that the horse would be easy to reach; Big Bear simply had to walk through the herd. "The horses will rear up and kick at you," said the spirit, "but if you show no fear, they will move aside and let you pass. But if you show any fear, you won't get to the horse in the middle." Big Bear left the spirit and entered the cave full of horses. There were animals from wall to wall, bunched together, but as he approached them and showed no fear, they moved aside to let him pass. He was doing well and was nearing the centre of the cave when suddenly a huge black stallion reared up as though to strike him. More out of surprise than fear, Big Bear raised his arm to protect himself and crouched down. Instantly, the entire herd disappeared, and Big Bear found himself alone with the spirit man. "It's too bad you crouched," he said. "You had your chance but now you'll never be rich in horses as long as you live."[16] When he awoke, Big Bear interpreted the vision to mean that he should never try to own a large herd of horses, so whenever he was successful on a raid he gave the animals away, keeping only enough for his personal needs.

In spite of his success as a warrior, visions and religion remained important elements in Big Bear's life, and he was remembered as much for the supernatural powers he possessed as for his political acumen. In later years he was not just a chief, but a holy man as well. His most famous vision was one associated with war. While still a young man, perhaps seeking a vision, he left the camp of his family near the mouth of the Red Deer River and sought an isolated place to fast and pray for guidance from the supernatural powers that could help and protect him in war. The vision came in the form of a bear spirit, a son of the Great Parent Bear, which offered to be his protector. The bear was considered to be the greatest of all animal spirits, because the Cree believed it was much like man himself. When the creature stood upright, it was called "the bear that walks like a man"; and when its carcass was skinned, it looked disturbingly like a human body. To the Cree, it was *neoko-teonshin,* "four-legged person."[17]

When Big Bear returned to his camp, he fashioned the war medicine according to the bear spirit's directions. He wrapped it in cloth to form a bundle, called the holy men together to sanctify it and said that no woman should ever be allowed to witness the ritual. Then, with the bundle lying on the altar in front of them, he told a holy man to take some sweet grass and sprinkle it on the glowing embers placed at the altar. A thin curl of pungent smoke rose into the air, purifying all it touched and driving away any evil spirits that might be hovering around. On Big Bear's instructions, the holy man took a stone pipe and passed it unlit through the smoke, pointing its stem upward towards the mighty *Manito,* asking the great spirit to notice that this was being done as directed in Big Bear's vision.

Next, the holy man had his assistant take an ember from the fire to light the pipe, and after taking four puffs, the shaman rotated the pipe counterclockwise so that its mouth made a complete circle. He then lowered the pipe slightly and prayed to the Great Parent Bear, signifying that the bear spirit was powerful, but not as lofty as the mighty *Manito.* As he prayed, the holy man explained that the bundle was new and was being opened so that it could be purified and sanctified.

The place where Big Bear had received his vision was then considered to be a source of supernatural power, a place where the sons of the Great Parent Bear might visit or dwell. Therefore, the pipestem was pointed in that direction, while Big Bear told the hushed audience the details of his vision. When he had finished, there was utter silence, for everyone feared and venerated the bear spirit. That this greatest of all supernatural beings had bestowed its powers upon a member of their camp was a cause for jubilation and awe.

Big Bear instructed the pipe man to rotate the stem and point it to the ground in four places, as though indicating the four legs of a bear. He acted as if the bear spirit was in the lodge with them and the Great Parent Bear was listening from the ground in front of the altar. Then the pipe was returned to its place, while the holy man took a wooden bowl of saskatoon berry broth and held it aloft over the incense. Berries were the bear's favourite food. The purified pipe and berry broth were passed around to the other holy men. Each had brought his own small bowl and spoon, so as one side of the lodge was busy taking their broth, the other was smoking in the fashion that Big Bear had instructed. At last, when the broth was eaten and the tobacco was gone, all eyes turned to the bundle lying in front of the altar. Only Big Bear knew what it contained, for he had fashioned it alone and in secret, according to the instruction of the bear's son.

"You got your power from the Manito and now give it to the people," the holy man said, speaking directly to the bundle. "I am going to untie you now. We pray for good luck in two ways — one for this man who owns the bundle, and one for us who are gathered here. That is why I am going to untie you."[18] The holy man passed his hands through the smoke of the incense to purify them, then carefully untied the thongs and folded back the cloth to reveal its contents. There, with all its fearful implications, was a bear's paw, its savage claws still attached. It had been tanned and fastened to a square of scarlet flannel, so that it could be worn around the owner's neck whenever he went to war or participated in ceremonies.

This, Big Bear told them, was *okimaw-okusisaw-ochichi,* "chief's son's hand," or, more simply, "bear's hand." Before putting it around his neck, the owner had to dig a deep hole in the ground, scoop out some clay and plaster it over his face. Then, with outstreched fingers, he made streaks through the wet clay on his face as though they were bear scratches. Finally, he donned the war medicine while he sang its holy song: "My teeth are my knives; my claws are my knives."[19] Then he was ready for war.

The holy men realized that the power of the bundle would protect the camp from harm, particularly from attack by enemy warriors. At the same time, the Cree in the group were aware that the bear figure among the Ojibwa also had vicious powers; if offended, it could wreak havoc upon those who insulted it.

A man who knew Big Bear was sure that his use of the bear bundle against enemy tribes was of great help to him "when he was getting to be a chief."[20] Yet the war medicine was primarily a protector of the man himself. Some people believed that he even had the power to make himself invisible in times of danger.

On one occasion, Big Bear's family was camped on the South Saskatchewan River, not far from Red Deer Forks. Each day the hunters went out in search of buffalo, while the women dried the meat and began to make pemmican. The hunters always went east of their camp to avoid any Blackfoot who might be hunting in the area. A few warriors were instructed to stay at home to protect the women and children, in case the camp was discovered by an enemy. Big Bear was taking his turn in camp one afternoon and told his friends he would ride west for a few miles to see if there were any buffalo in that quarter. They would have no problem guarding the camp. Big Bear had gone a considerable distance looking for signs of buffalo and was just starting to climb a small ridge when he heard something behind him. Turning, he saw a dozen or more riders coming after him at full gallop. As they shouted their war cries, he knew they were Blackfoot. Quickly, Big Bear dug his heels into his horse's flanks and darted up to the top of the ridge and down the other side. He then noticed a large clump of wolf willows at the bottom of the ridge, so he spurred his horse in that direction and rolled off the animal as it sped by the bushes. From the ridge, the Blackfoot could see neither rider nor horse, but suspecting the hunter had taken refuge in the bushes, they surrounded the willows and began a systematic search. As people said afterwards, they should have found Big Bear, but they did not. At last, convinced that he was not in the clump, the Blackfoot warriors mounted their horses and rode off towards the sunset. When he knew they were gone, Big Bear crawled out of his hiding place and walked back to his camp, arriving long after dark. He was told that his horse had come back and that everyone feared he had had an accident or been killed by the Blackfoot.[21] There can be no doubt that Big Bear's adventure had saved his camp from possible attack, yet the mystery of why a dozen Blackfoot warriors could not find him in a small grove of wolf willows was never answered.

As a young warrior, Big Bear went on many expeditions against the Blackfoot nation; the Blood tribe in particular was a favourite target. Not only were they richer in horses than the neighbouring Blackfoot tribe, but they seldom made peace with the Cree. When Big Bear was between the ages of thirteen and twenty — the most common time for a Cree youth to devote all his attention to war — there were few significant peace treaties to curb his use of his war medicine.

In 1847, when Big Bear was twenty-two, he was caught up in a revenge raid that affected his entire family. Early that year, the Blackfoot had pounced upon a Cree camp and killed four relatives of a leading chief, The Man Who Gives the War Whoop, who was a close friend of Big Bear's father. That fall, The Man Who Gives the War Whoop organized a huge revenge party, which he personally led. A raiding expedition was made up of only a dozen or so men who were intent on capturing enemy horses, but a revenge party was different. It was organized for the sole purpose of killing any enemy it encountered in retribution for the loss its members had suffered. The victims of the vendetta did not need to be the actual perpetrators of the earlier killing, though attempts were made to gain vengeance from the same tribe. Once the revenge party had killed an enemy — even one person — their vengeance was satisfied.

In this instance, the party had no sooner reached the plains than an illness struck, causing the deaths of several persons. Fearing this was a bad omen, the revenge party turned back, but The Man Who Gives the War Whoop was not to be dissuaded. During the winter, with Big Bear's father as his companion, he set out to organize another revenge party for the spring. Together, the pair went from winter camp to winter camp along the North Saskatchewan, haranguing the chiefs and trying to convince the warrior lodges to take part in the raid. Each time a war leader agreed, he turned his medicine pipe over to the two chiefs as evidence of his vow to join. This medicine pipe consisted of a long pipestem, ornamented with feathers, porcupine quills, fur and beads. There was no bowl, for it was used for religious purposes rather than for smoking. Although possessed by an individual, it belonged to the whole band and served as a protector and symbol of honesty and truth. By the time the men reached the Cree camps near Fort Pitt, they had nine medicine pipes besides the ones owned by Black Powder and The Man Who Gives the War Whoop.

Early in June the various Cree bands came together, forming a large camp of ninety lodges. Doubtless, Big Bear was there, close to his father. About three miles (5 km) from camp, a site was chosen for a Thirst Dance to be held before the revenge party set out for the south. Each band recovered its medicine pipe, and together they used the occasion to perform the Medicine Pipe Dance, calling upon the spirits to help them in their coming fight with the Blackfoot.

Unknown to the people in the camp, the Blackfoot were equally anxious to gain satisfaction in blood for the losses they had suffered the previous year. When the grass was green, and long before their own Sun Dance was scheduled to be held, a combined party of five hundred Blackfoot, Blood, Sarcee, Peigan and Gros Ventre Indians set out for the north. Near Fort Pitt they met some traders and told them that "they were in pursuit of the Crees and Assiniboines, whom they threatened totally to annihilate, boasting that they themselves were as numerous as the grass on the plains."[22]

Shortly after the Cree Thirst Dance ended, Blackfoot scouts found their deserted, brush-covered lodge, and one of the men who clambered to the top of the centre pole to take some sacred offerings saw the smoke from the Cree camp in the distance. As the scouts prepared to go back to the main party, they were sighted by a Cree, but he assumed that the group was simply a small horse-stealing party. As soon as the news that horse raiders were near was announced in the Cree camp, a group of warriors boldly dashed out to meet them. But instead of meeting a handful of young boys, they rode directly into the face of overwhelming odds. Most of the Cree withdrew to a more advantageous fighting position, but one leader, *Pehothis,* refused to retreat and galloped forward; he charged among the Blackfoot, knocking warriors from their horses with his stone club, while arrows and musket balls whizzed around him. At last, after being wounded several times, a ball broke his arm, and he was no longer able to control his horse, which carried him away to his own camp. There, badly wounded, he lay down to die, while terrified women and children fled into the bushes.

Although taken by surprise, Black Powder and others in the camp fought back bravely and succeeded in killing ten of their enemy, including the leading chief of the Sarcee. However, the defence of the camp had been costly; by the time the Blackfoot withdrew, they had killed eighteen people besides the brave *Pehothis* and wounded forty more. The Cree had been forced to fall back from their camp during the height of the battle, so the raiders also took whatever booty they could find among the lodges.

Neither Black Powder nor Big Bear was injured in the melee. Had the Blackfoot not struck when they did, the Cree would have handed out the same treatment to the first enemy camp they encountered. As it was, The Man Who Gives the War Whoop had suffered two setbacks in his efforts to organize a revenge party, so the plan was abandoned.

Why had the two attempts failed? In the minds of the Cree, there could have been any number of reasons. Perhaps there was a Blackfoot shaman who had greater power than anyone in the village of The Man Who Gives the War Whoop. Perhaps the chief had an adversary within the Cree or Ojibwa camps who had made incantations against him. Perhaps a spiritual protector had been offended by some action or by a failure to leave an offering at the right place or at the right time. There were many possibilities, all rooted in the supernatural; in fact, very little that happened to the Cree or Ojibwa was perceived as accidental. The supernatural spirits were always at work: some good, some bad. But always they were there, giving help, taking vengeance, controlling the destiny of man. In this instance, the powers acting against The Man Who Gives the War Whoop were so strong that not even Big Bear's war medicine could stop them.

Big Bear was now in his mid-twenties, a seasoned warrior who was recognized for his visions and his involvement in religious life. He was not a big man, being somewhat short and stocky. The pockmarks on his face were barely visible, but even his best friend could not say he was handsome. Rather, he was plain, if not ugly, but had a personality and a charisma that superceded his physical appearance. He was good-natured and respected by all who knew him. At about this time, Big Bear married an Ojibwa girl named *Sayos*.[23] She was the first of five wives but always remained his favourite during the long years they were together. She was the only one of his wives known to be an Ojibwa; the rest likely were Cree. Born in the Pembina region south of Fort Garry, she had, with others of her tribe, drifted west and intermingled with the Cree, just as Big Bear's father had done.

After the marriage, Big Bear and *Sayos* moved into their own lodge, but they stayed in the camp of Black Powder. Here the young husband found new responsibilities and new pleasures, as he shifted away from warring activities and took up the task of beginning a family. No longer could he while away the hours with other bachelors in the warriors' lodge or dart away to war at the slightest pretext. He now had a wife to look after and, as he did throughout his life, took his responsibilities seriously. His hunting was not just to supplement what his father killed, but was for his own household; when he helped to guard the camp, his own lodge was among those he protected.

When *Sayos* gave birth to their first child, a girl whom they named *Nowakich,* Big Bear undoubtedly was pleased with his daughter, for he was fond of children, but the major event in his family life was the birth of his first son sometime before the end of the decade. This boy was called Twin Wolverine, a woodland name that may have been passed down through Black Powder's family. Boys were usually named by a grandfather or elder, the choice made either as a result of the giver's own war experiences or, more commonly, because the name had once belonged to an ancestor and was no longer in use. If the previous owner had been a renowned hunter or warrior, then the good luck associated with his name was believed to pass down to the child. Girls, on the other hand, were usually given names by grandparents. In 1851, while camped for the winter in the Little Hills, Big Bear's second son was born. He was named *Imasees* (or, more correctly, *Ayimasees*), variously translated as Wild Child, Bad Child or Mean Boy. This boy's second name, which had once been used by his grandfather, was *Apistakoos,* or Little Bear.

Big Bear was still too young to be a member of the council, but his war record entitled him to be a Worthy Young Man and a member of a warrior society. The society's duties were to guard the camp, control the buffalo hunts, and maintain law and order within the village. It had its own lodge pitched within the camp circle, where rituals were performed and where some younger unmarried members lived.

In many ways, Big Bear's life was uncomplicated during the next several years. As a family man, he did not go to war so often, but was always prepared to defend his camp from enemies. Food was usually plentiful, there were no serious epidemics and the white man was present in such few numbers as to be inconsequential. Big Bear had no particular grievance with the Hudson's Bay Company; he might not be as close to the traders as his father was, but he found them honest and reasonable in their dealings. He knew a number of the men personally, particularly those at Fort Pitt and Carlton House, where he and his family normally traded.

By now the Plains Cree had a firm foothold on the lands south of Fort Pitt, and though altercations still occurred with the Blackfoot, neither tribe experienced the massacres so common when Big Bear was a boy. The River Cree — a general name used to describe those living between the North Saskatchewan and Battle rivers — and the Beaver Hills people farther west had undergone subtle changes in their hunting grounds during the southward withdrawal of the Blackfoot. The bands from the Edmonton area now camped as far south as Buffalo Lake, while wood-land people who normally stayed near Saddle Lake and Smoky Lake began to make regular forays out onto the prairies. Those from the Fort Pitt area hunted all the way to the Red Deer River and were the ones who most often had to take the brunt of Blackfoot warfare.

Black Powder and his band were accustomed to the plains, but were not prepared to give up their life in the forest. Not only were they safe in the woods, but winter gave them the chance to trap fur-bearing animals to trade at Fort Pitt for cloth, musket balls, powder and much-needed supplies. Big Bear tended to think like his father, and though he may have been more oriented to the plains, he still sought the protection of the woodlands as long as the buffalo were within reasonable distance of the Little Hills.

The early 1860s saw a rise in turbulence and discord along the North Saskatchewan River.[24] Angered by the killing and scalping of one of their chiefs in 1860, the Blackfoot attacked a Cree village near Fort Pitt, killing twenty people. The following year, a trader noted in exasperation that the Blackfoot "now threaten openly to kill whites, Halfbreeds or Crees wherever they find them, and to burn Edmonton Fort. All this is owing to the Blackfoot Chief that was killed here last Fall by the Crees."[25]

Leading chiefs among the Cree near Fort Pitt tried to conclude a treaty in 1862, but it lasted for only a short time, and by the following spring they were at war again. The Blackfoot considered the Hudson's Bay Company to be in league with the Cree, so their relations with the traders became tenuous. In 1863, the Blackfoot began to raid Fort Pitt itself, crossing the river and creating a state of fear and concern among those who had considered the region to be safe. On one such raid, the Blackfoot threatened a Métis who was on the trail to Fort Pitt south of the river and then trapped four Crees just across from the fort. Big Bear was at the trading post with eight companions when this incident occurred, and the trader was angry when they refused to go to go to the aid of their tribesmen. At first, the factor offered to let them use his rowboat to cross the river, as Big Bear and his friends were afoot; when they demurred, he was willing to make the Hudson's Bay Company horses available to them. In the trader's mind, Big Bear "was thought to be rather cowardly," yet for nine men to ride out on strange horses against a well-armed and mounted army would have been virtual suicide.[26] Not only that, but Big Bear must have understood the situation better than the trader, as all four Crees escaped unharmed.

However, just when the whole problem of Cree-Blackfoot warfare was becoming intolerable, nature again interceded. In the winter of 1864–65 a savage epidemic of scarlet fever raced through the Blackfoot camps, killing more than a thousand people, particularly the very young and the elderly. At the same time, an epidemic of measles erupted among the Cree and half-breeds near Edmonton and quickly spread throughout the district.

Sometime during the holocaust of scarlet fever, measles and bloody warfare, Black Powder died. The Ojibwa leader had been a faithful friend of the traders, a good warrior and a respected chief of his camp for many years. Now his successor would take over the band on the eve of dramatic changes in the lives of everyone in the Cree nation.

Like many other events in the tribe, the selection of a chief was done by consensus. By their actions, the people made known their wishes to be led by a certain person; if anyone else aspired to the position, he would probably move away with some followers and form his own group. In Black Powder's band, Big Bear had been groomed for the job and stepped easily into the role. At the age of forty he was still a young man compared with other chiefs, yet he was old enough to command respect. His band was a small one, consisting of about twelve lodges, or close to a hundred men, women and children.

With his father's death, Big Bear put aside the security of his own home and family to take his first steps along the perilous and ill-fated trail of leadership, first of his band and then of the tribe. He had many of the qualities of a good chief. His exploits on the war trail were admired, as were his abilities as a hunter. And, as everyone knew, he was warm-hearted, with a good sense of humour, and generous to a fault. He was a gifted orator and could speak in a loud, booming voice for three or four hours at a time. As one Cree elder commented: "Big Bear was a great leader and people thought a lot of him. He was respected by everyone and he was known as a kind man. He did not have a bad temper but was easy to get along with. He was particularly remembered because he liked children. He used to gather them around him, not just his own, but those in the camp, and he would lecture them about being good. He explained the difference between good and bad, told them about the kind of work they should do, how to be responsible, and to do things that were good."[27]

An important element in Big Bear's leadership was his mysticism. Not only did his war medicine give him an aura of power, but his association with the bear spirit made him respected and feared. An active ceremonialist, he sponsored the Thirst Dance and other religious activities of the tribe. Although these may have enhanced his position as chief, he did them for reasons of personal conviction, rather than political gain. Like his father before him, his feelings for the supernatural were deeply rooted in his Ojibwa heritage.

As chief of the band, Big Bear became the owner of a medicine pipe, perhaps the one his father had used to make war against the Blackfoot. This pipe, wrapped in a bundle with other sacred objects, was cared for by a medicine pipe man, and though it was controlled by the chief, it influenced the whole camp. The bundle could be opened and used to cure the sick through incantations, or used in the Medicine Pipe Dance if good luck was needed to find buffalo herds. Most often, however, it was used for peace or war. "One time the Crees and Blackfoot had been fighting each other for a long time," recalled an elder, "and Big Bear decided to stop it. So he got the medicine pipe bundle, *oske'chee*, and he got the chiefs together and made them all take an oath on it that they would have a peace treaty. They all had to put their hands on it when they made their oath. Then Big Bear took the medicine pipe to the leading chief of the Blackfoot and he told him what he had done. So the Blackfoot leader got his men together, and they went with Big Bear to meet the Crees and to make the treaty."[28]

Big Bear continued to have visions, revealing those that could be told and placing great faith in their interpretations. He was particularly sensitive to omens, both good and bad, and patterned his life in accordance with these signs. At the time Big Bear became chief, Christian missionaries were already active in the district. The Roman Catholics and Methodists were often among the Indians, trying to convert the chiefs in the belief that the others would follow. Big Bear had no interest in these white medicine men, but could not help noticing the influence they had in some of the Cree and Assiniboine camps. The Cree who traded at Edmonton had welcomed the Methodists, who had been labouring out of that fort since the 1840s. *Lapotac,* a leading chief of the Beaver Hills Cree until his death in 1861, had become a convert to Methodism, as had one of his lesser chiefs, Broken Arm, or *Maskepetoon.* Near Buffalo Lake, the warlike chief Bobtail supported the Oblates, perhaps because his father, a Métis named Piche, had been instrumental in bringing the first Catholic clergy to the region twenty years earlier. Only a few of the lesser chiefs in the Edmonton–Buffalo Lake area, like *Passpasschase,* *Kominikoos* and *Takoots,* seemed unaffected by the missionary influence. Among the Woods Cree who ventured onto the plains, the Methodists had made significant inroads. Little Hunter, the principal chief, became a convert, as did *Pakan,* The Nut and *Kehiwin,* or The Eagle, who wintered in the Saddle Lake region. These men had been influenced by an educated Ojibwa missionary, Henry Bird Steinhauer, who had been among them since 1855. The Plains Cree trading into Fort Pitt were the only major group in the area not affected by the missionaries. This was due, in part, to the fact that there were no resident missionaries at the fort, so there was no ongoing influence over the camps.

In 1865, Sweet Grass, *Wihaskokiseyin,* was the leading chief of the Fort Pitt Cree, while Little Pine ranked second. Although their hunting grounds were in the same general region, Little Pine's followers tended to go farther southwest on the plains and were more frequently at war with the Blackfoot. Sweet Grass hunted near The Nose, Sounding Lake and south to Red Deer Forks. As a minor chief, Big Bear allied his following to Sweet Grass, camping with him, joining him in the hunt and generally recognizing him as his superior chief. It was a strange anomaly that none of the three chiefs at Fort Pitt was entirely Cree. Big Bear, of course, was at least part Ojibwa; Little Pine's mother was a Blackfoot, and Sweet Grass was not a Cree at all, but a full-blooded Crow Indian.[29]

Sweet Grass was about ten years older than Big Bear and, like his companion chief, was not a big man. Rather, he was a diminutive warrior who was noted for being fearless in battle. Like so many other warriors, once Sweet Grass became a chief and was responsible for his people, he began to seek peace. During the 1860s, he made several attempts to end the war with the Blackfoot, but succeeded only in bringing about a brief period of tranquility. Big Bear, too, became a proponent of peace once he was chief, but in times of war both leaders were always ready to defend their camps or to raid an enemy. Any thought of peace was out of the question during this unsettled period, so when Sweet Grass suggested they go on a horse-raiding expedition, the younger chief agreed. Sweet Grass and Big Bear were firm friends by this time, the latter admiring his leader for his bravery and the guidance he received from his spiritual helper, the mosquito. That lowly insect had taken pity on Sweet Grass and had used its powers to help him to become a chief.

The two chiefs organized a war party of eighteen young men and set out on foot for the Blackfoot hunting grounds. Several days later they were camped by a stream when a snowstorm halted their journey, and a young man was sent out to kill a buffalo for food. No sooner had he left the hidden camp than he spied a lone Blackfoot on the prairie, rounding up his horses. Quickly, the young man went back to the others, and they all rushed out to kill the man and take his herd. But luck was not with the raiders that day. The Indian saw the Crees coming, so he stampeded his horses towards the valley of a nearby river. When the raiders followed him over the bank, they almost stumbled onto the main Blackfoot camp, which lined the river bottom amid the cottonwoods and the snow.

Sweet Grass, Big Bear and the others now became the hunted instead of the hunters. As the Blackfoot warriors raced to their horses, the Crees made their way on foot to another gully, but found it, too, was filled with Blackfoot lodges. Turning to the open, snowswept prairie, they got only as far as a small grove of spruce trees when they were surrounded. Nothing could be done but to dig rifle pits, pile logs in front for protection and fight for their lives. In this kind of battle there were two types of men: the fearless warriors who stood exposed and fired shot after shot into the enemy lines, and the untried young men who remained under cover, reloading the flintlocks passed down to them. That day there were only three warriors: Sweet Grass, Big Bear and a man named Half Sky. "They fought for a long time," recalled Coming Day, a son of Half Sky. "At last night came. At nightfall some more Blackfoot arrived, and these too joined in the fight against the Cree. Finally, they built fires all around, intending to bring it about that the Cree should not leave that place."[30]

Next morning the battle continued, and many Blackfoot were shot, but not one of the Crees was hurt. Although vastly outnumbered, the Cree warriors kept their enemy at bay; each time the Blackfoot tried to attack, they ended up dragging away their dead. The second day ended, and then "late in the night, Big Bear got tired; he went into the pit, wearied from having fought two days and almost two nights. Then only two Crees were fighting."[31] At one point some Blackfoot threw burning sticks at the embattled war party, setting fire to their log defences. Before morning, the logs were ablaze, and during efforts by the Crees to protect themselves, Half Sky was shot in the shoulder, breaking the blade. That left Sweet Grass alone to carry the fight until morning.

At daybreak a Blackfoot chief crept to a burned-out tree, and using it as a shield, he began shooting at the men in the pit. Behind him, more Blackfoot warriors gathered to storm the trenches. Realizing that the tree was just a shell, Sweet Grass fired a ball right through it, striking the Blackfoot chief in the heart. The killing of their chief took all the fight out of the Blackfoot, and they decided to withdraw.

"Who are you?" one of the Blackfoot called out to the entrenched enemy.

"Cree."

"I recognize some chiefs."

"There are no chiefs here," the Cree warriors replied with amusement. They had no intention of letting the Blackfoot know that they had trapped two chiefs, or the enemy would never give up the fight.

"How many of you have been slain, O Cree?"

"None at all," they answered truthfully. "And you?"

"Seven great chiefs of the Blackfoot you have slain; and six Blood chiefs you have slain; and four Sarsi chiefs you have slain, and two Piegan chiefs. There are not many Piegans here, but of those whom I have named, of them you have killed many chieftains. Now they will cease; they fear you now."[32]

During the parley, one of the young Crees became curious and wanted to look at the Blackfoot. "Do not!" his comrades shouted to him, but he paid no attention and climbed out of the trench. At once a shot rang out, and a bullet shattered his spine. "If you had obeyed," they said, "you would not have been wounded."[33]

After waiting for some time, the Crees heard no more sounds of the enemy, so a young man went to investigate. He found that the Blackfoot had struck camp and left. The beleaguered Crees, who had not eaten, slept or had anything to drink for two days, prepared to flee.

"Are you going to leave me?" plaintively asked the wounded boy.

"No," his companions answered him. "It is only that we are thirsty. When we have found water, you will be fetched."[34] But they deceived him, for they were all leaving for home. When they got back to their camp, they found that Sweet Grass's coat and blanket had thirty-two bullet holes in them, but he was unharmed.

That is the story, as told by Coming Day. When the men abandoned their comrade in the field, they realized that his spinal wound could not be treated and that he would soon die. Their parting words would give him faint hope in his last hours. The warriors could not stay with him, for they were deep in enemy territory and their presence was known.

In spite of intermittent warfare with the Blackfoot, life was good for the Cree. Buffalo were never far out on the prairie, massive epidemics had not decimated their numbers since the smallpox of 1837–38, and the traders were happy to take dried meat, buffalo robes and furs in exchange for the manufactured goods that had become part of Cree daily life. Guns, ammunition, knives, copper kettles, beads, paint, blankets — all were on the traders' shelves. During these good years, the presence of the white man was felt only when Big Bear and his followers visited the trading posts. Most of the time the Cree were a free people in their own land, untrammelled and at liberty to wander where they pleased. There was no one to place a halter over their heads or to imprison them in corrals like captive horses. All they knew was a life of freedom.

The Cycle of Life

ACH YEAR WHEN spring arrived, Big Bear abandoned the wastes of winter that had collected around his camp and journeyed to the open prairies. Along the way, he often met Sweet Grass, who had wintered some distance upstream near the mouth of Dog Rump Creek. As they travelled, snow still lay huddled and grimy in the coulees, shrinking before the warm rays of the sun. On the nearby hillside, pussy willows proudly displayed their furry coats, while delicate crocuses cast colourful patches of purple amid the dry, brown prairie grass. By midafternoon, water trickled through the gullies, and high overhead, V-shaped flocks of ducks coursed noisily northward.

Spring and its harbingers were part of the endless cycle of life for all creatures on the prairies, including the Cree. They had shaken themselves loose from the confinement created by winter blizzards and snow-filled trails to join with the rest of nature in exulting in the glory of the new season. After a few days on the trail, they found their first buffalo, an old bull hanging about near the main herd; his shaggy winter coat, coming off in huge clumps, gave him the appearance of an ill-kempt rug. This aging and fallen monarch had been ejected from the herd by a younger and more virile bull who had taken his harem of cows. That, too, was a part of the cycle of nature.

If the main herds were near, Big Bear and his people ignored the old bull, for his meat would be tough and stringy. What they wanted were the succulent young cows, whose back fat and ribs were a meal fit for a chief. When one of the scouts riding ahead saw the dark, moving mass of animals, he galloped to a nearby hill to signal the news. His index fingers, hooked like horns on either side of the head, formed a sign that could be read from a great distance.

The soldiers in the band kept the hunters back until everyone was ready. Then the scouts checked the wind direction, the lay of the land and the drift of the herd to determine the best direction for an attack.

Excitement rose as hunters changed from their riding horses to buffalo runners, tightening the saddle pads and checking their bows and arrows. Flintlocks sometimes were used, but the process of reloading at a dead gallop amid a thundering buffalo herd was often too much trouble. Besides, the feathered arrows protruding from the side of a dead buffalo could easily be identified after the hunt, and no one could question who had made the kill. If a gun was used, the hunter had to hurl down some object, such as a whip or kerchief, to identify his kill after the confusion of the chase.

Often using a shallow coulee or a hill to hide them, the hunting party came within a few hundred yards of the herd before a whooping cry gave them the signal to attack. Then, it was every man for himself. Big Bear and his hunters dashed forward, their bows or flintlocks held high, as they galloped into the stampeding herd. Urging a horse along by the pressure of his knees, a hunter like Big Bear would ride alongside a fat cow and fire pointblank just behind the shoulder, aiming directly for the heart. If the horse was sure-footed and the hunter calm, he might be brushing against the buffalo itself when he fired the shot. A good running horse then immediately swung wide in case the buffalo swerved and fell, and horse and rider were off to seek their next prey. If the hunters were lucky, they might kill two or three animals each before the herd stampeded away.

Even as the earth still rumbled from the hundreds of thudding hoofs, Big Bear's wives and the other women were moving forward with travois and carts in the dust, each looking for a sign of her husband's kill. A distinctively marked arrow in the side of a dead animal here, a red kerchief on the ground near a gunshot animal there — each was evidence to the women that their men had been successful. Happily chattering, they soon had a buffalo properly positioned for butchering, and with a lifetime of experience behind them, they methodically and skillfully skinned the beast and cut it into manageable chunks. Arms and hands streaked with blood, they hauled out the entrails to be cooked later over an open fire, then gloried in the kidney, which they ate raw, still warm from the body. Other parts — the boss ribs, tongue, heart, front and hindquarters — all took their place in a neat pile ready to be hauled to camp.

If it was the first kill of the season, a holy man would take a choice morsel to a nearby hill to give thanks to Old Man Buffalo, the spiritual protector who controlled the herds. If the hunters happened to be near an ancient monument, a pilgrimage was made during prayers of supplication. These monuments, though many miles apart, were on high hills, usually within sight of each other, so that a man standing beside the Iron Stone near the Battle River could see the hill holding the Rib Stone far to the southeast. These monuments were like sentinels on the prairie, each one a tribute to Old Man Buffalo, guardian of the herds.

In the summer, Big Bear and his followers ranged far out onto the prairies, choosing favourite campsites where the buffalo were plentiful. Because of the ongoing war with the Blackfoot, they tended to travel farther east than usual, stopping at Sounding Lake, where some of the Eagle Hills people came to hunt. From there they wandered south, staying close to the buffalo, until they came to the banks of the South Saskatchewan. There they remained, living off the herds, drying meat and tanning robes for sale to the traders.

Once in a while, a warrior strode through the camp, singing his holy song and inviting others to join him in a raid on the Blackfoot horse herds. They were at war, so Big Bear and the camp soldiers only smiled approvingly as preparations for the expedition began. Had there been peace, the warriors would have stopped the demonstration and patrolled at night to be sure that no one slipped away. But this time, the women prepared extra moccasins for the raiders, who would be setting out on foot, and the night before they left, the men gathered for ceremonies in a warrior's lodge. Each person was painted according to his own society or spirit helper, as they all performed the War Dance that had come to them from the Sioux. There was jubilation among the men and crying from the women as the raiders set off at daybreak. Among the party were at least one or two boys who were barely into their teenaged years and were going out for the first time. The leader may have been a mature man in his twenties or thirties, but most of the group was made up of teenaged boys, young but with eyes and minds hardened by the bloodiness of previous raids.

As the days passed and sometimes turned into weeks, wives and mothers anxiously looked westward for signs of the returning party. The men, too, were concerned but tried not to show it. At last, a shout came that the war party was coming back, and everyone rushed out to search the hills for the advance scout. He was riding a horse now, not walking, and silently made his way to a rise within sight of the camp. There, he took his blanket and waved it. Once. Twice. Or perhaps he dismounted, picked up a rock, held it aloft, then put it down. He did it once, then once again. A cry went up from the camp, for they knew that of the men and boys who had gone on the raid, two were dead. Soon the other survivors arrived, their faces painted black to show they had had a successful raid; in front of them were thirty Blackfoot horses.

When the camp crier determined who had fallen, he walked among the lodges, calling out their names and telling everyone that they had looked upon their faces for the last time. The relatives of the dead wailed in mourning, yet they were proud that their men had fallen in battle. As the others gathered around the returning heroes, the warriors called out the names of relatives and friends, and in front of everyone, gave them most of the horses they had captured. "Listen, everyone!" a warrior may have called out. "I give to Little Child the bay stallion I captured. He is my wife's brother, and I honour him now!"

"Ho!" another may have said, "Little Badger shall receive my pinto mare. I remember his gift to me from his last raid. He is my relative, so I honour him."

That night, a Scalp Dance was performed so that the women could praise the returned heroes. During the ceremony, each man stepped forward and told of his deeds — how they spied the Blackfoot camp, crept in at sunset and took the best horses; how a skittish mare alerted its Blackfoot owner, and how they made their escape with guns blazing all around them. One warrior told how he had shot a Blackfoot in the chest, killing him instantly; another raider immediately jumped up and confirmed it, saying, "I saw it happen." Another told how he had ridden down one of his assailants, crushing him beneath the hoofs of his horse as he galloped away. The dance carried on far into the night, but four men did not join. They were soldiers, members of the warrior society; their task was to guard the camp after sunset whenever there was danger of enemy attack. On this night, the Blackfoot might have followed the raiders and be somewhere in the darkness.

As the days became shorter and the ice began to gather on the edges of the ponds, Big Bear's camp made preparations to move on. They were more intent now on killing as many buffalo as possible, both for their winter supply and to sell to the traders. Big Bear knew all the ways of hunting buffalo, for this had been part of his life since he was old enough to hold a bow. He could hunt by himself, crawling along until he was within range, sometimes covered with a calfskin to hide his true appearance; then, a single shot might bring down a cow before the rest of the herd ran away. When they were going into their fall hunt, Big Bear might find an appropriate area to build a pound. This consisted of a huge corral that had a slight incline at the mouth of its only gate. The buffalo were driven towards it along parallel rows of brush and fences; the space between the two lines gradually narrowed, and the herd found itself being pushed into a smaller and smaller area. When the bulls leading the herd could see the trap ahead, they might try to turn back, but were pushed on by the wild-eyed stampeding creatures behind them. Once in the corral, there was no way to get out, and the buffalo quickly died at the hands of hunters, little boys and old men, all armed with bows and arrows. Forty or fifty buffalo might be killed at a single run, giving the camp plenty of meat to start the winter. They tanned the buffalo robes they needed for themselves and set aside those that they could exchange for trade goods. Soon their travois were heavily laden with dried meat, pemmican, fat and robes, as they wended their way slowly to the north.

The grass had lost its lushness and was again a dull brown. In fact, the whole landscape was painted with the drab colours of autumn. For a few days, the trees in the coulees and along the river beds had been brightly mantled with leaves of red, yellow and orange, but the first prairie breeze had whipped them away, and they had come to rest amid the dry grass of the valley floor. By this time almost everything was brown or grey — the grass, the bare trees, rocks and hills. Here and there an alkaline lake offered an unwelcome glaze of white, and farther north a few spruce trees stood like green statues among the bare poplars. Only the sky remained aloof from the drabness of the earth. During the cool autumn days, it was a crystal blue, with fleecy cumulus clouds breaking the awesomeness of its intensity. The sun, its rays weakened by the lateness of the season, still yielded a comforting warmth to the caravan of horses, travois, dogs and people picking their way across the prairie grass.

And then there were the autumn sunsets. As if to compensate for the greyness of the countryside, the spirit of daylight seemed determined to paint the whole sky during its fading hours. Clouds were fringed with flaming pinks that softened to paler tones as light was cast over their billowy surfaces. Streaks of magenta, orange and yellow swept out from the western horizon, reflecting off the prairie lakes and colouring the distant hills in purples and blues. The Cree believed that the spirit of daylight saw everything that happened and heard all that was said during the hours of sunshine, and to let the world know it was leaving, it created a spectacle for everyone to see. As the fingers of darkness edged over the land, the colours paled, then faded into the shadows of oncoming night.

After their fall trade at Fort Pitt, Big Bear's followers stayed on the prairies south of the fort, killing more buffalo and making final preparations for winter. At last, when the snows began sweeping down from the north, they moved to the Little Hills, Jackfish Lake or the mouth of Vermilion River to winter in the protective confines of the woods. Some men went out to trap, going north to Lac la Biche, Loon Lake or Meadow Lake to seek beaver, muskrat, weasel, mink or other fur-bearing animals. These trappers went alone or in small family groups, and were isolated from the rest of the band until spring. They were the ones who had never completely abandoned their woodland ways and were content to live off fish and small game during the cold weather. Others in the camp were pure plainsmen who would disdain to eat moose or deer and considered buffalo to be the only proper food for an Indian. If the winter was mild, they ventured onto the edge of the plains to live off the herds and remained there as long as the weather would allow. Some stayed away all winter, but those in Big Bear's band usually preferred the safety and comfort of the woodlands.

Winter also was the time to visit other villages up and down the river, hold ceremonies, and tell stories about war, adventure and the supernatural. As children listened in breathless silence, an old man might tell of his raid against the Crow, acting out the events, singing his war songs, describing in detail what their enemy wore, how they were beaten and how the spirits had smiled upon the Cree. Another might tell of a mystical event, like the boy who was raised by bears, or of the "little people" who dwelled near the riverbanks and made stone arrowheads for Cree hunters. Then, as signs of spring began to appear in the sky and among the trees, the whole cycle was ready to start again.

Big Bear and his camp were so much a part of the land that they were sensitive to all its moods and changes. Their world of prairies, forests, rivers and skies gave them everything they needed: food, shelter, clothing and life itself.

In 1866, an event occurred that was the first step in a series of incidents to shatter the complacent life of Big Bear and other Cree leaders along the Saskatchewan River. That summer, they learned that the Iron Stone was missing from its hill near the Battle River. Of all the monuments dedicated to Old Man Buffalo, the Iron Stone was the greatest and most venerated. It was a meteorite composed almost entirely of iron so soft it could be cut with a knife. A total of 386 pounds (176 kg) in weight, it was believed by the Indians to have been placed there after the flood by *Nanebozo*, the great spirit of the Ojibwa. Not only did the stone have protective powers, but the holy men said it grew in size as the years passed. At one time, a person could lift this sacred stone, but now it had grown so that even if someone wrapped his arms around it, he could not raise it from the ground. The Iron Stone was not just a protector of the buffalo; it was the guardian of all the Indians in the region. Offerings were left beside it when the Cree went to seek the buffalo, for they knew that as long as the stone stayed in their hunting grounds, there would be food. Now it was gone.

"The medicine men," observed a visitor several years later, "with unbroken faith in the creed of their fathers, prophesied dire evils to follow the removal of the stone which Manitou had placed on the hill. The buffalo would disappear, there would be a pestilence and fierce war. At the time the prophecy was made, I am told, the plains were black with buffalo, 'whose ponderous tramping made the prairie quiver'; there were no indications of disease; war, though not unknown, was infrequent."[1]

Where had the Iron Stone gone? The Indians soon discovered that Methodist missionaries had loaded it on a cart and taken it a hundred miles (160 km) north to Victoria mission, where it sat in the churchyard. Later, it was shipped to a Methodist college in Ontario, far from the land it had once protected. Missionary George McDougall knew what he had done by taking the stone, for he commented that "for ages the tribes of Blackfeet and Crees have gathered their clans to pay homage to this wonderful manitoo." He also noted that the taking of the idol had "roused the ire of the conjurors. They declared that sickness, war, and decrease of buffalo would follow this sacrilege."[2]

Big Bear, the vision seeker, and holder of the bear bundle and a sacred medicine pipe, often hunted in the area of the Iron Stone, as did his fellow chiefs Little Pine and Sweet Grass. Until that year, the missionaries had been little more than a divisive element, causing some Indians to turn their backs on the old ways and to separate themselves from those the missionaries called pagans. But in taking the Iron Stone, the white medicine men showed themselves to be a threat and a danger to the traditional life of the Indians.

Leaders like Big Bear had heard how white men and half-breeds at Red River were killing all the buffalo, so that the Ojibwa and Cree in the district had to travel for days before finding any game. Other white men were breaking the land and living from the soil without ever going on a hunt. Were missionaries the advance scouts for these people? In war, scouts went ahead to find if it was safe to travel, and the others followed behind. Perhaps the white man was doing the same.

Three years earlier, Broken Arm and Little Hunter had gone to a missionary, complaining that they were poor and hungry. He had told them to give up buffalo hunting and to use their horses for farming. "How can I get my young men to take a hoe and dig up the new sod?" protested one of the chiefs. "I cannot get the young men to work at new ground while the good buffalo meat is so near."[3] So now, as though in answer to the chief's question, the missionaries had taken the stone that protected the herds. This action sowed the first serious doubts in the minds of Big Bear and other chiefs about the intentions of the white man. Until then, neither fur trader nor missionary had done anything to upset the daily lives of the Indians. Now, their motives were in question.

Pestilence, War and Starvation

I N SPITE OF vast distances and problems of communication, news could travel like a prairie fire across the plains. In 1869, when the Hudson's Bay Company made arrangements to transfer its authority to the new Dominion of Canada for £300,000 and certain land grants, Big Bear, Sweet Grass and other chiefs were hearing garbled accounts of the sale within a few weeks. "A rumour reached them," said missionary George McDougall, "that a power greater than that Company [the Hudson's Bay Company] will soon be here to treat with them for their lands. Injudicious parties have informed them that their old neighbors have received a large sum for these lands, and the Indian is not so ignorant but to enquire to whom has he ever ceded his hunting grounds."[1] This action, taken without consulting either the half-breed settlers at Red River or the natives within the territories, resulted in a confrontation at Red River that erupted into rebellion under the leadership of Louis Riel.

As the Red River Rebellion continued, half-breeds began moving among the Indians, telling them stories of what would happen once they became subjects of Canada. Some Indians refused to pay their debts to the HBC and threatened to break into the company's stores. In the Qu'Appelle Valley, news of the troubles spread rapidly "in every form of distortion and contortion, and as it was further spread by rumour all over the plains, produced a state of such unrest and excitement that the business of hunting came almost to a stop."[2] In order to stem the unrest, missionary John McDougall set out from Victoria mission to visit Big Bear, Sweet Grass, Bobtail, Little Hunter, *Pakan* and others who were hunting on the plains. "I would stop for days," he recalled, "alone with the Indians, going from lodge to lodge attending councils, and when I could, holding meetings and giving lectures, which you may be sure were at the time packed full of English history and Canadian experience and fair play, justice and liberty."[3]

Big Bear heard these outpourings, just as he heard the words of the anti-British priest Constantine Scollen and the half-breeds who supported Riel's provisional government at Red River. He had no way of knowing who was telling the truth. He and other chiefs understood only that strangers were buying and selling their lands without permission, that the Cree were in danger of being robbed of their hunting grounds, their buffalo and their way of life.

Big Bear could not help but remember his first vision — that the white man would someday come and take his land. The signs were not good, and Big Bear was worried. He and Little Pine were the only leading chiefs who had not come under the influence of the missionaries. Even Sweet Grass was having his head turned by the priests, as were *Kehiwin* and Bobtail. The Methodists had a firm hold of Little Hunter and *Pakan*; they had previously had Broken Arm, but he had been killed that spring when he had gone to a Blackfoot camp to try to make peace.

In the spring of 1870 the worry of white encroachment was replaced by the terror of smallpox. In the previous autumn a Blackfoot had stolen a blanket from a disease-ridden Missouri River steamboat, and before winter the scourge was racing through his people's camps, wiping out whole families and sending the survivors fleeing over the prairies. When warm weather came, small war parties of Cree went south, where they were surprised to find enemy camps deserted, clothing and possessions abandoned, and wolves gnawing on the corpses of men, women and children. Heedless of the cause, eager young warriors took scalps, blankets and other objects, then returned to their villages singing their victory songs. Within days, the songs turned to wails as the pestilence appeared in their camps. By summer, more than a hundred Crees had perished around Fort Pitt alone. Out on the plains, hundreds more died in agony, while still others succumbed to starvation because they were unable to hunt. The summer was hot and dry, so that prairie fires swept through the Indian camps, burning to death those who were too weak to flee.

Big Bear's camp was struck down by the disease like all the others, but the chief himself was immune, having survived the contagion in his youth. His people and others along the river were quick to blame the whites for the disease. Some tried to infect the traders at Fort Pitt by rubbing their open sores on door handles and windows, while others sought to revenge themselves on the missionaries by leaving infected clothing near Victoria mission.

People began to avoid each other on the trail, camping alone and shunning those who were sick. A small party of Cree travelling near Fort Pitt saw an abandoned village, and as they swung wide to pass it, a beautiful young woman emerged from a tepee and told them that she was the only one left. Then she began to sing, ending with the words, "How I used to love to hear this song when we were all alive."[4] Some wanted to help the survivor, but others were afraid, so they continued on until nightfall. Then two young men decided to go back to rescue the girl, taking a change of clothing so that she would not infect the camp. When they got to her lodge, they called for her, but she did not answer. Inside, they found that she had hanged herself.

When the Iron Stone had been taken, the holy men had predicted three disasters: sickness, war and starvation. The first of these had come to pass in the form of smallpox exactly four years after the theft had taken place. This was significant in itself, as four was a sacred number in Cree religion. In ceremonies, the pipe was pointed in the four cardinal directions; the four Thunders were commemorated on the altar at the Thirst Dance, and many holy songs were repeated four times. In later years, Big Bear placed great emphasis upon the holy number four.

In the meantime, events at Red River continued to have an unsettling effect upon the Indians of the plains. The news that Riel had executed an Ontario troublemaker, Thomas Scott, gave credence to rumours that the half-breeds were now running the country. In the spring of 1870, the half-breeds called a mass meeting at Qu'Appelle, giving an opportunity for free traders from Edmonton, Carlton and other regions to stop on their annual trip to Red River. Their objective was to determine whether the Métis farther west would now play an active role in siding with their friends at Red River, including taking possession of the various trading posts across the prairies. At the meeting, Hudson's Bay Company officers read a proclamation circulated by its commissioner, Donald A. Smith, urging everyone to remain loyal to the Queen, but the Métis responded by saying "it was wrong for Canada to seek to impose her rule over the country without first making terms with its people,"[5] and nothing was resolved. When the meeting was over, the Cree chose to side with the Hudson's Bay Company, and a leading chief, Loud Voice, placed a protective circle of tepees around the fort at Qu'Appelle.

Canadian and British troops under Col. Garnet Wolseley arrived at Red River in the summer of 1870 and ended the threat of a half-breed uprising. By then, Big Bear and other leaders were already far out on the plains, fleeing from the spectre of smallpox, carrying out their summer hunts and fighting with the Blackfoot.

Realizing that the Blackfoot had been more weakened by the epidemic than the Cree and Assiniboine, a number of leaders decided to form a large revenge party to strike at the heart of their enemy's lands. The idea originated with chiefs in the Qu'Appelle Valley, and from there messengers were sent with tobacco to villages near Carlton and along the North Saskatchewan. Little Pine and Big Bear both agreed to go, as did

Little Mountain and *Piapot*. Following the South Saskatchewan River, they sent their scouts ahead to find the main encampments of Blackfoot, Bloods or Peigans. At last, they discovered a small Blood camp on the Belly River about three miles (5 km) from Fort Whoop-Up. Believing it to be an isolated village and an easy target, the revenge party swept down on it just before sunrise, killing a leading warrior and a number of women. However, the Crees had no way of knowing that a large number of South Peigan, all heavily armed, were located just a few miles away. Normally, they would have been far south along the Missouri River, but a massacre of more than two hundred of their people by American soldiers had driven them north. The Cree had only flintlocks and bows and arrows, which were no match for the repeating rifles of the enemy. When the Peigan arrived after dawn, the raid against the Blackfoot turned into a rout. The water of the Oldman River ran red with blood, as enemy warriors standing on the banks fired into the ranks of the retreating Crees. One group of about fifty Crees made a stand in a grove of cottonwood trees and was completely annihilated. Many Blood and Peigan warriors were killed or wounded, but the losses to Cree and Assiniboine ranks were catastrophic. Between two hundred and three hundred men were said to have died that day.[6] It was the last major battle between the Cree and the Blackfoot tribes; never again would either side suffer such severe losses.

The second of the three calamities predicted after the theft of the Iron Stone had now occurred. Big Bear, who had taken part in the ill-fated battle, must have pondered with increasing unease the effects of the white man's intrusion. Their tragic defeat had not been the fault of Cree and Assiniboine warriors, for they had fought brilliantly, but with the white traders who had supplied the Peigan with repeating rifles and the white soldiers who had driven them away from their usual hunting grounds. White people had also brought the smallpox that had slain almost four thousand Crees, and white people were selling Indian land. To make matters worse, Big Bear, Sweet Grass and their followers had not been able to gather a winter food supply during the epidemic. For the first time, their people were unable to seek safety and seclusion north of the river when the cold weather came. Instead, just about every camp that hunted buffalo was obliged to stay out on the plains for the entire winter. Not only that, but the buffalo did not come north that year, so they had to go far beyond the Battle River and into the Hand Hills before they found a few scattered herds.

As one calamity piled upon another, the Cree gathered in the wooded valleys of the Hand Hills, where their chiefs, including Big Bear, discussed the deteriorating political situation. The Hudson's Bay Company was no longer their guardian, and the half-breed rebellion had been defeated; hundreds of soldiers occupied Fort Garry and might invade their lands at any time. A man whom the traders called "Canadian government" now ruled them, just as the Queen had ruled them in the past. And this "Canadian government" person had paid hundreds of pelts to the Hudson's Bay Company for lands that belonged to the Cree.

On hearing of the large gathering at Hand Hills, the Hudson's Bay Company and missionaries assumed that a grand council had been called to discuss the Canadian takeover of the West. Fearing that "evidently they meant mischief,"[7] missionary John McDougall was sent from Fort Edmonton to allay the Indians' fears. This was the first of many meetings in which Indian intentions were misinterpreted from the outset. The Cree had not gathered to agitate against the government, but to survive the winter. If they had been given their choice and the white man had not upset their lives, they would be happily nestled in their winter camps along the North Saskatchewan, instead of suffering on the open plains.

McDougall called a meeting of the fifteen bands that were there and extended to them the goodwill and friendship of the Edmonton people. Sweet Grass was the leading chief and the others undoubtedly included Little Pine and Bobtail as secondary chiefs, followed by Big Bear, *Kehiwin,* Half Blackfoot Chief and those who normally hunted in the area.

Sweet Grass, the negotiator of several peace treaties with the Blackfoot during the 1860s, had now come fully under the influence of the Roman Catholics and been baptized by Father Lacombe. A friend of the whites, he had succeeded Broken Arm as the peacemaker of the region. "We are thankful that our friends in the north have not forgotten us," Sweet Grass told McDougall. "In sorrow and in hunger and with many hardships we have gathered here, where we have grass and timber, and, since we came, buffalo in the distance, few, though still sufficient to keep us alive. We have grumbled at hunger and disease and long travel through many storms and cold; our hearts have been hard, and we have had bitter thoughts and doubtless said many foolish and bad words. . . . Your coming has done us good; it has stayed evil and turned our thoughts to better things. We feel today we are not alone."[8]

McDougall found the meeting to be a friendly one; even Little Pine, who had earlier threatened to kill McDougall's father, George, was reassured. However, the chiefs raised a number of questions that the young missionary could not answer, so arrangements were made for them to send messages directly to the new Canadian government. Such an action would reinforce the efforts of the McDougalls. As soon as the first announcement had been made back in 1869 that Canada would be acquiring the Hudson's Bay Company territories, the elder McDougall had urged the immediate negotiation of treaties. In January of 1870, not realizing that Riel had captured Fort Garry, he had advised the intended lieutenant-governor that "no time be lost in meeting them at their councils, treating with them for their lands, and by patient explanation allay the present excitement."[9] Six months later he advised the government to keep any surveyors away and stressed again "the importance of sending a Commissioner to visit the Crees. I would not advise that their lands should be treated for now: this might be premature; and they would be satisfied for the time if informed that they would be justly dealt with. If this is delayed, trouble is before us."[10]

In the spring of 1871, Sweet Grass and other chiefs went to Edmonton to transmit a frank message to the lieutenant-governor. It is possible that Big Bear accompanied them, though he was not an important enough chief to sign the document. "We heard our Lands were sold and we did not like it," said Sweet Grass flatly. "We don't want to sell our Lands; it is our property and no one has the right to sell them. Our Country is getting ruined of Fur-Bearing Animals, hitherto our sole support, and now we are poor and want help. We want You to pity us." He then spoke of the need for farming equipment, their concern about starvation and smallpox, and the problems caused by American traders selling whiskey on Canadian soil. "We invite you to come and see us," he concluded, "and to speak with us. If you can't come yourself, send some one in your place."[11]

The lieutenant-governor of the territory responded to the appeals with words, but not with action. No response was made to the request that someone in authority come to see them; in spite of the fact that two white representatives of the Canadian government — Captain McDonald of the Ontario Rifles, and Col. William F. Butler on special assignment — both travelled as far west as Edmonton in 1870 and 1871. However, neither visited the Cree to allay their fears about the intentions of the new government. Consequently, in the long period since the Indians had learned of the Hudson's Bay Company sale and the arrival of troops in Red River, rumours had continued to circulate. As each month passed without the appearance of an official representative, suspicion mounted that they were to be ignored and their lands stolen from them.

★ ★ ★

By 1871 Big Bear had been chief for six years, during which he had seen warfare, disease and hunger. He was now forty-six years old, with a partially grown-up family. His eldest daughter, *Nowakich,* had married an outstanding warrior named Lone Man, and the two men became close friends that transcended a father-in-law/son-in-law relationship.

Like so many other followers of Big Bear, Lone Man saw in his father-in-law the qualities of leadership that gave him confidence to follow the chief without question. Besides, Lone Man found Big Bear to be a likable man — jovial, wise and an engaging storyteller. The chief liked being with children, so when Lone Man and *Nowakich* had a family, the bonds of companionship became even closer as the older man visited and doted upon his grandchildren.

Lone Man was the son of a Blackfoot woman who, together with her sister, had been captured by the Cree. His father had married one of the women, and Lucky Man, a prominent leader in Big Bear's camp, had married the other.

Big Bear's oldest son, Twin Wolverine, had been to war and was now settling down as a family man. His father was proud of him and looked to him to carry on the family tradition of leading their band. From the time he was small, Twin Wolverine had been groomed for the role of chief, just as Big Bear had been. The second son, *Imasees*, had just turned twenty, and in both appearance and demeanour was much like his father. In fact, their similarity of temperament may have been the reason they later had so many disagreements. But at this age, *Imasees* was still going to war; only later did he marry one of Lucky Man's daughters and begin to settle down. Another of Big Bear's daughters married a Cree named French Eater, but of them little is known, except that they chose to remain in Big Bear's camp rather than to move to her husband's band. The camps of Big Bear, Sweet Grass and Little Pine were closely inter-married, particularly among the leading families. And these alliances went even further afield, with Little Pine being a brother-in-law of the great southern leader *Piapot*.

Big Bear had three wives with him now. *Sayos* had borne him two boys and two girls, and his second wife had given birth to King Bird, *Okimowpeeaysis*, when Big Bear had become chief. His youngest wife, who had just joined his lodge, gave birth to a son, Horse Child, and after that to his last child, Earth Woman.[12]

Big Bear had proven to be a good family man and a good chief. He was well liked and respected, firm in his decisions and expected to be obeyed. Meetings of his council were held as often as they were needed, and if a dispute had to be settled, the matter was brought to him. It could be the question of ownership of a horse, the alleged theft of firewood, a dog stealing meat, or a woman who had run away from her husband in another camp and sought sanctuary with her lover in Big Bear's camp. In times when their enemies were far away, Big Bear had undisputed control of the village. The soldiers carried out his edicts without complaint, controlling the hunts, meting out justice to those who broke the laws and acting as the police force of the camp. However, if the village was in danger of attack, the leader of the soldiers' lodge immediately became the war chief and ruled with complete authority. Big Bear, as the political leader, could voice his opinions, but the war chief was in charge. Once the danger passed, control reverted to the political chief. This custom was rooted in the logic of survival, for the political chief of a camp was often an old man, who was interested only in peace. In times of conflict, he would have neither the energy nor the ability to lead his followers into battle. For that, a younger and more aggressive man was needed; someone who might be ill suited for leadership in peace time, but who could act quickly and ruthlessly when lives were at stake. The delicate balance between the chief and the leader of the soldiers' lodge was recognized by everyone in the camp, so it was rarely the source of conflict or jealousy.

★   ★   ★

After a difficult winter on the plains, Big Bear's followers were pleased to see the buffalo return north in large numbers in the spring of 1871. Not only that, but everyone had become tired of war, and both the Cree and the Blackfoot had agreed to keep the peace. By autumn the followers of Big Bear had their travois loaded with dried meat and robes, as they wended their way north to their wintering grounds.

On this trip Big Bear took his goods to the Hudson's Bay Company post adjoining Victoria mission, and after the trade was finished, his people settled in the pleasant valley, hunting buffalo south of the North Saskatchewan River. When they had been in the camp for several days, some of Big Bear's people began stealing potatoes from the mission fields. To resolve the problem, the chief met with missionary John McDougall, who suggested the Cree help with the potato harvest and take any surplus potatoes for themselves. The idea of a camp of buffalo hunters digging in the earth may have seemed strange, but Big Bear heartily favoured the plan. They had always dug up wild turnips and other roots for food, so potatoes would not be much different. Also, its meat was much like their own roots, except it was bigger and more tender.

"The next day we went at it," recalled McDougall, "men, women and children. Soon the potatoes, in piles, and heaps, and bags, were all over the ground. The whole thing was new to these buffalo-eaters; the wonderful crop, this strange four-wheeled iron-bound cart, this most obedient team of horses. Some of them had never taken part in such sport in all their history, and all day I took the fertility of the soil, and the response to agriculture, industry, and the beneficence of the Creator as my texts, and from the vantage ground of the waggon, with reins in hand and rushing things, I lectured and preached every little while to listening crowds." At the end of the day, with a quarter of the field still untouched, the missionary told Big Bear that his followers could harvest the rest of the crop for themselves. "There were loud acclaims at this announcement, and the chief sent the people home on the jump, promising a fair start for all in the morning."[13]

True to Big Bear's word, they all came back the next day and happily carted back to camp all the potatoes they could carry. This was Big Bear's first exposure to agriculture, and it was a good one. He knew that *Pakan* and his people had gardens at Goodfish Lake, and that the priests at St. Paul des Cris tried to encourage farming, but he now had the experience of taking enough food from the ground to last for weeks. Perhaps there was an alternative to buffalo after all.

During the winter of 1871–72, the buffalo grazed in the neighbourhood of Big Bear's camp, though their numbers were far fewer than in earlier years. In the past, when the chief had found the main herd, he had seen a sea of moving buffalo right to the horizon. Now the herds were smaller and scattered, but they still provided enough food for everyone. The good hunting extended into the summer, when Big Bear took his people to The Nose and from there across the Battle River. Because they were at peace with the Blackfoot, some other bands, particularly those under Little Pine, crossed the Red Deer River and found the main herd near the Three Hills. It seemed that more and more buffalo were congregating closer to the foothills inside Blackfoot country, leaving many parts of the Cree range abandoned and bare.

One problem that season was not a shortage of buffalo, but an abundance of American whiskey traders. For two years, these merchants of rotgut and death had been trading with the Blackfoot, creating havoc and poverty in their camps, and in 1872 they extended their operations, opening a small post at the mouth of the Bow River, another on the Bow itself and still others in the Cypress Hills. From there, they loaded their wagons with whiskey and visited Indian camps far out on the plains. One enterprising merchant even went farther north to the Hand Hills, where he traded whiskey to a Cree clientele. The results were the same all over the prairies. If whiskey was not available, the people did without it and were unconcerned. But if it could be bought anywhere in their region, they moved heaven and earth to get it. They hunted buffalo they did not need, simply to get the robes to sell to the traders. They left carcasses rotting on the prairie and spent their time preparing hides instead of drying meat. And once they got the whiskey, they quarrelled, killed each other and sometimes poisoned themselves. In many instances, if their hunger for alcohol was great enough, they sold their horses, lodges, anything they had in order to get the fiery brew.

All the Cree camps had trouble with whiskey that year, some worse than others. Those who normally hunted near the South Saskatchewan were the most severely affected, as their camps were within easy reach of the Americans. The chiefs, even if they opposed the traffic, were powerless to stop it. One leader went to Fort Pitt to see if the Hudson's Bay Company could do anything about it, asking why "the Americans were allowed to come into their Country bringing with them quantities of Liquor for Trade."[14] As a result of the liquor traffic, the Cree were ill prepared for winter, their camps having too little dried meat and too few horses. They hoped that the buffalo would stay in the north as in the previous year; if the weather was mild, they could keep themselves provided all winter. But it did not happen that way. In the early fall, while Big Bear and others were taking their few provisions to Fort Pitt, the buffalo left the country. They just disappeared, as though someone had opened a hole in the ground and driven all the animals into it. One week the area around Battle River was dotted with animals; the next week there were none. Some had gone across the Red Deer River to Blackfoot country, while many more had wandered south to the Missouri River and beyond. The hunting grounds of Big Bear, Sweet Grass and Little Pine were virtually barren.

Big Bear was camped at The Nose when his hunters reported the strange absence of buffalo. As with their situation two years earlier, the chief realized that they would not be able to withdraw into the woods for the winter, but would spend another season on the plains. Resignedly, Big Bear had his camp crier tell everyone that he was striking his lodge in the morning and leaving for the south. Those who wished could go with him. This was the way with the chiefs; they did not order their people to move, they simply told them their own plans. A good chief had a faithful following, and they would go with him; but if for any reason his people disagreed with him, they were free to make their own decisions. Big Bear's people followed him. They travelled south, a long line of horses, travois and carts along the trail, while the soldiers went ahead, behind, and on the flanks, watching for signs of danger. Periodically, scouts galloped to the far hills to see if they could find the buffalo herds. But there were no curved fingers at the side of the head to signal that buffalo were near. There was nothing but open prairies, bleached bones and the odd eagle circling overhead, its lonely cry echoing through the still autumn sky.

After several fruitless days on the trail, Big Bear's camp was savaged by a blizzard that swept down from the north. The winds shrieked through the upper poles of the lodges to announce that Cold Maker was coming; a few minutes later snow was battering against the walls of the tepees and causing the ponies to turn their backs and huddle together for protection. The prairies, once crackling and brittle underfoot, were transformed into huge carpets of white, which disappeared from view into the raging blizzard. Snow covered the open land, piling up in coulees and building strange nodules around any obstruction of brush or rock that stood in its path.

Inside his lodge, Big Bear relaxed and waited. Winter and blizzards were as much a part of his life as the pleasant days of summer. At times like this, a man could visit with his friends, tell stories and reminisce about the glories of hunting and war. A woman could finish some intricate quillwork on a pair of moccasins, repair her husband's leather shirt or teach a girl child a variety of beadwork stitches. When they were running short of firewood, the younger girls ventured from the lodge to collect buffalo chips. These burned quickly, too quickly, but if their mother had a bit of fat, she could suspend it above the fire so that it slowly dripped on the dung, making it last longer and creating a better heat. At night, when the fire burned low and then went out, everyone was wrapped snugly in his buffalo robe and stayed there until the morning campfire poked its tongues of heat into every part of the lodge. Even on the coldest mornings, some of the men insisted on stripping to their breechcloths and going outside to rub snow over their bodies. Trim, fit and hardened by a life in the outdoors, they adjusted to the cold so that they could more easily withstand the rigours of the trail.

Usually, when a fall blizzard ends, the warm weather returns, bringing with it the beauty and tranquility of an Indian summer. That year it did not happen. The first blizzard was the beginning of a winter that was "the severest and longest ever witnessed by the oldest inhabitants."[15] Four days later, when Big Bear's camp moved on, the leading riders had to bully their way through snowdrifts, breaking the thick crust and plowing a channel for others to follow. The temperatures plummeted until a trail of vapour could be seen behind every horse and rider. Frost glistened on the muzzles of the animals, and snow clung tenaciously to their long winter coats.

And still there were no buffalo. Along the trail, families began slipping away from the main camp, hoping to find an old bull that might feed them for a while. Others turned back towards the north, remembering the dried meat they had sold at Fort Pitt and hoping to recover some of it by giving up their horses. Or, if they were lucky, hunting and fishing might be good north of the river. The others stayed with Big Bear, going farther and farther south, killing a buffalo here and there, but slowly seeing their hunger change to starvation. In the valley of the South Saskatchewan River they found some protection from the savage winter and a few buffalo, so there they remained.

The story was the same throughout the Cree hunting grounds. Starvation lurked in every camp, and bands split up into small family groups in the frantic search for food. In the north, one group was lucky. It had just crossed the Vermilion River when a deaf old man had a vision in which a spirit dressed in pure white buckskins told him they would not find what they were looking for if they continued to go south. After some discussion, the people decided to heed his advice and turned back to the Big Timber Hills on the edge of the plains. There they lived comfortably on deer, elk and rabbits throughout the winter and saved their horses by clearing away the deep snow so that they could feed. In the spring, these fortunate people saw their friends and relatives coming back from the plains. "They were sure a pitiful sight," said one of the winterers. "Among them, numbering about 50 people, they had only one horse left. This miserably skinny animal was hauling its owner, a crippled old fellow, as well as a number of small bundles belonging to those who were too weak to carry anything but their own wasted bodies. These poor people had eaten all their horses and dogs, besides all rawhides and even portions of their tepees. My mother and the rest of the women of our camp spent the night boiling meat and chopping bones with which to make soup for those who continually came in asking for more. It was rather pathetic the way each man grabbed at what was extended to him and took a big bite off the dried meat or fat. When a person is hungry, pride is forgotten."[16]

Another group was not so lucky. Four people — a man, his wife and a teenaged son and daughter — left the band and went hunting on their own. In one place they found an abandoned camp where there were some buffalo heads with bits of meat still attached, but it was not enough to satisfy them for long. Finally, the man died of starvation, and in desperation the other three turned cannibal and devoured his body. Then, crazed with hunger, the two women killed the boy while he slept and used his flesh to sustain themselves in hopes of finding game. At last, when there was nothing left to eat, the mother offered to sacrifice herself so that her daughter might live. Her remains kept the girl until spring, when at last she reached a friendly camp. She stumbled into the village, her face black and swollen. Some small boys took one look at her and ran away, screaming "*Wetigo!*" the name for a person who has been possessed by a cannibal spirit. People tried to talk to her but she would not speak or look anyone in the face. Finally, an old man decided to test her by feeding her some raw fresh meat. When he handed it to her, she grabbed it and tore it to pieces with her teeth as she devoured it. A few minutes later she began to vomit. "In this way," said a Cree elder, "they knew beyond a doubt that she had been eating human flesh. Then they gave her some medicine which revived her to the extent that she could talk coherently. Alas, her mother's sacrifice was in vain, for she only lived long enough to tell in detail her awful story."[17]

One of the families that left Big Bear's camp was that of Thunder Child and his parents. With seven in their party, including three young children, they tried without success to trap wolves; when their dogs chased the animals, the wolves turned on them and killed them. For a while the family lived off dog meat, and after that they started to kill their five horses. Starvation can have strange effects upon people, as they discovered after their last food had been eaten. Just as they were pondering where they would find their next meal, they met the families of two old friends, Night Scout and *Semakan,* who had five horses and were on their way back to Fort Pitt. They camped nearby and killed one of their horses for food but refused to share the meat with Thunder Child's family. The spurned family may have had some satisfaction later when they learned that all the men in Night Scout's party had starved to death on the way to the trading post.

Meanwhile, Thunder Child's family barely survived the winter and were just skin and bones as spring approached. The men could not move about and had trouble breathing, and only the women had strength enough to keep the campfires burning to boil marrow bones for soup. One day, Thunder Child had a dream in which a good-looking man came to him and said, "I come to tell you how you can save yourself. Look south." As the boy looked to the south, he saw that everything was green. Then he was told to look north, and there he saw darkness. "Go south," the spirit said. "Try to flee there. Try!"[18] Next morning the boy told his parents about his dream, and they decided to follow the spirit's advice. By now the snow was starting to melt, but they were so weak they could travel only a few miles a day. After four days, one of the women saw some buffalo in a nearby coulee, but when Thunder Child's father went to stalk them, he was too weak to make a good shot. At last, Thunder Child's aunt took the gun and was gone all night. The next morning she came back with meat. They were advised to eat only blood soup at first, for their stomachs were too shrivelled up to hold solid meat. Two of the party who ignored the suggestion were violently ill and almost died. Soon, however, they were all feeding off the dead buffalo and felt some strength coming back to their bodies. Then they set out for the Red Deer Forks, where they stayed with a camp of Assiniboines who had plenty of food. After the Crees had fully regained their strength, they set out to look for Big Bear, using a lodge and horse that the Assiniboines had given them.

Travelling west along the river, Thunder Child's family finally discovered the village of Big Bear; he had stayed near the South Saskatchewan all winter. There had not been enough food to sustain them, and they, too, had eaten many of their horses and had seen some of their people die. Now they were beginning to move west, those with horses carrying the weak who could not walk. They were a pitiful sight, some being wasted away to mere skeletons; yet their spirits were high, because their hunters were beginning to find buffalo. Most of the herds were farther west, so Big Bear decided to test his tribe's peace treaty with the Blackfoot.

A small group, consisting of Big Bear and some scouts, went on ahead of the main party and succeeded in finding the Blackfoot camps. There they were greeted in a friendly manner, and the chief was assured that the peace pact was still firm. "Don't starve," they told Big Bear. "We have a great number of horses and plenty of food. We invite your people to visit us."[19] Big Bear was pleased with the news, and when his band straggled into the camp, he was gratified to see Blackfoot families welcome them and invite them to their lodges. A Blackfoot who owned a large tent took in Thunder Child and his family, and though neither group could speak the other's language, they communicated by signs and became good friends. Thunder Child's older brother gave his name to the Blackfoot boy, and when they finally left, the two Cree boys were each presented with a horse. These were the same people who would have slaughtered one another a few years earlier, but now the problems of starvation, whiskey traders and the ever-encroaching white man had made them allies against these greater foes. Big Bear, like most older chiefs, preferred peace to war and was happy to establish friendships among this tribe of fellow plainsmen.

In 1866 the holy men had predicted sickness, war and starvation when the Iron Stone had been taken. Now, in the spring of 1873, the third and last of these predictions had come to pass. Ever since the *Manito* guardian of the buffalo had been hauled away in a white man's cart, one tragedy after another had befallen the Cree tribe.

Big Bear recalled his first vision, which had told him that the white man was coming and would take his land. Perhaps when they got there, no Cree would be left to oppose them; they would all be dead from smallpox, poisonous whiskey or starvation. Big Bear learned that even Little Pine, who had hunted close to the Blackfoot all winter, had seen forty of his band starve to death. Big Bear's followers were still scattered over the plains, but he knew the mortality rate would be great among them as well.

As soon as his people were fit to travel, they headed north towards Fort Pitt, hoping to find buffalo along the way. But soon they were hungry again, and by the time they reached the fort in April, many of them were destitute. "Indians have been arriving here every day," said the Hudson's Bay Company trader, "and all Starving. Several old men and old women died on the road coming in, owing to Starvation. They were left by their friends where they were, not able to walk. A grate [sic] many of the men, women & children scarcly [sic] got to the Fort, they were so week [sic]. One woman arrived here alone starving with a Child on her Back nearly dead and during the night the Child died and was eaten by the Dogs. The skull of the Child was found next morning about the horse guard."

"It was pityfull [sic] to see them when they first arrived," he continued. "There are now 70 Tents about the Fort and all living out of the Company's Store. I am Spending all the provisions we had in Store, all our pounded meat and Scraps; wheat & Barley is done with the exception of a little Barley that I am Keeping for Seed. They bring Horses, Robes, Guns & Clothing to trade provisions. I have been now a long time in the Company's service and never had so much trouble with Indians as we are having this winter."[20]

Shortly after arriving at the fort, Big Bear saw a fight break out between two brothers over a bag of pemmican. The younger brother lost the argument and stalked away from the camp; a short time later, he crossed the river to the place where the Hudson's Bay Company cattle herd was grazing and angrily began to shoot at them. By the time Big Bear raced to the scene, the man had already killed one of the bulls and was still firing wildly at the herd. Firmly, the chief ordered the man to stop and lectured everyone about respecting the traders' property. During the next few weeks, even though they were starving, Big Bear discouraged his people from causing trouble. He knew that the traders were doing their best to feed the hungry camps.

When it became obvious that they would die if they stayed in the north, Big Bear took his followers out to the plains again. There were no buffalo between Fort Pitt and Red Deer River, so he turned to the southeast to join the bands from Eagle Hills. There he learned of a large herd farther east of the hills, but it was being controlled by a camp of half-breeds from the St. Laurent settlement.

Big Bear resented the half-breeds for their incursions into Cree lands. Many of them were intermarried with the Cree, but they hunted in their own fashion, travelling in large companies and using a militaristic type of organization that went far beyond the Cree idea of co-operative hunting. Before leaving their settlements, the half-breeds elected a captain and drafted a set of laws that everyone had to follow during the entire hunt. Anyone who joined them on the trail was also bound by these laws and could not leave the company once he had joined. Big Bear knew about their rules, but he thought laws should be made only by those who controlled the land, and he saw the half-breeds as interlopers living off Cree buffalo. Not only that, but with their trains of Red River carts and their organized system of hunting, they could slaughter thousands of buffalo and decimate an entire region.

However, the only herd accessible to the starving Crees was the one being followed by the St. Laurent hunters, so Big Bear had no choice but to go to their camp. Yet in his mind, he was going on his own terms, not theirs. When he got there, he found three other Cree bands, amounting to forty lodges, but most of the hunters were half-breeds from St. Laurent, with others from as far away as Wood Mountain and Qu'Appelle.

Big Bear was in a surly humour when he entered the camp at the head of his small band. He rode directly to the lodge of the leader, Gabriel Dumont, where he was invited to eat. However, no sooner had he sat down than he put a request to the half-breed captain, probably that his people be allowed to hunt on their own without interference. *"Nemoia!* No!" thundered Dumont.[21] Without saying another word, Big Bear angrily wrapped his blanket around him, still determined to achieve what he believed was fair and just, and stalked out of Dumont's tent.

Thwarted in his first attempt to hunt without interference, Big Bear dispatched six young men to secretly split the herd and drive some of the animals across the river towards his own camp. This would still leave plenty for the half-breeds, and he could hunt the second herd without interference or restriction. The fact that he would be breaking their rules by leaving their camp was of no consequence to him. Shortly afterwards, a half-breed scout reported that the main herd was moving westward, and that only small bands remained near the camp. He was sure that they were being deliberately hazed away.

Dumont called a meeting of the half-breed leaders and sent for the four Cree chiefs. At first, Big Bear refused to appear, so the messenger was ordered to get him. The Cree chief finally arrived, "his humped-up shoulders set in defiance."[22] When Dumont demanded to know if all the young Crees were in camp, the three other chiefs nodded, but Big Bear was evasive. "I can't be sure. My young men come and go as they please."

"You are the chief, are you not?"

"Yes, but I have not much control over them."

"You're not much of a chief, then."

"I am chief . . ." protested Big Bear, rising to his feet.

"Oh yes," answered Dumont. "I know what sort of chief you are. You're a dirty thieving chief, that's what you are; and if any of your young men have had a hand in this, it won't be well for you."[23]

Insulted and humiliated, Big Bear stamped out of the council, followed by the other equally perturbed chiefs.

The next day, Dumont, his cousin Petit Jean and trader John Kerr set out to search for the herd and came upon Big Bear's young men, who were urging a few buffalo across the river. Only a small part of the herd had actually gone to the other side. The trio galloped down the hill, firing their guns in the air to stampede the entire herd away from the river and back towards the half-breed camp. During the round up, they caught one of the young Indians, who told the half-breed council that Big Bear had instructed them to cut out only a few hundred animals so they would not be missed, but they had failed and inadvertently moved the entire herd.

When Big Bear was confronted with the evidence, he admitted his plan, but stressed that no one would have been bothered if his instructions had been followed and that his starving band could have hunted without interference from the bigger camp. Big Bear was neither apologetic nor cowed by the blustering threats of the councillor, and "when his back-talk became too saucy for Gabriel, [the half-breed] jumped up, grabbed a gun from an onlooker, and jabbed the chief in the stomach with the butt-end, telling him if he didn't know how to talk decently, he'd soon show him."[24]

The whole episode was a bitter experience for Big Bear and created a rift that never healed. In the end, the half-breed council seized a horse, cart and harness belonging to the recalcitrant chief and gave them to a Wood Mountain half-breed. The six young men were then ordered to drive back as many as possible of the scattered animals to rejoin the main herd.

The ugly incident raised the whole question of who controlled that region of the West. Was it the Canadian government, which had paid money to the Hudson's Bay Company but had never sent a representative to deal with the Indians? Was it the half-breeds, who seemed to practise the idea that "might is right" to enforce their laws? Or was it the Cree, who considered themselves to be the aboriginal inhabitants of the land?

Prelude to Treaty

E VER SINCE 1870 the Canadian government had been talking about signing treaties with tribes along the Saskatchewan River but had initially postponed taking action because of the Red River troubles. Another
reason for the delay was that the government knew treaties signed in 1871
in Manitoba already were the basis for criticism and unrest. "The Indians
treated with in 1871 are dissatisfied with the treaty," commented a member of parliament in 1873. "Unaccustomed in the interior to the use of
money, they formed a very incorrect idea of the value of the bank bills in
which they were paid. [They] found that three dollars [treaty money]
only represented three pounds of tobacco, or two and a half pounds of tea,
or five yards of print. Dissatisfaction was the result."[1]

Officials in the West were sure that the Saskatchewan Cree would
want more money, and the Indian commissioner observed, "I have little
hope that they will be satisfied with $3 a year. They have already said
that the white people are killing their only means of living and that they
see nothing but starvation before them."[2]

Relations between the Cree and the government continued to deteri-
orate, as the Indians heard many rumours about a treaty but received
very little direct information. Each spring, traders returning from Red
River would say that the Big White Chiefs were coming to make a treaty
with the Cree, but no one would come. "They now have the idea," said
a traveller, "that no treaty is to be made with them, but that settlers are
slowly moving west, occupying their country, killing their game and
burning the woods and prairies."[3]

In spite of warnings from missionary George McDougall not to send
surveyors into the West before treaties were made, the advice was
ignored, adding to the Indians' unsettled state. In 1872, W. S. Gore came
out to survey the property around each Hudson's Bay Company post,
causing some Indians to believe that they were already starting to lose
their land. A year later, Robert Bell began a geological survey west from

The Elbow of the South Saskatchewan River. His presence caused much unrest, and one Cree chief, Little Bear, even travelled ahead of him "to announce to the Indians of the region to which we were going, that we were enemies of the Indians."[4] The surveyor complained that "on several occasions Indians threatened to steal our horses & outfit & even to kill us all; and finally ordered us to turn back."[5] In addition, surveyors of the international boundary between Canada and the United States had started near Lake of the Woods in 1871 and were moving steadily westward towards the hunting grounds of the Plains Cree.

Seeds of doubt and suspicion had been cast everywhere by each action or inaction on the part of Canadian officials. Had the government acted promptly in 1870, relations would have been amicable enough to sign a pact, but as each passing year saw a decrease in buffalo herds, an increase in destitution and more unauthorized incursions by surveyors, the Indians became fearful and defiant. Even the peaceful Sweet Grass was obliged to think of possible war with the Canadians. When the chief had once travelled to Winnipeg with Father Lacombe, he had seen the military force at Fort Garry and "imagined that the soldiers he saw here were all that Canada could turn out, and, upon his return, impressed his people with the belief that 'they could clean the Canadians out.' "[6]

But as Little Pine told a white visitor, his people "would be sorry to have to open a war with us," and the whites should stay at home where they had plenty of food to eat, instead of robbing the Indians of their only food.[7]

During this period of unrest and hardship, Big Bear was forced to stay out on the plains all the year round in order to survive. After his humiliating experience with Gabriel Dumont, he took his band southward to hunt the buffalo herds northeast of the Cypress Hills and went north in the fall only to trade. At long last, his transition from the woodlands to the plains was complete.

In the eight years he had been a chief, Big Bear had proven to be such a dynamic and effective leader that many families were gradually drifting to his camp. From twelve lodges, or about a hundred people, the band had grown dramatically to sixty-five lodges containing more than five hundred men, women and children. His band was even larger than that of the peaceful Sweet Grass, whose following had slipped to fifty-six lodges since he had embraced Christianity. Although Big Bear commanded the largest camp in the Fort Pitt region and was surpassed only by Bobtail in the entire upper Saskatchewan region, he still acknowledged Sweet Grass as spokesman, and the two men remained close friends. He was concerned, however, that the priests were constantly with Sweet Grass, counselling him and advising him about the forthcoming treaties. More and more, Sweet Grass was prepared to accept the inevitable and, like the other Christian Indians, to turn to farming, even while the buffalo still coursed the plains.

To Big Bear, this was a mistake. A keenly intelligent man, the chief could see, like Sweet Grass, that the buffalo herds were dwindling and that starvation was becoming commonplace. Big Bear's solution, however, was not to give in and settle on a small plot of land but to find some way to protect the herds and keep the land inviolate for the Indians. He despised the American hide hunters who were using repeating rifles to kill hundreds of buffalo and then putting strychnine in their carcasses to kill prairie wolves for their skins; too often, an Indian camp dog found the animal first and died in agony. He also objected to the half-breeds who came from as far away as Manitoba to destroy the last of the herds, and he even saw the Hudson's Bay Company itself as a detriment to the Indians because of the tons of dried meat it needed each year to feed its servants. Some method had to be found — perhaps a treaty with the government — that would let the Christian Indians farm but would save the buffalo and the prairies for those who wanted to keep their freedom and retain the old ways. Thousands of buffalo still roamed the plains, and each spring the cows gave birth to a new herd of orange-coloured calves, but the cycle of nature could remain intact only if the white man with his repeating rifles and insatiable greed could be controlled.

Big Bear was a good-natured, friendly man, but when the survival of his band demanded it, he could be shrewd, stubborn and unyielding. And more and more, during those early years of the 1870s, he realized his people were hurtling headlong into chaos and tragedy, unless something could be done. And he, Big Bear, was determined to try.

Now that his band had grown so large, he had some good men to help him. His two oldest sons, Twin Wolverine and *Imasees,* had their father's dogmatic strong will, which had carried them on successful war expeditions against the Blackfoot. They had heard his discussions with fellow chiefs about the problems with the white people and shared his concern for the future, even if they were still too young to command the respect of the elders.

Wandering Spirit, who had an Ojibwa heritage, was a leading warrior who joined Big Bear's band sometime during this period and aspired to leadership. He had taken thirteen scalps in battle, more than Big Bear himself. On one occasion, he had pursued a Blackfoot hunter on foot across the open prairie until he killed and scalped him in the trees.

Little Poplar was another member of the camp who was rising in popularity. Among his many wives was *Imasees'* sister-in-law, so he was related to Big Bear; among the Cree, relationships across marriage lines were often considered to be as close as blood lines. Little Poplar, a handsome young man and a dandy around the camp, had a keen mind and an aggressive nature, which commanded respect and attention wherever he went. A wanderer, he had spent considerable time with the Crow Indians and had a wife from that tribe.

Lucky Man was older than the rising young leaders in the camp, and he too was associated with Big Bear's family through marriage. Not as hotheaded or temperamental as Wandering Spirit and Little Poplar, he was a firm but conservative leader who inspired confidence among his own small group of followers.

Another man associated with Big Bear's camp, though he often travelled separately, was Half Blackfoot Chief, who once had been a leading warrior. His spiritual power came from a frog that had spoken to him in a vision and told him where to find a Blackfoot horse herd. The Indian had led a raiding party to the place, and sure enough, the animals were there ready to be taken. On another occasion, Half Blackfoot Chief was given a song that enabled him to strike his target every time he fired his gun.

Most of Big Bear's active followers — the ones who would ultimately become leaders — were young men in their late twenties or early thirties: Four Sky Thunder, The Singer, Strong Eyes and Black Star had all been to war and were now married and raising families. Still too young to serve on the councils, some tended to be wild and outspoken, believing that all their problems could be solved through war or a show of force. The older men were more conservative, both within and beyond Big Bear's camp. This in itself created a problem, for many Cree leaders had become too old, too Christianized, or both, to want to confront the Canadian government. Little Hunter was well on in years, while old *Kehiwin* was already showing signs of blindness. Sweet Grass was ten years older than Big Bear and, because of the influence of the priests, he now considered his years on the warpath as evidence of "what evil I once did."[8]

Little Pine was perhaps the only older chief prepared to bargain openly and firmly with the government. Like Big Bear, he was not affected by the influence of the clergy, and while essentially a man of peace, he had a keen sense of what was just or unjust. Big Bear and Little Pine seemed to be the only two willing to speak for the vast majority of Saskatchewan River Crees who wanted to save their land and their buffalo.

★ ★ ★

In 1873, the Canadian government finally began to act on its western policies. John A. Macdonald, the prime minister, organized a police force for the West: some of the men had wintered south of Winnipeg, training for their forthcoming duties, but the rest were still being recruited in eastern Canada. In the meantime, officials found it expedient to sign a treaty with the Ojibwa Indians east of Winnipeg, near Lake of the Woods. On foot, by cart and by steamboat, soldiers and other Canadians had been using the Dawson Trail to travel through Indian lands and causing considerable unrest among the native inhabitants. Aware of the dissatisfaction over the two earlier treaties, the government increased the annuities to five dollars per person for Treaty Three and added agricultural equipment though the basic terms remained the same.

Next, in the summer of 1874, the authorities headed for the prairies to negotiate Treaty Four with the Cree, Ojibwa and Assiniboine in the Qu'Appelle region. The meeting proved to be a stormy affair; the Ojibwa in particular were hostile about the previous survey of lands around the trading posts and the payment made by the Canadian government to the Hudson's Bay Company. This money, they said, should have gone to the Indians, because the territory belonged to them. They refused to start the negotiations until the meeting was moved away from Hudson's Bay Company property and then said that the government offer was too niggardly. Instead of five dollars per person, the Cree asked for twenty dollars, while the Ojibwa wanted their debts with the Hudson's Bay Company cancelled. When this was rejected, they tried for fifteen dollars a year. However, the commissioners were not there to negotiate but to offer a previously prepared deal, and in the end the Indians agreed to accept the same terms as had been given to the Lake of the Woods Indians.

Piapot, brother-in-law of Little Pine, had not been informed about the treaty and was disappointed when he finally saw the document. Later, when he was asked to sign his adhesion to the treaty, he requested additional items; since he did not get an outright refusal, he believed his request had been granted.

Some politicians thought the government was acting irresponsibly in the whole treaty-making procedure, and one member of parliament questioned its basic ethics. "Our laws declare him a minor," he said of the Indians, "and yet we drive as hard a bargain with him as though he were a land-jobber, and when other arguments have failed to make him accept the terms, we plainly give him to understand, in a spirit of civilized barbarity, that might is right, and that we will have his lands."[9]

When the North-West Mounted Police were ready to set out to establish posts near Edmonton and Fort Whoop-Up, Big Bear at last had a chance to meet his first government-appointed official. To prepare the way for the peaceful passage of the force, the authorities selected two men to visit the Indians to let them know the police were coming. But they were not officials from the federal government in Ottawa or the territorial government in Winnipeg. Rather, William McKay, the Hudson's Bay Company trader at Fort Pitt, was chosen to contact the Cree, and missionary John McDougall the Blackfoot.

After travelling for five days south from his fort, McKay arrived at Big Bear's camp — the first of six he contacted on his tour. "On my arrival," said the trader, "I explained the reasons which have induced the Queen (our Great Mother) to send a troop of Police men into Her North West Territories, and to send also a portion of Her troops with a party of American Soldiers to mark out the line between Her Territories and those of the United States, so that Her Indian & White subjects might know where the lands of the Queen begins."[10] Big Bear was asked to regard this expedition with goodwill and a friendly eye. He also was told that the Mounted Police would preserve law and order and drive away the American whiskey traders, but that they did not have a military purpose. After delivering this message, McKay gave out presents of ammunition, tea, sugar, tobacco, pipes and, oddly enough, fifteen scalping knives.

There were some violent reactions to the presents from people in Big Bear's camp, who were immediately suspicious and protested that these items were "given them as a bribe to facilitate a future treaty."[11] In subsequent visits to the camps of Sweet Grass, Bobtail and other leaders, however, McKay found that the Indians were pleased to at last have had some word from the government. The news that the troops were coming in friendship was greeted with relief.

With the arrival of the North-West Mounted Police in the West in 1874, everyone believed that the treaty along the Saskatchewan would be negotiated in the following year. There was no further excuse to vaccilate, and all the Indians knew of the treaty signed at Qu'Appelle. Now they were the last of the Plains Cree and Assiniboine who had not treated with the government. However, in spite of the urgency of the situation, the federal government informed the Crees in 1875 "that it is impossible to make a Treaty in August of this year owing to other pressing matters and that it may not be possible to do so this year."[12] Inevitably, the result of this postponement was a further wave of hostility and suspicion. As for Big Bear, the delay convinced him that the government was a man in faraway Ottawa who could not be trusted. Like most Indians, he saw the government not as a faceless gaggle of bureaucrats, but as a single man, elderly (hence his prestige), rich (hence the gifts) and desirous of owning the Cree lands. This man, Government, was second in rank only to the Queen, a chief woman who lived across the great sea in the same village as the man they called the Hudson's Bay Company. They must live in the same place, for how else could the Queen tell the Hudson's Bay Company he could sell the Cree lands to the government?

From this point on, Big Bear believed that the government was capable of being a fork-tongued liar and that anything officials said had to be treated with caution. No longer could Big Bear hear their words and believe them; instead, he had to search for the real meaning, look for trickery and wait for evidence to prove they were speaking with a straight tongue. If a man broke his word once, he was capable of doing it again and again.

The Christian Indians were more trusting than Big Bear, but even their patience was stretched to the limit when a train of carts, mowers, rakes and cattle arrived at Carlton House in the summer of 1875, destined for the West. When the chiefs inquired, they were told that the caravan was going to build a government telegraph line through Cree lands to Edmonton. Along the way, they would be cutting Cree timber for poles and using Cree grass to feed their cattle.

Star Blanket and Big Child, the two leading chiefs of the Carlton area, protested this incursion. No treaty had been made. No one had told them that the contractors were coming, and no permission had been sought to travel across their lands; they had no intention of letting anyone cut trees or grass until a treaty was made. After some discussion, however, the two suspicious chiefs agreed to permit the men to cross their area, doing no building but leaving caches of wire and supplies along the way so they could work more quickly once the treaty was made.

Neither Star Blanket nor Big Child realized how far the telegraph line would go, and when they learned that the men were leaving their hunting grounds and going into the territory of Sweet Grass, Big Bear and Little Pine, they sent three of their soldiers to stop them. These men caught up with the caravan near Grizzly Bear Coulee, directly south of Fort Pitt, and saw for the first time how the telegraph wire would be laid across the prairie.

"My chief is Big Child," said the leading warrior. "He told me to tell you not to go any farther until a treaty is made. I never saw wire like that before. If we allowed you to put it up, it would frighten all the game away. We want the government to send a man to tell us what their intentions are, whether the government likes us or hates us. It is going to make a treaty with us or it is going to take our country by force?"[13]

Fortunately for the contractors, Big Bear and his followers were out on the plains and did not hear of the incident until after it was resolved. Otherwise, hotheads like Little Poplar and *Imasees* might not have hesitated to take more direct action to see that the caravan left their hunting grounds in a hurry. Big Bear was far south of Fort Pitt, for the buffalo

had drifted to the east and he had been obliged to follow them. He could
see that the herds were thinning out more each year, but once his band
found a good concentration of buffalo, they lived well.

Meanwhile, the measures taken by Star Blanket and Big Child to turn
back the telegraph party shocked the government into action. It was one
thing for Indians to talk endlessly about broken promises, but it was
quite another to halt a government-sponsored caravan and order it out
of the territory. By this time, government officials had commissioned
missionary George McDougall to tell the Indians the treaty meeting
would take place in July 1876 at Carlton House and Fort Pitt. He was in
the field before the telegraph incident took place, so Supt. L. N. F. Crozier of the North-West Mounted Police was appointed a second emissary
to the same Cree camps. Now, instead of one messenger from the
government, the Cree suddenly had two who came to their villages
within months of each other, both reassuring the Indians about the
government's good intentions.

McDougall was the first to go, spending the late summer and early
autumn visiting twenty-two camps all the way from Green Lake to the
South Saskatchewan. Big Child and Beardy, in the Carlton area, were
reassured by the missionary's words, but his real test came when he
went to the plains to see the Fort Pitt Crees. Unfortunately for him, the
docile Sweet Grass was absent, so Big Bear was the leading figure there.
McDougall saw Sweet Grass's young son, Little Man, who was only
twenty-six years old, and received from him and the head men in the
band "their thanks for the presents received and they expressed the
greatest loyalty to the Government."[14] But Big Bear was not impressed
by these promises from the government or by its generous gifts. In his
first vision as a youth he had been warned about the "bounteous presents
from the Great Mother," and here they were now being proferred amid
assurances that the government would treat them justly.[15]

"We want none of the Queen's presents!" Big Bear exclaimed to the
missionary. "When we set a fox trap we scatter pieces of meat all around
but when the fox gets into the trap we knock him on the head. We want
no baits! Let your Chiefs come like men and talk to us."[16]

In his report, McDougall derided Big Bear, calling him "a Soto
[Ojibwa] trying to take the lead in their Council," when in fact, with
sixty-five lodges, his band was in the majority at the camp. With Sweet
Grass away, he was the proper spokesman, but the missionary painted
him as an outsider who "formerly lived at Jack-fish Lake and for years
has been regarded as a troublesome fellow. These Sotos are the mischief
makers through all this Western country and some of them are shrewd
men." He also discounted the importance of both the chief's position and
his speech, saying that "Big Bear and his party were a small minority in

camp. The Crees said they would have driven them out of camp long ago but were afraid of their medicines as they are noted conjurors."[17]

Although McDougall ridiculed the idea that Big Bear's speech had any validity, he conceded that all the Cree and Assiniboine on the plains were united on one point: "That they would not receive any presents from Government until a definite time for treaty was stated."[18] Of course, this was simply another way of phrasing Big Bear's own words.

This report brought Big Bear to the attention of authorities in a significant way for the first time. It was unfortunate, therefore, that he should be painted as an obstreperous Ojibwa who had no support from the Cree camp. In truth, he was considered to be a Plains Cree, and the increasing size of his own band was mute testimony to his leadership and reputation. Yet the die had been cast, and instead of being regarded as a brilliant leader who was trying to find an equitable solution to his people's problems, he was tagged simply as a troublemaker.

The problems that lay before Big Bear were formidable. On one hand, he wanted to preserve the buffalo as long as possible, but he also appreciated the fact that many Indians were beginning to live by agriculture. At this stage, he did not want his people to be tied down to farms but preferred to let them range free across the open plains as long as there were buffalo to sustain them. When the end came, he knew they would be dependent upon the government to mold a new life for themselves, but already Ottawa had proven itself to be untrustworthy. He bore no hatred toward the police and others in authority; he simply wanted to be treated fairly and honestly.

Some politicians from the West appreciated the problems faced by Big Bear and other chiefs. "We know that our occupation of the Saskatchewan valley means the disappearance of the buffalo and other prairie animals," said a member of parliament. "We know that to the prairie Indians these animals are more than manna was to the wandering Israelite; their flesh feeds him, their skins clothe him, and their hides form the house he lives in. The question, then, to consider is: What are we to give him in compensation for his hunting grounds?"[19]

An estimated 160,000 buffalo a year were being slaughtered on the Canadian plains, mostly by American hide hunters from Montana and half-breeds from various settlements on the prairies. Yet neither the government in Ottawa nor the North-West Territories Council was prepared to implement and enforce hunting restrictions. Rather, they seemed to accept the rapid extinction of the buffalo as inevitable and directed their attention to providing "farm instructors and cattle and implements and opportunities to become agriculturists or herdsmen."[20]

The second government emissary, Superintendent Crozier of the North-West Mounted Police, set out in the autumn of 1875 to convince the Indians of the Saskatchewan region not to interfere with federal telegraph lines or roads. He brought with him further presents from the government and a solemn promise that the treaty session would take place as scheduled. But he had come too late in the season, and by the time he reached Carlton House, the only Indians left there were the aged and the sick. Crozier then set out for Fort Pitt, but the only chief still there was Big Bear, who had come in with his family to trade. The chief adamantly refused to accept any gifts from the government, saying that he and his followers "wished to take nothing until the treaty was made."[21] It was a strange anomaly that a year later, Crowfoot, who would not accept presents for the same reason as Big Bear, was lauded for his actions. "I could not help wishing," said Commissioner David Laird of Crowfoot at that time, "that other Indians whom I have seen, had a little of the spirit in regard to dependence upon the Government exhibited on this occasion by the great Chief of the Blackfeet." Yet when Big Bear refused the gifts, he was simply "a troublesome fellow."[22]

Big Bear spoke with Crozier and "did his utmost to persuade me not to take out the presents, saying the Indians were already satisfied with the presents and promises of the Treaty they had received. He, as well as others of experience in the Country, said it would be all but impossible to see the Indians at such a season as they would be greatly scattered, many of them already having gone south of the Red Deer River."[23] Obviously, Big Bear would not encourage the officer to embark upon a mission that the chief believed was morally wrong, so when Crozier asked him to go ahead to round up the camps, he again refused, claiming that it could not be done. Crozier found the chief's comments "to be true, having heard so many discouraging accounts from every person of the impossibility at that season of reaching the Indians."[24] But the officer set out for the plains in spite of Big Bear's opposition and managed to contact only one camp near the Eye Hills before he suddenly became deranged. His interpreter sent an urgent message back to the factor at Fort Pitt, saying that "Captain Crozier was Crazey [sic] and for me to go out and see him or tell him what to do with the Captain."[25] Still, the officer persisted in his mission, going to other Cree camps as far south as the Hand Hills and west to Buffalo Lake. He wandered about "in most wretched health" and must have been an awesome spectacle in the prairie camps.[26] Crozier finally showed up at Big Gully, where a trader said, "I think the man is almost out of his mind."[27] Unwilling to leave him in that condition, the trader contacted Col. James Macleod, the assistant commissioner, who arranged to escort the officer to Fort Macleod. There Crozier made a rapid recovery and a month later was able to write a clear and lucid account of his journey.

The Indians did not believe that incidents like this occurred by mere happenstance. Most often, a man went temporarily insane due to the incantations of a powerful shaman, or because a supernatural spirit had inhabited his body. The fact that the Queen's representative had been afflicted would have been perceived by some — the non-Christian Indians in particular — as an ominous sign, or warning. If Crozier's condition had been caused by a Woods Cree or Ojibwa shaman — the ones with the greatest powers — there would have been incantations made and a secret mixture of roots and herbs placed into the claw of a hawk or eagle from the man's medicine bundle. If possible, the shaman would have a nail cutting or a lock of hair from the policeman to more effectively cast the spell. Then, during the darkness of night, the bird spirit would fly to the poor unfortunate and render him insane. The curse usually remained effective only as long as the medicine itself was believed to be potent, or while the afflicted subject remained close at hand. The elders still talk about the time such medicine was used by a Woods Cree upon Emile Petitot, a Roman Catholic priest at Fort Pitt. The curse the shaman placed upon him was to remain effective as long as he and the priest were not separated by water. It is recorded that Petitot did indeed become insane late in 1881 and not until he returned to France did he effect a full recovery.

So it was with Crozier. As he wandered in and out of prairie camps, the Indians must have wondered who had used their magic powers to render him insane. Coincidentally, at the very time that Crozier was experiencing his problems, missionary George McDougall — the first messenger to the Crees — died on the prairies near Fort Calgary, less than three months after he had completed his task of informing the Indians about the treaty meeting. These two representatives of the Queen, bringing news of the forthcoming treaty, seemed to be harbingers of disaster.

The treaty of 1876 was to be the last of six involving Cree and Ojibwa bands that would be immediately affected by white settlement. The first three, all in Manitoba, had extinguished the claims of Indians who had been affected by the growth of the Red River settlement. Treaty Four at Qu'Appelle had gained the surrender of the southern Saskatchewan prairies, and in 1875 a treaty had been concluded with the trapping and fishing Indians of northern Manitoba. They had presented no problem, the terms accepted by them being even more niggardly than those given their southern relatives. However, the government had no illusions that the Saskatchewan Cree would be as docile as the other Indians had been. They knew the chiefs had strong ideas "as to the conditions and stipulations whereby they would conclude a Treaty at all with the Commissioners, and seemed quite indifferent on the matter, unless they received better terms than had been given to other Indians."[28] The long and unnecessary delays had given Indian leaders time to learn of the dissatisfaction in other treaty areas and to gain some appreciation of the government's need to settle with them. The Cree were also aware that prospectors were seeking gold in their western territories and that the region contained vast areas of valuable agricultural land. Some chiefs were familiar with United States treaties and believed that tribes like the Sioux had received better deals from their government even though they had been at war with them.

On the other hand, many Indians who had accepted the fact that the buffalo were being exterminated were terrified about the future. They already had experienced one season of starvation because of the scarcity of buffalo and wanted assurance of government help until they learned how to farm. So the pressures both for and against a treaty were present within the camps.

A number of Crees north of the Saskatchewan had already accepted the inevitable and were starting to farm near mission stations, though a shortage of plows, seed and other supplies limited them to tiny plots of land, which were little more than gardens. But, clearly, they were ready to create a new food base for themselves once the buffalo were gone. Those who spent part of their lives in the woodlands could make the transition fairly easily, as they already were accustomed to using a variety of food resources to sustain themselves. During some parts of the year they fished, at other times they hunted big game or went to the plains to hunt buffalo; digging in the soil for wild turnips and other edible roots had already made them aware of the benefits of agriculture.

The Plains Cree, on the other hand, knew only the prairie herds. At times they might deign to eat lesser foods, but just until they could return to the red meat of the buffalo. Some, like Big Bear, had known both the woodlands and plains but had gradually adopted more and more ways of the prairies; they saw farming as a possible future life, but not as long as buffalo were still wandering the plains. Big Bear made no attempt to till the soil and had no intention of doing so until driven to it in order to survive. Even Sweet Grass, who had embraced Christianity and had spent considerable time at the mission at St. Paul des Cris, was more willing to let the priests do the cultivating than to have his hunters take on what was considered to be demeaning work.

On the date appointed for the treaty negotiations, the commissioners were on hand at Carlton House for the first round of discussions. They consisted of Alexander Morris, lieutenant-governor of the North-West Territories; William J. Christie, a retired Hudson's Bay Company factor, and the Honourable James McKay, a well-educated Métis who was minister of agriculture in Manitoba. All had had previous experience in treaty negotiations.

Most of the Carlton House Indians were there, led by Big Child and Star Blanket. Of the eight chiefs in attendance, four of them, including the two leaders, were Christians. Prominent among those missing was Beardy of the Willow Cree, who had had a vision in which he had been told to discuss treaty only on a certain hill near his camp. He had asked for a change in venue for the sessions but had been curtly refused.

Also in attendance was a large contingent of Mounted Police, who paraded with their brass band through the Cree camp. "They were quite excited," commented a policeman, "never having seen or heard a band before. A number of squaws were running into their tepees crying, 'We are losing our country.' "[29] Others at Carlton included a flock of missionaries representing the Methodists, Roman Catholics and Anglicans of the region and many traders, some of whom had come all the way from Manitoba and Montana to share in the bonanza when the Indians spent their treaty money. Big Bear did not attend these sessions, but he was aware that the discussions would have a major impact upon the bands in the Fort Pitt area. The acceptance or rejection of the treaty at Carlton would put pressure on the Fort Pitt bands to follow suit.

The Carlton House Crees set aside two days before the negotiations to meet among themselves to discuss their views and to choose their spokesmen. Then Commissioner Morris took two days to make his presentation, the first day being confined to explaining why treaties were being made across the land and to assure everyone of the Queen's interest in their future. On the second day, he lauded some of the bands for beginning to farm and said they should sign the treaty and choose reserves before large numbers of white people came. In that way, the Indians could have their pick of the best land. He told them that they would get the same as the Qu'Appelle Indians: 640 acres (256 ha) for every five persons. He also promised schools; farming and carpentry tools; cattle; liquor prohibition; uniforms, medals and flags for the chiefs; $1,500 a year for ammunition and twine; a twelve-dollar bonus to every man, woman and child for agreeing to the treaty, twenty-five dollars for chiefs, fifteen dollars for head men, and an agreement to pay annually forever, five dollars to each man, woman and child, twenty-five dollars for chiefs and fifteen dollars for head men.

The Cree took an entire day to discuss the terms among themselves. The next day, Sunday, the Anglican and Roman Catholic missionaries held services, mingled freely with their respective flocks and undoubtedly pressed the chiefs to accept the treaty and take reserves. The Reverend John McKay commented a few days later: "By gathering them into settlements we shall have the opportunity of enlightening them on

the one all important point, their need of the Gospel."[30] From the beginning, it was apparent that Big Child and Star Blanket favoured the
treaty, but some others opposed it. These included Poundmaker, Badger
and Joseph Toma, speaking for both a Cree minority and many of the
Ojibwa. None was a leading chief, but together they represented a
goodly number of people in the camp.

Poundmaker was unmoved by the favourable response of the senior
chiefs, exclaiming during the sessions: "The governor mentions how
much land is to be given to us. He says 640 acres, one mile square for
each family, he will give us. This is our land! It isn't a piece of pemmican
to be cut off and given in little pieces back to us. It is ours and we will
take what we want."[31]

Similarly, *Nuswasoowahtum,* an Ojibwa leader from Quill Lake,
believed that the Crees were being exploited and should take more time
to consider the consequences. "All along the prices have been to one
side," he said, "and we have had no say." He told them that the Indians
should remain with their old way of life, given by "He that made us,"
rather than become like the white men, who seemed to believe that the
world was created for their convenience.[32]

Later, when discussions with the commissioners resumed, Poundmaker, Badger and several other Indians asked for promises that the
government would help them to make a living and give assistance until
they could fend for themselves. Commissioner Morris would not give
an unequivocal answer until Big Child and Star Blanket came to the
support of the dissidents and sought similar assurances. One Indian
expressed it this way: "If all the buffalo were allowed to be killed they
would expect the Great Mother to feed them."[33]

Commissioner Morris was unwilling to make such a commitment and,
in fact, had come with the intention of offering them the same terms
accepted by the Qu'Appelle Indians, and nothing more. When that was
made plain to the chiefs, they asked for a further postponement, so that
they could draft their reply in writing. Unfortunately, the chiefs then
started to quibble over details and made no attempt to address the larger
issues before them. The possibility of introducing controls to preserve the
buffalo was never mentioned, nor was the value of the land examined in
comparision to the gifts being offered. Poundmaker was the only one
who seemed to grasp the broader questions of their loss of freedom and
their complete dependence on the government if they accepted.

The chiefs were satisfied with the $1,500 for ammunition, which was
twice as much as the amount offered at Qu'Appelle, and using this as a
guide, began to double as many of the offers as possible: four hoes
instead of two; two scythes, spades and axes instead of one; one plow for
three people instead of for ten; one harrow for three people instead of for

four; four oxen instead of two. They also added a boar, two pigs and a hand mill per band, as well as two hayforks, two reaping hooks and a whetstone. For the chiefs, they wanted a horse and harness, with either a wagon or two iron-rimmed carts.

To these requests, the commissioners readily acceded. They also agreed to give the Carlton people $1,000 a year for three years to help while they were getting established on their farms.

The main point of concern of the Indians was the threat of starvation, and the commissioners realized that without some general assurance, they probably would not sign the treaty. So after some deliberation, they added a phrase to the treaty that should the Indians be "overtaken by any pestilence, or by a general famine, the Queen . . . will grant to the Indians assistance of such character and to such extent as her Chief Superintendent of Indian Affairs shall deem necessary and sufficient to relieve the Indians from the calamity that shall have befallen them."[34]

In making these various concessions, the commissioners suspected that they would incur the wrath of Ottawa, as indeed they did. But as the Honourable James McKay noted, "it actually appeared at the time of negotiations that a Treaty could scarcely be concluded owing to the various demands of each Tribe."[35]

After Commissioner Morris had cited the list of changes he would accept, a few half-hearted efforts were made to negotiate further, but without success. The only man to clearly voice his displeasure was *Nuswasoowahtum,* who told the commissioners: "I would have been glad if every white man of every denomination were now present to hear what I say; through what you have done you have cheated my kinsmen."[36]

Yet the leading chiefs accepted the treaty and appeared to be satisfied with it. Their concern had been with the immediate threat of starvation, and the agreement had set their fears to rest. Interestingly enough, when they chose their reserves, the commissioner noted that "with one or two exceptions all these bands are cultivating the soil."[37]

In that respect, they were vastly different from the bands of Sweet Grass, Big Bear, Little Pine and others around Fort Pitt, who still were entirely buffalo-hunting Indians. Had the commissioners gone to Fort Pitt first, the negotiations might have taken a different turn. As it was, there was little concern at Carlton House about the buffalo, and not until a separate meeting was held with Beardy and his Willow Crees did the question arise. Both Beardy and his head man were worried about the rapidly disappearing herds and appealed to the commissioners to preserve them. Morris's answer was political and noncommittal, saying only that the North-West Council would "see if a wise law can be passed, one that will be a living law that can be carried out and obeyed."[38]

While the commissioners were at Carlton House, a priest told Morris that Sweet Grass had gone to the prairies to hunt and would not be at Fort Pitt for the negotiations. In the priest's opinion, "his absence would be a great obstruction to a treaty,"[39] so a messenger was sent to fetch him for the conference on 5 September. No one, however, tried to notify Big Bear or Little Pine to assure their presence.

As a result, when the negotiations were held at Fort Pitt, there were one hundred and seven lodges, but only twenty-five of them were Plains Crees under Sweet Grass. Most of the others were Wood Crees, Chipewyans and a few transitional people. According to census figures, Big Bear alone commanded a following of sixty-five lodges and *Sayakimat* another twenty, so the majority of Fort Pitt Crees were still out on the plains.

The chiefs who were present included *Kehiwin,* who with Sweet Grass was under Catholic influence; *Pakan* and Little Hunter, who were Methodists; Cut Arm, Frog Lake Chief and Thunder Companion, the leading non-Christians; and White Fish, from farther north, a chief of six lodges of Catholic Chipewyans. The bishop and a priest were there to represent Catholic interests, and there were also missionaries from the Methodist and Anglican churches. As well, many of the traders who had been at Carlton House had followed the commissioners' trail to Fort Pitt in hopes of more quick profits.

Sweet Grass had not yet appeared, so the sessions were postponed. Indians who were arriving daily brought news that the messengers had found the chief on the plains hunting buffalo and that he was now on his way in. He finally reached Fort Pitt late on the following day and the sessions were scheduled to begin on the seventh. However, before the treaty negotiations started, Sweet Grass and other leading chiefs met to find out what had happened at Carlton. One of their number, Little Hunter, had witnessed the affair, as had Peter Erasmus, an educated half-breed who lived in *Pakan*'s camp and had served as an interpreter at the Carlton sessions. Erasmus gave them a detailed account of the negotiations and, in an attempt to influence them to support the treaty, saved the acceptance speeches of Big Child and Star Blanket until last and "swung the whole opinion of the assembly in favour of the signing."[40] Little Hunter, too, gave a favourable report. Sweet Grass seemed to be more interested in what the Carlton chiefs had decided than in the terms themselves, and before the sessions even started, he made up his mind. He believed that Big Child and Star Blanket were far wiser then he, "therefore if they have accepted this treaty for their people after many days of talk and careful thought, then I am prepared to accept for my people."[41]

As a consequence, the sessions themselves were almost a formality. They began with an impressive parade, the Indians singing and drumming as they approached the commissioners' tent. At their head came a group of riders, all bedecked in their finery and so painted that one policeman thought they looked like devils. They went through the intricate paces of a sham battle and then retired, as the chiefs walked forward to take their places on the ground in front of the three commissioners. Four chiefs had brought their medicine pipes to Fort Pitt, and after a smoking ritual, Commissioner Morris tried to assure those present that "we wish to help you in the days that are to come, we do not want to take away the means of living that you now have, we do not want to tie you down."[42] He also said he was aware that Big Bear, Little Pine and others were not there and that they would be offered the same terms as those who were present.

The chiefs took the next day to discuss the specific details of the treaty. During this time, the clergymen spoke earnestly to their own converts. Bishop Grandin told Sweet Grass that he would send missionaries to all the reserves that were established and that the Chipewyans need not make any decisions without him being present. Methodist clergyman John McDougall told the chiefs about British justice and "Canadian Government fair play" and strongly advised them to accept the proposals as offered.[43]

When the session reassembled and the commissioners asked the chiefs if they had any questions or comments, no one answered. Morris feared that they were being obstructive and secretive, but he soon found out that their concurrence was such a foregone conclusion that no one had anything to say. At last, Sweet Grass arose and accepted the treaty. "I have pity on all those who have to live by the buffalo," he added, alluding to the missing chiefs, and said that "We will commence hand in hand to protect the buffalo." But as for himself, he intended to turn to farming in the spring.[44]

During these sessions the Christian Indians had dominated the treaty proceedings, just as they had at Carlton. "It was very gratifying to notice," commented missionary John McKay, "that the influence of the Christian Indians, although a small minority with regard to numbers, seemed to preponderate in the deliberations of the whole body."[45] Bishop Grandin agreed, reporting that "Sweet Grass requested that missionaries be provided for each reserve, and a school where children could learn to read, to pray, and to write. I must insist on the word pray as I have recognized that this expression was not taken into consideration during the drafting of the treaty. This word, in the Indians' mind means no more or no less: Christian Instruction. I do not know if the interpreter was faithful in his rendition of Sweet Grass' words, who spoke on behalf of all the Catholic chiefs."[46]

One result of the missionary involvement was, of course, that the feelings and concerns of the non-Christian buffalo hunters were not expressed. Intimidated as they were by the scarlet-coated Mounted Police, the richly uniformed commissioners and the stream of white men currying the favour of the Christian chiefs, such leaders as Thunder Companion and Cut Arm were reluctant to open their mouths. Neither wished to appear foolish in front of the dignitaries, nor more importantly, to be made to look silly in front of their bands. Cut Arm came closest to expressing a concern when he acknowledged that what he "once dreaded most is coming to my aid and doing for me what I could not do for myself."[47] It was, in effect, an expression of resignation, of accepting the inevitable.

Big Bear did not reach Fort Pitt until after the treaty had been signed, the reserves selected and the Indians given their presents. Not only had he learned of the meeting too late, but unlike Sweet Grass, he had been holding conferences with various camps of Crees and Assiniboines so that he could carry their messages as well as his own. He was understandably angry that Sweet Grass and the other chiefs had not waited for him. "I find it difficult to express myself," he told the commissioners in the presence of the treaty chiefs, "because some of the bands are not represented. I have come off to speak for the different bands that are out on the plains. It is no small matter we were to consult about. I expected the Chiefs here would have waited until I arrived. The different bands that are out on the plains told me that I should speak in their stead, the Stony Indians as well. The people who have not come stand as a barrier before what I would have had to say."[48] In effect, he did not believe that he could speak freely to the commissioners until he had delivered the messages from the other camps. But with the treaty discussions over, he had no forum in which to present their views.

Sweet Grass, somewhat defensively, tried to persuade Big Bear to accept what had already occurred. "My friend," he said, "you see the representative of the Queen here, who do you suppose is the maker of it [i.e., the treaty]. I think the Great Spirit put it into their hearts to come to our help. I feel as if I saw life when I see the representative of the Queen; let nothing be a barrier between you and him; it is through great difficulty this has been brought to us. Think of our children and those to come after; there is life and succor for them. Say yes, and take his hand."[49]

Big Bear did not share his fellow chieftain's gratitude for having the treaty offered to him. He had come to discuss specific terms, particularly the preservation of the buffalo, and was not prepared to take any deal without fully talking about it first. When *Pakan,* too, urged him to accept the treaty, he felt pressured and pushed their words away from him. "Stop, stop, my friends," he cried. "I have never seen the Governor before; I have seen Mr. Christie many times. I heard the Governor was to come and I said I shall see him. When I see him I will make a request that he will save me from what I most dread, that is: the rope to be about my neck (hanging)."[50]

During the negotiations at Carlton House and Fort Pitt, the commissioners had engaged the best interpreters they could find. The leading one was Peter Erasmus, who had a keen understanding of the finer points of the Plains Cree dialect. However, he had left for Whitefish Lake as soon as the Fort Pitt treaty was signed, so it is likely that the Reverend John McKay acted as translator of Big Bear's words. But McKay spoke Swampy Cree, and at Carlton he had become so confused while translating that he had been obliged to sit down. "I knew that McKay was not sufficiently versed in the Prairie Cree to confine his interpretations to their own language," complained Erasmus.[51]

What resulted from Big Bear's words at Fort Pitt was a classic example of a mistranslation creating a chain of confusion. When Big Bear spoke of having a rope around his neck, he was not talking about a fear of being hanged, as the interpreter indicated. Rather, he was using a common expression on the plains that denoted a person giving up his freedom. It was analogous to a wild horse having a rope placed around its neck so that it could no longer wander unfettered and free, making it a prisoner of the one who held the rope. Years later, when Poundmaker complained about being drawn into the Riel Rebellion, he said, "I felt as if there was a rope around my neck dragging me on to do it."[52] Similarly, at Treaty Seven, an old Indian medicine man predicted that in future "the whites will lead you by a halter."[53] Commissioner Morris had used a similar expression in his opening address when he told the Indians that "we do not want to tie you down."[54] And Big Bear alluded to the same theme again in 1884, when he said, "I feel sad to abandon the liberty of my own land."[55] Presumably, Big Bear's interpreter had confused the term *ay-saka-pay-kinit* (lead by the neck) with *ay-hah-kotit* (hanged by the neck).[56] Had the words been properly translated, Big Bear might have received an assurance from Morris that could have changed the course of history.

In his speech, Big Bear added a note of friendship when he said, "It was not given to us by the Great Spirit that the red man or white man should shed each other's blood."[57] Coupled with the mistranslation of his earlier statement, Morris concluded that Big Bear was opposed to capital punishment, that the white man should not be permitted to execute an Indian. He therefore launched into a long tirade that good Indians need not be afraid of hanging, that a person had a right to kill someone in self-defence but not in cold blood.

Big Bear must have wondered what in the world the commissioner was talking about. The chief did not even try to pursue this convoluted line of discussion but politely changed the conversation: "What we want is that we should hear what will make our hearts glad, and all good people's hearts glad." Then, he added, returning to his original theme, "There were plenty of things left undone, and it does not look well to leave them so."[58]

"I do not know what has been left undone," said Morris.[59]

With a shrug, Big Bear indicated that he would have to speak to his people before he could continue. The words he brought with him were meant for discussion prior to the treaty, not for argument afterwards. He could only repeat that he did not want to lose his freedom, but again it was mistranslated: "I have told you what I wish, that there be no hanging."[60]

"What you ask will not be granted," said Morris, adding with puzzlement, "Why are you so anxious about bad men?"[61]

Exasperated that Morris kept talking about good and bad Indians, Big Bear made another attempt to put the conversation back on the right track. He restated the core of his message, the reason for his discontent and concern of the Indians for whom he spoke: "Then these Chiefs [i.e. those who uphold the law] will help us to protect the buffalo, that there may be enough for all.[62]

"The North-West Council is considering the framing of a law to protect the buffaloes," replied Morris, "and when they make it, they will expect the Indians to obey it."[63] That was all: no promises and no assurances. He went on to invite Big Bear and the other missing chiefs to sign their adhesion to the treaty next year. Then, as he rose to say farewell, all the other chiefs rose respectfully and shook his hand.

Big Bear remained seated until the last of them had left and then spoke confidentially to the commissioner, trying earnestly to make him understand his position. And with a poor interpreter, this was not easy. "I am glad to meet you," he said, rising and shaking the commissioner's hand. "I am alone, but if I had known the time [of the meeting], I would have been here with all my people." He did not mention that though Sweet Grass had been summoned by special messenger, the other Plains Cree chiefs had not. "I am not an undutiful child. I do not throw back your hand [offered in friendship], but as my people are not here, I do not sign. I will tell them what I have heard, and next year I will come."[64]

Commissioner Morris left Fort Pitt with the understanding that Big Bear had agreed to accept treaty in the following year, though his speeches had made it perfectly clear he would not make a decision until he had spoken with his people and the other chiefs still on the plains.

Perhaps, like many other parts of his speech, his final words had been misinterpreted.

Certainly, the chief's actual intentions had been distorted in the translation so as to be unrecognizable and ineffectual. Big Bear was a highly intelligent political leader who saw the immediate problem as one of buffalo preservation and, coincidentally, of Indian freedom. He was shrewd enough to realize that the day would come when the buffalo would be exterminated, but with careful management they could last for many years. He also was aware that the Indians were giving up valuable hunting grounds and were getting little in return.

Even a few Canadian politicians agreed with Big Bear. When the first treaties were being negotiated, the Honourable John Schultz gave the House of Commons a mathematical breakdown. "East of the Rocky Mountains," he said, "we have acquired an Indian territory of three million square miles; on it there is a population of thirty-eight thousand Indians; the individual Indian, then, in an average treaty, cedes to the government forty square miles of country; this forty square miles of country at present supplies him with his food, his clothing and his house, the smaller fur-bearing animals on it give him the means of acquiring what he needs of European manufacture."[65] To this member of parliament, the amount being offered in the treaties was entirely inadequate.

Because Big Bear had arrived after the treaty was concluded, he had no chance to negotiate and discovered that the door seemed closed to further discussion. He knew, however, that the Indians who had signed Treaties One and Two had become dissatisfied and that the government had altered the terms four years later. If the government could renegotiate those treaties, he saw no reason why they could not do so with Treaty Six, particularly if all the Plains Crees could speak with a unified voice. Stubborn and intractable when he believed he was right, Big Bear was not willing to meekly accept what the Christian chiefs had taken. He would try, with determination, to get a better deal for his people.

Four Years to Wait

THE CREE PLACED great faith in signs that indicated supernatural forces were at work. Before Treaty Six, two white messengers had travelled the plains to tell the Indians about the meetings: one had gone temporarily insane, and the other had died soon after completing his mission. Then, shortly before the treaty session, a meteorite had been seen hurtling through the sky, reminding everyone of the Iron Stone taken from its resting place a decade earlier. The holy men had predicted disasters, and four years later, they had started to happen.

When this new meteorite had flamed its way through the night sky, the holy men had gathered to discuss its significance. They concluded that it was a warning to Indians not to sell their lands, for they did not belong to them but to the Great Spirit. If they sold even a portion of their hunting grounds, the wise men said, it would surely bring disaster. But Sweet Grass and the other political chiefs had not listened and had signed the treaty. Then about four months after signing, Sweet Grass died, or rather, was killed by the accidental discharge of a pistol. Such accidents, the Indians knew, did not simply happen by themselves; they were caused by forces more powerful than any mere human. Years later, Big Bear's granddaughter explained the situation as it was understood by her people. "One day," she said, "our great chief Sweet Grass, the chief of many tribes of Prairie Indians, was invited by the Whites where a meeting was to take place. Our Chief Sweet Grass was told through an interpreter that the Great White Queen, who ruled over all this land, had long arms and would therefore take care of all her children and make sure that none of them ever went hungry. Chief Sweet Grass signed the Treaty and was given a beautiful gun. Upon his return, Chief Sweet Grass was killed by his brother-in-law."[1] She believed that the chief's death was punishment for the treaty he had made. "It must be further explained," she said, "that the Prairie Indians were not consulted before this Treaty was signed.

Therefore, it is obvious that our people resented being sold out of land which rightfully belonged to us all."[2]

On the death of Sweet Grass, the leadership of the Fort Pitt Crees shifted to Big Bear. Little Pine was a possible contender, but he now confined his hunting to the Bow River region, trading at Fort Calgary or at smaller posts in the south. Another successor might have been Sweet Grass's son, Little Man (later called Young Sweet Grass), but he was only twenty-seven years old. A few close relatives decided to stay with him, but the majority of Indians now considered Big Bear to be their chief. Leaders like Thunder Companion, Half Blackfoot Chief and *Sayakimat* also accepted him as the leading chief of the region.

When the government became aware of the change in leaders, officials were worried, for they realized that they would no longer be dealing with a missionary-dominated Indian who would comply with their wishes. "I fear," said Lieutenant-Governor Morris, "that the loss of the influence of Sweet Grass will render the task of obtaining the adhesion of the Plains Crees who were not present at Fort Pitt, much more difficult than it otherwise would have been, and will lead to their making new and exaggerated demands."[3] In essence, Morris was correct, though a strong feeling of dissatisfaction had already existed before Sweet Grass's death, particularly among the bands on the plains. Morris suggested that Commissioner W. J. Christie, who knew Big Bear, should go to the treaty meeting scheduled for 1877 to convince him to sign. Instead, the government appointed a stranger, M. G. Dickieson, a clerk in the Indian department. Dickieson was described as not having "the slightest qualification for the important and delicate position he fills, other than that he is the sometime private secretary of a sometime member of the late Grit Ministry."[4] He was given the authority to pay annuities to all of those who had already accepted treaty and to gain the adhesion of any holdouts at Carlton or Fort Pitt.

Meanwhile, the North-West Council finally took some action to preserve the buffalo, though the terms were not what Big Bear had expected. He wished to have the buffalo left for the exclusive and unrestricted use of the Indians, but the council prohibited the use of buffalo jumps or pounds, introduced a closed season for cows from mid-November to mid-August and banned the killing of calves. The slaughter of buffalo for tongues or hides was forbidden, as was their hunting for pleasure purposes. Only when Indians were facing the threat of starvation could they violate these rules, and then only to meet their immediate needs.[5]

Dickieson reached Battleford a week late to begin paying treaty money and received his first insight into the attitudes of the dissident Indians when he spoke to Yellow Sky, an Ojibwa who led a mixed camp at Big Bear's old stamping grounds at Jackfish Lake. This chief's reasons for rejecting treaty were common to many holdouts in the area and probably reflected some of Big Bear's thinking. "After some little time their spokesman rose and said they desired to be independent," reported Dickieson, "that they did not wish to take anything from the Government, or to come under the law. He said I was not to think it was because they were unfriendly to the Government or to the white man that they do not join with the other Indians but they wished to remain as they were. They had likewise been told that by holding out, 'better terms' would be granted to them."[6]

When Dickieson reached Fort Pitt, he was several days late and was met by a large camp of Indians, many of them dissatisfied because they had not received their promised agricultural equipment. A journalist who was present noted that "some of those chiefs were foolish enough to think that they were not treated well last year and caused some useless talk," but to no avail.[7] When Dickieson refused to alter the terms, the treaty chiefs grudgingly accepted their annuities. The only new adherent was Half Blackfoot Chief, who came to the treaty table with 169 followers.

Big Bear had ridden in from the plains for the meeting, but had brought only three or four head men with him. The buffalo were near the South Saskatchewan River that year, and a hunter could travel for fourteen days south of Fort Pitt without encountering any herds, so it seemed pointless to bring his large following. He knew he had a mandate to sign the treaty if the terms were suitable, but otherwise he would not act without their consensus.

Dickieson told them about the buffalo ordinance, and though Big Bear and the others were pleased that some action had been taken they believed it was too strict in its application to Indians. They shared the common belief that the buffalo had been placed on earth by the Great Spirit, and while the government should restrict the activities of half-breeds and white men, it should not interfere with the Indians. For example, Indians killed buffalo calves to provide soft, thin robes for their children; now the government was telling them they had to stop this age-old practice.

Big Bear took an active part in the discussions and arguments with Dickieson, but in the end, all the other chiefs backed down before the unyielding clerk. Only Big Bear remained firm.

In his report, Dickieson played down the role of Big Bear and implied that the reason the chief did not sign an adhesion to the treaty was that the clerk felt the man was too unimportant to be considered. "The 'Big Bear' was at Fort Pitt," he acknowledged, "but as he had no band his adhesion was not taken. This chief's influence has apparently declined

very much."[8] The opposite was actually true. As the buffalo herds concentrated in the south and the Indians who stayed behind were reduced
to eating rabbits, fish and any game they could find in the forests, they
began to review the terms of the treaty as they understood them. In
particular, many suspected that the clause dealing with the threat of
starvation had been altered without their knowledge. They were sure the
government had promised them food whenever they needed it, but now
they were told that a general famine had to exist throughout the land
before they could expect help. They also discovered that the thousand
dollars for assistance to farmers, offered both at Carlton and Fort Pitt,
had sounded like a lot of money, but divided among hundreds of people
it was a mere pittance.

As the unrest continued to grow, both among those who had signed
the treaty and those who had not, Big Bear emerged as a solid rock of
determination against the tidal waves of government rhetoric and
unfulfilled promises. "I hear 'Big Bear' is trying to get all the non-treaty
and some of the treaty plain Indians to assemble," noted Lieutenant-
Governor Laird, "and demand a new treaty or at least to ask for better
terms." Then, as an indication that the mistranslations of two years
earlier were still dogging the chief, Laird added, "He still, I am
informed, entertains the idea that Indians should be exempted from
hanging. It is said also that he thinks Indians should not be imprisoned
for any crime and though he asked Lieut. Gov. Morris in 1876 that the
buffalo should be protected it appears he did not intend that any law of
the kind should apply to Indians."[9]

The recurring references to hanging served to undermine Big Bear
and his mission, for they gave the impression he was an eccentric leader
who should not be taken seriously or was a devious man who feared the
rope. Either way, the topic distracted government officials from the real
grievances Big Bear expounded: that the treaties did not provide a fair
exchange for surrendering their land and that the Indians had no guaran-
tees they would escape starvation if they could not adjust to farming
once the buffalo were gone.

Although officials might give the impression that Big Bear was unimportant, they knew that his influence was growing day by day. Therefore, when he suggested the 1878 treaty payments be held not at the
Hudson's Bay Company posts but out on the plains among the buffalo,
his advice was accepted. He recommended Sounding Lake as a good
central location for both the Carlton and Fort Pitt Indians and said that
"he and the other non-Treaty Cree chiefs expect to meet Commissioners
near that point this summer."[10]

As the Sounding Lake meeting approached, Big Bear turned fifty-
three years of age. That was old for a man on the prairies, where life was

harsh. Living in a skin tepee, where the morning temperatures differed little from those outside, riding for hours at a time searching for buffalo, then dashing after them at full gallop during the chase — all of this became more difficult as Big Bear grew older. There were lines in his wind-toughened face, and his slight body was less sinewy than it had been when he was a youth. In manhood he stood only four feet five inches tall (135 cm), with a chest measurement of forty-two to forty-eight inches (105 cm to 120 cm). He was described as a "short, black and shaggy-looking creature . . . wearing a large bearskin cap, surmounted with three black plumes."[11]

The chief's two oldest boys, Twin Wolverine and *Imasees*, had become increasingly interested in their father's mission, but because of their youth, they tended to gravitate to the young hotheads who opposed the treaty, not because of its terms, but because it came from the white man. They believed their problems of starvation and destitution stemmed directly from the invasion of the whites, so their simple solution was to get rid of the invaders. If there were no white people, there would be plenty of buffalo and no need for a treaty.

Their approach was diametrically opposite to that of Big Bear, who, with the insight and intelligence of a skillful politician, saw the situation in its true light. He did not hate either the white man or the government, for they were facts of life. He knew also that he could not turn back the clock; the best he could hope for was to delay the inevitable and get the best deal possible for his followers. For this, he was prepared to negoti-ate and to wait. As a politician he could become angry at times and harshly honest in his opinions, but his usual demeanour was pleasant, sometimes laced with a bit of sarcastic levity. On one occasion an official came to him and said he would provide a troop of Mounted Policemen to escort Big Bear and his starving followers, supposedly to protect them but really to see that they did not cause any trouble. Instead of becoming angry, Big Bear looked around to see if the policemen were near, then commented: "Thanks. I don't see the escort and it's just as well, perhaps. We are hungry and might eat their horses!"[12]

After spending the winter of 1877–78 near the mouth of the Red Deer River, Big Bear realized there was no point in going north in the spring, for the country all the way to Fort Pitt was devoid of buffalo. Many Carlton House Indians had camped on the edge of the plains that winter, and before spring starvation was common in their villages. The chiefs, remembering the treaty promises, went to officials in Battleford for help, "but the Government did not consider their circumstances of last winter to necessitate relief, and none was given."[13] This only added to the dissatisfaction of the treaty Indians and brought more support to Big Bear's camp. By spring, the chief had a massive village of four hundred lodges, which included most of the leading plains bands from Fort Pitt, with many more from Edmonton, Carlton House and a few from Qu'Appelle. In order to feed them, he moved south of the river and into Blackfoot country on the west side of Cypress Hills.

By this time, the whole region near the hills was teeming both with buffalo and Indians. Northwest of Big Bear's camp were the Blood and Blackfoot, while just over the hills were the Qu'Appelle Cree and Assiniboine. Beyond them, yet uncomfortably close, were the refugee Sioux who had fled to Canada after defeating the American cavalry at the Battle of Little Big Horn two years earlier. The Sioux chiefs, Sitting Bull and Crazy Horse, both had camps within a few days' ride of Big Bear, and worried Americans were convinced the Cree leader was ready "to embrace Sitting Bull with a fraternal hug."[14] In fact, the last thing that Big Bear wanted was any association with that chief, for not only were the enemy Sioux despised, but their method of dealing with the white man was completely opposite to his own peaceful negotiations.

In August, when Big Bear began the two hundred–mile (320-km) journey to the Sounding Lake treaty grounds, he knew his role as chief negotiator for the prairie Crees was critical. Late in the previous year, the Canadian government had successfully negotiated Treaty Seven with the Blackfoot nation, giving them terms that were virtually the same as Treaty Six, or perhaps a little less, for they omitted the promise of aid in times of famine and offered no money to help them to begin farming. Treaty Seven was the last in the series that had started near Winnipeg in 1871 and now encompassed the entire prairies. The way was clear to grant land concessions to the Canadian Pacific Railway and to open the West for settlement.

Consequently, in the eyes of politicians in Ottawa, the reluctance of Big Bear, Little Pine and the other Cree chiefs to sign their adherence to Treaty Six was of less importance now. The need for granting further concessions was, therefore, unnecessary. It was not a question of determining the validity of Big Bear's claims, but rather the realization that anything further would cost the government more money. Prime Minister John A. Macdonald and his Conservatives, who had been out of power since 1874, had just returned to office and had no wish to incur added expenses or to tamper with a task they believed was completed. "It would not be advisable to alter the terms of Treaties," commented the prime minister flatly.[15]

Another problem facing Big Bear was the growing restlessness of the nontreaty people. When he got to Sounding Lake, the tents, stores and the carts of twenty-three traders were already there, some with goods that the Indians had never seen before. Nearby were rope corrals holding five hundred horses, including race horses and buffalo runners, which the traders had for sale. A nontreaty man with a family of five could collect thirty dollars for that year alone if he accepted treaty, and his bonus would give him another seventy-two dollars. Moreover, keen competition among the traders had caused prices to fall lower than anyone had ever seen before: a man could buy a Winchester rifle for forty-five dollars, a blanket for five dollars or an unbroken cayuse for as little as thirty-five dollars. Even Red River carts were going for the unheard-of price of twenty dollars each. Someone with a hundred dollars in his hands could leave the camp with enough supplies to last his family for an entire winter.

Big Bear knew if he failed to win concessions at Sounding Lake, he would have trouble keeping the people away from the pay tables. Even if their chiefs refused to take treaty, individuals could move to the camp of a treaty chief and accept their annuities with him. Big Bear astutely avoided this problem by leaving his own band back in the Cypress Hills, taking only two or three lodges with him to the meeting.

When he arrived, more than twelve hundred Indians had pitched their tepees along the valley of Sounding Creek on the east side of the lake. The chiefs came out to greet him, wanting news about the treaty and whether the government was willing to reconsider its terms. Big Bear could not tell them; the commissioner was a new man, the Honourable David Laird, whom he had never met. But the treaty chiefs agreed to prevent their followers from accepting annuities until after the nontreaty faction had held its meeting.

During the next couple of days, another six hundred Indians came to the valley, pitching lodges near their friends or finding open areas among the hundreds of tepees that lined the valley. The smoke hung heavy in the mild summer air, as children played, dogs romped through the short prairie grass and hunters returned with meat. A year earlier, when Big Bear had suggested the site, the buffalo had been thick around the lake, but this year the closest large herds were two days' travel away towards the Red Deer River.

On 13 August, Lieutenant-Governor Laird arrived at the camp with a contingent of Mounted Police. They pitched their bell tents and drew their supply wagons around them to make an improvised fort. The police were apprehensive, as the rumours of discontent over the treaties made them think that an uprising was imminent. The officer in charge, James Walker, was prepared to be firm with anyone who threatened discord or trouble. He had concluded that Big Bear was "one of the most troublesome Cree Indians we have in the territories."[16]

When the meeting was called, Laird met Big Bear for the first time, and was surprised to find him a "rather old and weazened Indian with very few words."[17] But as the sessions extended over the next three days, he heard more and more from the chief, for both treaty and nontreaty Indians had appointed him to be their spokesman. Big Bear told the commissioner that the treaty did not give their people enough to live on; when Laird responded that it was intended to help them only until they could fend for themselves, the chief was unimpressed. "The Great Spirit has supplied us with plenty of buffalo for food until the white man came," said Big Bear. "Now as that means of support is about to fail us, the Government ought to take the place of the Great Spirit, and provide us with the means of living in some other way."[18]

In trying to find a common ground with the commissioner, Big Bear asked what would happen if the Indians tried to live within the terms of the treaty and found they could not survive: would the government then reconsider? But Laird was in no position and in no mood to bargain. As he recalled later, he did not like Big Bear and "came to the conclusion that he was an untrustworthy and bad Indian."[19] Like his predecessors, he was caught up in the mistaken notion that Big Bear was an evil man who was afraid of hanging.

A white woman who went to the treaty with her trader husband came to know the chief by sight, and her impression of him was rather different from Laird's "old and weazened" Indian. "He was to be seen every day riding round the camp on an Indian pony," she said, "haughty and defiant, his face and body adorned with war paint, and his long black hair decorated with eagle feathers, while he carried a gaudy colored parasol over his head. He was the typical red Indian in all his savage glory and was a striking figure, with his brown body well tanned by the sun, exposed to view as the weather was warm, and he had allowed the blanket which was always carried to fall down behind him on the horse."[20]

During the discussions, Big Bear learned that the commissioner had no power to change the terms of the treaty. This news took him by surprise, for he knew that in 1876 the commissioners had come with their terms but had altered them in the face of Indian demands and that the government had altered Treaties One and Two after they were signed. As a result, Big Bear terminated the conference in disgust and asked the commissioner to pass the requests of the nontreaty chiefs to someone who did have the authority to make the changes. He would be back a year later to hear the government's answer.

The treaty chiefs were as fed up as Big Bear; they had held off accepting their annuities for several days in the belief that Laird had the right to alter the terms. When this proved not to be the case, the people rushed forward to receive their money and to shop for bargains among the traders' tents. Only two chiefs broke ranks with Big Bear and took treaty; these were Winning Man and *Makaoo*, both transitional people whose bands spent most of their time in the woodlands. However, many individuals from the nontreaty camps succumbed to the lure of the calicoes, rifles and fancy mirrors at the traders' wagons and accepted their annuities with one of the treaty chiefs.

Sadly, Big Bear withdrew from other chiefs and went alone to contemplate his situation. What little confidence and trust he had in the government was shaken by Laird's unsympathetic reception. The chief believed that his requests were just and reasonable; all he wanted was assurance that his people would be cared for. Yet Laird's reply, coupled with the government's failure to meet the promises already made, caused him to wonder whether the Cree would simply be abandoned to starve.

Perhaps this was when Big Bear had another vision. "I saw a spring shooting up out of the ground," he said. "I covered it with my hand, trying to smother it, but it spurted up between my fingers and ran over the back of my hand. It was a spring of blood."[21] Such a vision could be a warning that further agitations on Big Bear's part could lead to war. Always mindful of the omens from the spirits, he then decided he would stop trying to organize the nontreaty bands; he would stop making long speeches about the rights of his people; he would stop appealing to the government for a better treaty. Instead, he would turn to He Who Made Us — the Great Spirit — and ask him to carry on the fight.

Four: that was one of the sacred numbers of the tribe. The pipe was passed four ways. Four thunderbirds marked the cardinal points of the world. For four years the holy men had waited for the predicted tragedies after the theft of the Iron Stone, and then they had come. Now, Big Bear vowed to the Great Spirit that he too would wait for four years; not for disaster, but for good luck.

The chief went back to Laird's tent to announce he would not be attending any more annuity meetings; he could be contacted on the plains if Ottawa decided to change the terms of the pact. But, regardless of the outcome, he would wait four years before he would consider accepting treaty. During that time, "he would watch to see whether the Government would faithfully carry out its promises to the Indians."[22] At the end of that period, if he was satisfied, he would expect the commissioner himself to hand him the paper to sign.

With the failure of the Sounding Lake meeting, Big Bear shifted from the role of a dynamic political spokesman to that of a mystical leader. He believed that if the treaty was to be changed and if conditions were to improve, his people would need to rely upon those supernatural forces that had guided their destinies for generations. Big Bear would now give the spirits a chance to exert their healing powers upon the prairies.

Only the Great Spirit owned the land; the Indians merely occupied it during their lifetime, travelling over his prairie and eating his buffalo.

Some holy men believed that their gods had abandoned the Cree as punishment for letting the white people in and giving away the land that did not belong to them. If this was true, perhaps the spirits would ignore the pleas of Big Bear during this time of hunger and confusion, but he prayed that this would not happen. He hoped that the white man would become honest and compassionate in dealing with his people and that in four years' time, if the buffalo had gone, the Crees would have become happy and contented farmers. *Chesqua.* Wait. That would become the byword in his life.

Throughout the years, Big Bear's faith in his visions and the signs given to him through omens had remained unshaken. His bear war bundle and his feathered medicine pipe were always in their traditional places in his lodge, as he faithfully carried out the daily duties of prayers, songs and the burning of incense. Whenever possible, he joined with the other holy men to perform ceremonies or to say prayers. Although his Ojibwa heritage made available to him some rituals that were feared by the Crees, there is no evidence that Big Bear's belief in the supernatural and his use of various medicine bundles was anything put positive. It was in keeping with his whole dedication in life that he would be more interested in good luck and a bright future for his people, rather than in casting dark spells.

Some of the young Crees at Sounding Lake were not as spiritual as Big Bear. When they learned that the commissioner would not alter the treaty, they galloped angrily through the camps, wheeling menacingly towards the wagonbox fort of the police and firing their rifles wildly into the air. Since Big Bear was the leading nontreaty chief in the camp, he was blamed for the incident, and the superintendent of the Mounted Police threatened to have him arrested unless the young warriors were controlled. Big Bear did manage to cool the spirits of the hotheads, even though the problem was not really his, for his own band was still back near the Cypress Hills. Having been tagged by the authorities as a troublemaker, however, he received the blame.

As for Commissioner Laird, he kept his promise to Big Bear in a half-hearted way. He dutifully wrote to Ottawa, but without clearly defining the chief's terms, and recommended that the authorities "do nothing for one band within the limits of a Treaty that is not done for all [and so] perhaps the Treaty ought to remain unchanged."[23] If Big Bear was expecting help from the spirits to make the authorities compassionate and understanding, he had no idea of just how much he was expecting them to accomplish.

Big Bear was not the only chief to protest the lot of the Crees. Little Pine had refused to accept treaty in 1877 because it would mean losing his freedom, and *Piapot,* complaining that the terms of Treaty Four were inadequate, would not take a reserve. Even the peaceful chief Star Blanket was concerned about insufficient help to start farming, while Beardy angrily demonstrated against the low rations. But Big Bear's dramatic appeals at Fort Pitt and Sounding Lake in 1877 and 1878 had made him the symbol of government defiance, both among disaffected Indians and the white people in nearby settlements. To the Cree, Big Bear was a determined, unyielding leader who was trying to unite the Indians and thus negotiate a better deal from the government. To many whites, he was an untrustworthy scoundrel who wanted to lead the plains tribes in a war of extermination. The growing community of Battleford feared the Cree chief, and wild rumours circulated that made it sound as though the plains would erupt in violence at any moment. In disgust, the Indian commissioner commented that "the inhabitants have shown a great amount of unnecessary nervousness."[24]

The stories persisted, however, all adding to Big Bear's reputation as a troublemaker and making peaceful negotiations virtually impossible. If people like Big Child and Star Blanket complained to the government, they were described as "well-disposed Indians" whose requests should be granted.[25] Even when a nontreaty spokesman patterned his words after those of Big Bear, saying, "I have not taken the treaty because I want to see how it works with the others. I am glad that the Government intends to help them farming but I do not think the land is enough and I want you to represent that to the Government," he was lauded by the Indian commissioner for making a very sensible speech.[26] Yet when Big Bear wanted to discuss terms with government officials, rumours circulated that "if the Governor did not grant them he would strike him," and that "if the police try to take him, he will kill them all."[27] Of course, enough young hotheads were joining Big Bear's band to give some basis for concern. Men like Little Poplar and *Imasees* already were aggressive and outspoken about their problems, so warriors who came to the band usually sought their company, not that of the older and more spiritual Big Bear.

From 1877 to 1879, the chief spent most of his time hunting near the Red Deer River and west of the Cypress Hills. Red Deer Forks was his usual campsite, and from there he travelled once or twice a year to take his buffalo robes and other goods to Fort Pitt. He had known the Red Deer Forks area since he was a child, for it was there that he had had the vision that gave him his war medicine. This area, once the southernmost point on his summer range, now served as his year-round headquarters, and his search for buffalo often took him far south of the river.

For that reason, Big Bear was upset on his return to the Forks one day in the summer of 1879 to find a team of surveyors busily at work. He learned that the land was going to be set aside as a reserve for one of the other bands; if this happened, the only good piece of wooded river bottom in the area would be closed to him, and he would be obliged to winter somewhere else. Accompanied by his sons and about a hundred warriors, he rode to the surveyors' camp and ordered them to stop work. This area, he told them, belonged to all the Cree, and they did not want to have it surveyed. "Under the circumstances," said the official, "I had no alternative but to report the matter to the officer commanding at the headquarters of the North-West Mounted Police."[28]

On receiving the news, Asst. Comr. A. G. Irvine of the NWMP expected the trouble might end in bloodshed, so he issued new Winchester rifles to the twenty-six men selected to go to the Forks with him and the surveyor. En route, they met a camp of Bloods, one-time enemies of the Cree, and when these Indians saw the size of the force and their weaponry, they too concluded that a fight was in the offing. Never ones to pass up the chance of a battle, especially one sanctioned by the Queen's soldiers, the Bloods asked permission to go along. Irvine seriously considered their request, but in the end he selected only the chief and his leading warrior.

"When we reached Big Bear's camp it looked ominous," said Irvine. "The women and children had all been sent away, which among the Plains Indians is always a sure sign that they expect to do some fighting." The officer proceeded directly to the surveyors' tent, where he found a chair and sat down, flanked by the Bloods and police on either side. If Irvine thought a camp of a hundred Crees was an intimidating sight, he might have considered the provocative picture he presented: a Queen's officer, accompanied by twenty-six scarlet-coated policemen — holding new carbines — and two well-known Blood warriors whose followers might be hiding nearby. To add to the tension, a Blackfoot messenger arrived during the parley, giving the impression that his tribe might be involved as well. Big Bear had no choice but to listen quietly to the police officer. "I did not waste many words with him," said Irvine, "but told him if he interfered with the surveyors, who were servants of the Queen's Government, as I was, I would have him arrested, taken to Cypress Hills, and locked up in the guard room."[29] Big Bear acceded to the directive and the surveys continued without any further interference.

Like many other such confrontations that occurred in those times, there were two viewpoints, but only one of them seemed to have any validity: the one reinforced by the Queen's law. Perhaps Big Bear had been wrong in stopping the survey, but his reasoning was logical; if the area was surveyed for the exclusive use of one band, all the others that used it, including his own, would be denied a camping place vital for access to the adjacent herds. There were many other river bottoms, of course, but as the surveyor commented, there was "but little or no wood to be found except at the Forks."[30]

This peacefully resolved incident was publicized, however, as another example of Big Bear's savage nature. An account in a Winnipeg newspaper claimed that Irvine had been pulled from his horse in a scuffle, and a Toronto newspaper reporter said that the surveyors' horses had been seized and that if Big Bear went to Battleford, the "outcome of the whole thing would be a bloody Indian war."[31] People in Battleford, still preoccupied with the idea that Big Bear was organizing a grand alliance of tribes, claimed Irvine's confrontation had been with "about three hundred warriors, comprising Assiniboines, Blackfeet, Crees, and a few Sioux, all eager for a fray."[32] Big Bear was becoming famous across Canada, not as a defender of his people's rights, but as a rebellious and dangerous man.

His reputation was not enhanced several months later when the soldiers' lodge in his camp took direct action against a party of half-breed hunters who interfered with the Cree hunt. Under the leadership of Wandering Spirit, the soldiers accused the hunters of violating the accepted codes of the chase, thus endangering the lives of those in Big Bear's camp. Then they meted out their own form of punishment, seizing the half-breeds' ponies, cutting up their harness and lodges and purportedly "committing assaults upon them and their women."[33] A party of sixteen Mounted Police went back to Red Deer Forks, where they found Big Bear camped a short distance up the river. No one offered any resistance when the police explained that only the Queen's men could enforce the law; two members of the soldiers' lodge, Big Squirrel and Two Teeth, were arrested and taken back to Fort Walsh for trial. The former was acquitted, but Two Teeth was given four months at hard labour.

In spite of the wild rumours of grand alliances, Big Bear stayed quiet and peaceful all winter, hunting near the Forks, where the herds were plentiful enough to feed his camp. A priest who saw him during this time said that he was "anxious to remain on good terms with the Government"[34] and that he "cannot be accused of uttering a single objectionable word."[35]

In the summer of 1879, Ottawa finally took steps to relieve some of the chaos among the Indians on the frontier. The Honourable Edgar Dewdney, former member of parliament and stalwart supporter of Prime Minister John A. Macdonald, was appointed to replace the ineffectual David Laird as Indian commissioner for the North-West Territory. His task, partly designated and partly self-appointed, was to set up a bureaucratic structure of Indian agents, farm instructors, government supply farms and contractors. He had no wish to let the Indians become

a permanent drain on the federal treasury, so he planned to transform
them into self-supporting farmers as quickly as possible. Those who
were on reserves would be encouraged to plant crops; those who had
signed treaties but still lived by the hunt would get as little support as
possible, so that starvation would ultimately drive them home.

Starvation also would force the nontreaty chiefs to sign, but in the
meantime the new commissioner planned to use every device available
to effect their compliance. Unlike the dour Laird, Dewdney was a
friendly, outgoing man, and hoped to win some of the chiefs over
through the sheer forcefulness of his personality. As a politician, he was
accustomed to friendly persuasion, but he also knew that the human
foibles of pride and avarice could be his best allies in the forthcoming
campaign. The treaties themselves or the revision of them were not
issues in his mind, as his prime minister had already stated these docu-
ments would stand as they were.

Before leaving Ottawa, the new Indian commissioner heard much
about the troublesome Big Bear, who stood at the head of all the disaffected Crees in the North-West. He knew of the difficulties at Sounding
Lake, the halting of the surveyors and the attack on the half-breed camp,
so he believed he would be dealing with a hardened warrior who might
take his people into battle at any moment. Yet the small, aging chief he
met at Fort Walsh on 2 July proved to be completely different from the
man describd in newspapers and official correspondence. "I have not
formed such a poor opinion of 'Big Bear' as some appear to have done,"
he wrote. "He is of a very independent character, self-reliant, and
appears to know how to make his own living without begging from the
Government."[36]

Dewdney encountered Big Bear quite by accident, while the chief was
travelling in search of buffalo; his large camp included his head men
Lucky Man and Thunder Child as well as his fellow chief Little Pine.
Seizing the opportunity of the chance meeting, Dewdney pointed out to
them that the buffalo had become scarce in their hunting grounds and
that as long as they did not take treaty, the government would not help
them. He told Big Bear that if he would not sign himself, then his
people would be permitted to break away and create their own bands.
The same could happen to Little Pine as well.

Although Big Bear had ceased to actively campaign for a revised
treaty, he could not resist expounding his views to the new commissioner. "He was anxious to obtain some concessions that the other Indians had not," Dewdney reported, "he wanted more land and more
money, and gave as his reason that he had not taken the treaty, that he
wanted to see how it worked with the other Indians."[37] Dewdney not
only had his prime minister's decision not to revise the treaties, but he

knew Indian opposition was crumbling in the face of starvation and an uncertain future. More and more individual Indians and head men were willing to leave their nontreaty leaders in order to receive much-needed money for food and supplies and for the assurances, albeit questionable, that they could turn to the government for help.

Big Bear remained adamant; he would not sign. But the resistance of others faltered in the presence of the voluble and persuasive Dewdney, and Little Pine agreed to accept treaty on behalf of his 272 followers, while Lucky Man and Thunder Child took 200 of Big Bear's people into the waiting arms of the great white mother. Big Bear's grandson, Four Souls, recalled the incident: "After Big Bear refused to sign the treaty, the Queen started going around him, appointing other men as chiefs. Big Bear's men were anxious to be made chiefs, so they listened to the Queen and signed."[38]

Dewdney noted that "Big Bear himself was present when both 'Little Pine' and 'Lucky-Man' signed. . . . He is now almost alone, only three or four followers having remained with him."[39] In fact, Lucky Man had taken less than half of Big Bear's band, but it still reduced the chief's following to a mere handful in comparison to the huge camps he had led a year or two earlier.

Dewdney left the session believing he had a commitment from Big Bear to accept treaty at the payments to be made at Sounding Lake the following month. Whether the chief was trying to be obliging or, more likely, whether he agreed to go if there was any word of a treaty revision, Big Bear had no intention of deviating from his vow to wait for four years. Keeping his promise to the Great Spirit, he would wait, watch and hope. His support might be crumbling around him and his people deserting him, but the mystic Big Bear had made his commitment to his gods. The only hope he could see for his people was for supernatural forces to intercede on their behalf.

Big Bear did not attend the Sounding Lake payments, but pursued the ever-decreasing buffalo. Later he learned some of the nontreaty people had gone there in the hope that the new commissioner would have some news about changes in the treaty. Disappointed, they still refused to take treaty and chastised the government for not fulfilling Laird's promise to reply to Big Bear's requests.

All season the buffalo were scarce, and by the end of the year the traders had taken in only eight thousand buffalo robes at Fort Walsh and five thousand at Fort Macleod, or less than half the amount bought the year before. "From these figures," observed a journalist, "it will be seen how rapidly extermination is overtaking the buffalo, and how terrible must be the suffering among the Indians who have to rely upon them for food."[40]

That fall, Big Bear took his scanty harvest of buffalo robes and meat on a long journey to trade at Fort Pitt. Where the land had been teeming with buffalo a few years before, he saw now only piles of bleached bones. The prairies were still painted in the drab colours of autumn and the sky was still a striking blue overhead, but after countless centuries, the cycle of nature had at last been broken. No more would the cows drop their orange-coloured calves in the spring. No more would the Indians leave their winter camps, strike their skin tepees and follow the herds. No more would the sun rise to the halting songs of a holy man praying to the Old Man Buffalo.

The buffalo and a way of life had come to an end. The land that Big Bear had known as a child was empty and silent. There were no buffalo at Sounding Lake, nor at the Battle River, nor in the Four Blackfoot Hills. In fact, the last buffalo that Big Bear had seen on the journey was away back at the Red Deer Forks. Big Bear knew, as he drew close to the valley of the North Saskatchewan and could see Fort Pitt in the distance, that he would never again come here with buffalo robes and dried meat. If he chose to stay with the last herds, he must do as the others in his tribe had done: follow them south, into the Land of the Long Knives, the United States. A number of Crees already had crossed the line, where they had been intercepted by military patrols and sent back. But there were too many small bands of Crees, Assiniboines, Sioux, Bloods and Blackfoot for the army to catch and so the creeks and valleys of northern Montana were rapidly being settled by Indians from the Canadian plains.

With regret and resignation, Big Bear, too, turned his back to the broad Saskatchewan River, not knowing if he would ever again see this land, where he had been born. His granddaughter, Isabella, was only a baby at the time, but in later years she heard the story of their journey south after trading at Fort Pitt. "Our people realized they had lost their land," she said sadly, "and so, scattered all over like little birds. We, who lived under that great Chief Big Bear stayed together and decided to follow the buffalo as far South as we had to go. Many were on foot while the more fortunate ones rode horses or travois." In her own family were her father, *Imasees,* her mother and an older sister. "Travel was slow and tiresome," she recalled, "and often our food ran out. In spite of many hardships we reached the land of the Big Knives way down south of the great line. Here we stayed a while."[41]

During the winter of 1879–80, Big Bear camped in the Milk River region of Montana, immediately south of Fort Walsh, and hunted into the Bearspaw Mountains. In his first few weeks in the United States, he came to appreciate the work done by the North-West Mounted Police back home. His old hunting grounds had been free of whiskey traders and renegades for the past five years, but in Montana he saw the grim days of the past return to his camp. Grizzled, unkempt white men pitched their tents amid the nearby cottonwoods and ladled out fiery whiskey in exchange for newly-tanned buffalo robes, while other whites stealthily approached Big Bear's camp at night and ran off with his horses. Virtually no law existed near the Cree villages. If the army arrived, it was only to send the Indians scurrying back over the line. If a United States marshal came, he was looking for a half-breed trader who had illegally brought his goods across the line. None of the law enforcement men was there to help the Crees, who were regarded as aliens trespassing on the Gros Ventre and Assiniboine reservation.

Under the combined weight of starvation, whiskey and thievery, the whole social structure of the Cree collapsed. Bands became fractionalized, and young warriors ignored both their chiefs and the camp soldiers. In some villages there seemed to be no controls, and the breakdown became moral and spiritual as well as social and political. To avoid these problems, Big Bear moved back into Canada whenever the buffalo wandered north, so that much of his time was spent in the Cypress Hills or close to Fort Walsh.

In Montana, Big Bear was faced with another problem that could have been disastrous. It involved the Métis leader Louis Riel, who had led the uprising at Red River in 1869 that resulted in the formation of the province of Manitoba. When British and Canadian troops occupied Red River, he had fled, then spent several years in asylums and with friends in the East. He had come to Montana in 1879 to recover his health and, ultimately, to try to form an alliance of Indian tribes and half-breeds to attack Canada. His goal, as stated by a witness to his campaign, was "nothing less than the invasion and taking possession of the North-West Territories, with the help of a general uprising of all the Indian tribes, united to the Half-breeds."[42] Over the winter, Riel held meetings at a large half-breed camp on Milk River, about a hundred miles (160 km) downstream from Big Bear. On one occasion, he took the treaty parchment Little Pine had accepted a few months earlier and trampled it under his feet, saying that it was no good and that he would give him a better one when the new republic was formed. To Red Stone, an Assiniboine leader, Riel gave a document that proclaimed western Canada rightfully belonged to the Indians and half-breeds and that he would help recover their lands.

While Big Bear was in his Milk River camp, he received an invitation from Riel to come to visit and to share food with him. Big Bear had never been enamoured of the mixed-bloods and had stayed aloof from them, particularly since his trouble with Gabriel Dumont a decade earlier, but curious about the militant movement, he decided to go. He was leaving to search for buffalo anyway, so he took a group of hunters and friends along the Missouri River to the Big Bend, where the half-breeds had built a colony of log cabins for the winter. "We were just gathering to have a feast," recalled Big Bear. "Riel had a lot of rum which he was selling but it ran out." The chief stayed for only one day, but during that time he joined with a large crowd of Indians and half-breeds to listen to the messianic leader. "Riel wanted me to raise all the men I could," he said, "but I wouldn't. Many wanted to fight in 1879 but I stopped them."[43]

In fact, the outbursts of the Métis leader held little interest for Big Bear. His goal was to obtain a better treaty for his people through peaceful means, either by intervention of the Great Spirit, or failing that, by continued negotiation. Bloodshed at this time would destroy everything he had worked for. As Big Bear's grandson commented, some of the chiefs "listened to Riel instead of Big Bear. Then they went to Big Bear and said let's fight the white people. Big Bear tried to talk them out of it. 'No,' he said, 'We should not fight the Queen with guns. We should fight her with her own laws.' "[44]

Apparently Big Bear convinced the other Cree chiefs his way was better, for over the winter each of them rejected the idea of a grand alliance, and Riel's plan withered away with the arrival of spring.

The chief made no further attempts to visit Riel or to receive his messengers at his camp. The Cree leader already had enough hotheads who would have liked nothing better than to make war on the Canadian government without having them stirred up by the half-breeds.

Besides, he had to face the more urgent problems of severe cold and blizzards, scattered buffalo herds and the constant threat of starvation. As spring approached, Big Bear began to hear pitiful stories about others in his tribe. Little Child had taken his camp farther down the Milk River, but the buffalo had avoided the area and savage blizzards had made it impossible for the hunters to travel. Over the winter, many of their horses died and thirty were stolen by the Bloods, so that when spring approached, most of the suffering people had to walk back to Canada. Farther south, Thunder Chief's band had been trapped by the severe winter near the military base of Fort Assiniboine. By spring they "were selling their guns and every other article of value to procure food, while the women were prostituting themselves to save their children from starvation."[45]

The treaty Indians in Canada were not doing much better during the summer of 1880; they spent most of their time hunting game in the woods, while those who were issued rations suffered even more. As Dewdney admitted: "The mortality among the Indians this year has been greater than usual, the Indians attributing it to the white man's food; and I have no doubt the sudden change from unlimited meat to the scanty fare they received from the Government has to some extent brought it about."[46]

Many problems were being experienced by those who tried to farm. The instructors, who were hired were mostly from eastern Canada, were political appointees with no knowledge of Cree and even less about western farming conditions. At planting time the authorities could not provide enough seed for the land that Big Child's band had broken, in spite of treaty promises; and the potatoes on Poundmaker's reserve, when harvested, were the size of marbles. Although there were some successes, the general feeling was that the government was being niggardly, so that the Indians had become discouraged. They wanted to farm, to become self-supporting, but bureaucratic inefficiency seemed to dog them at every turn.

"I will tell you as we understood the treaty made with Governor Morris," Big Child lectured Dewdney. "We understood from him that he was coming into the country to help us to live, and we were told how we were to get a living, and we put ourselves at work at once to settle down."[47] Big Child's head man then itemized their problems: not enough oxen to work the land ("With a band of a hundred families it would be perfectly ridiculous that we could get on with four oxen"), the choice of farm instructors ("I would prefer to have had men in the country who understood the language") and the rangy, unbroken Montana cattle given to them as milk cows ("It would have been better to have give us some buffalos").[48]

At the summer treaty payments, Poundmaker also complained about the inadequacy of the treaty provisions for oxen and said that his people were being prevented from farming. "We that are on the reserves now," he complained, "when we do set to work, have so few cattle that when one family goes to work lots of others remain idle and we cannot put in much crop."[49] He pointed out that the nontreaty Indians, like Big Bear, were watching those who had stayed on their reserves to see whether they could indeed make a living from the soil.

★　★　★

Two years had passed since Big Bear had made his vow. In that time the situation of the Indians had become worse. More than five thousand starving Indians were clustered around Fort Walsh, reluctant to go south but aware that "there is nothing whatever to keep them from starvation north of the line."[50]

In the autumn, Big Bear concluded there was no point in coming back into Canada any longer. The buffalo now were near the Missouri River, and herds were thick in the Judith Basin, so in spite of the chaos in Montana, he would have to join them or starve. As he prepared to leave, there was great excitement when a Cree, Little Fisher, was arrested for horse stealing and sentenced to six months in prison. His chief, *Piapot*, was shocked, for just three months earlier, a trio of raiders had served only fourteen days for the same type of crime.

Piapot called a council of the leading chiefs, and together they went to see Commissioner Irvine of the NWMP, Magistrate James F. Macleod and the local Indian agent. In their party were Big Bear, Lucky Man, Little Pine, Foremost Man, The Man That Took the Coat and Little Child. As spokesman, *Piapot* asked the officials if they intended to honour the promises made in the treaties and to help recover horses stolen from them. He noted the police were quick to arrest Crees, but those who stole from the Crees appeared to get away unharmed. "Our women have to carry their bedding and lodge poles when moving camp," complained the chief, "and our children that used to be well mounted before you came amongst us have to travel on foot. You deter our young men from stealing horses from their enemies by threatening to put them in gaol, and now that we are starving, what are we to do?" Magistrate Macleod explained that the police could not go into Montana after horse thieves and cautioned the Crees against stealing from ranchers or white settlers. However, if other tribes were stealing horses from them, why could they not simply steal them back? *Piapot* jumped up and pointed to Macleod. "You hear what the white chief says," he shouted. "He tells you that you can go to steal horses from Indians and that he will not punish you. Now, young men, you can do as you like, I won't interfere with you, either to encourage you or discourage you."[51]

Big Bear was silent during the meeting, but afterwards he voiced his displeasure and suspicion about the magistrate's statement. "The police," he said, "have bidden us to make up our losses by stealing from others. I think this is bad advice and is given because the whites want to have us killed off. The advice, if acted on, would very likely lead to collisions with other bands and result in bloodshed."[52]

After this unsettling meeting that seemed to counsel war, not peace, Big Bear set out with his massive camp of three hundred lodges to move to the United States. For the next two years he lived in Montana, dealing with the problems of hunger, intertribal discord and ranchers' hatred. He saw strange alliances formed and old ones broken as thousands of Indians congregated in central Montana to live off the last of the buffalo herds.

He selected a campsite at Carrol, a wood station for steamboats on the Missouri River, which had a cluster of trading cabins and makeshift saloons, all vying for the Indian trade. On the way there, scouts informed him that a large camp of Blackfoot already was in that valley and was prepared to greet the Cree in peace. When Big Bear arrived, he met with Crowfoot, a leading chief of the Blackfoot, and they agreed that the two tribes would camp side by side all winter. From there, Big Bear sent messengers with tobacco to the Blood and Peigan, asking that there be peace and a halt to horse stealing while everyone concentrated on the hunt. The former tribe reluctantly agreed, but the Peigan rejected the offer, claiming that the Cree were infringing upon their hunting grounds.

Before the onset of cold weather, a large caravan of carts screeched into the valley and stopped alongside the Indians. The half-breeds, too, had come for the winter. As it happened, there was buffalo enough for everyone; the herds were close to the river, and hunters could find fresh meat within a day's ride of camp.

The traders experienced their best season in years; one firm at Carrol alone took in four thousand robes and all the dried meat they could get. Other traders did as well, or better, dealing in whiskey. One trader sold two thousand gallons (9100 L) that winter to the Crees, Blackfoot and half-breeds, and prostitution became commonplace. "I think the Crees and Red Rivers loved liquor more than any other people I met on the plains," commented a Carrol trader. "The Blackfeet liked it, but not well enough to impoverish themselves for it. The former, however, would sell anything they had to obtain it, even their women, and it was rare for a family to have more than half a dozen horses. Many of the Crees were obliged to walk when moving camp, packing their few effects on dogs. There were nights when at least a thousand of them would be drunk together, dancing and singing around little fires built down in the timber, some crying foolishly, some making love, others going through all sorts of strange and uncouth antics." In Big Bear's camp, however, the trader noted: "There was very little quarreling among them, not half a dozen being killed in the whole winter. More than that number froze to death, falling on their way in the night and being unable to rise and go on."[53]

Big Bear himself experienced problems caused by liquor. On one occasion a member of his band named Blond Eyebrows, who was a distant relative, stole someone's horse, but the chief returned it to the rightful owner. A short time later the man in a fractious, drunken state staggered over to Big Bear's lodge and beat up the old chief, knocking him unconscious. Only Big Bear's daughter was at home at the time. She was so furious that she dashed over to Blond Eyebrows's lodge, slashed it with her knife and appropriated his saddles, hunting equipment and all his other possessions. When Big Bear regained his senses, he forced her to return all these things, but he never forgave the man for attacking him.

Another incident involving liquor wounded Big Bear more deeply than the injuries he received from the beating. Before leaving Canada, he had taken another wife into his lodge, a dark-eyed attractive girl who was less than half his age. She was the beauty of the camp and was regarded by Big Bear with pride and affection. However, during the period of prolonged drinking in Montana, the girl became involved with a warrior from Big Bear's band and started an affair with him. The younger man resented the fact that she was committed to someone else, and as the authority of all chiefs had diminished during the turmoil of social breakdown, he saw no reason to respect Big Bear just because he was a chief. Finally, in an angry drunken state, he set upon the chief with a club and knocked him to the ground. Big Bear's grandson swears that the blow was so vicious that it killed the chief on the spot. "But his wife *Sayos* had been instructed what to do in case he got killed," added Four Souls. "So she called a medicine man who followed the instructions and Big Bear was brought back to life. Big Bear didn't try to take revenge on this man right away, but later on he got the medicine man to use bad medicine on him and killed him."[54] Interestingly enough, Big Bear forgave his young wife, perhaps attributing her dalliance to alcohol. Later, when *Sayos* and his other wives died, this young woman became his only mate, but they had no children.

In addition to alcohol, problems with horse raiding continued for the entire time that Big Bear was in Montana. Not only were the Indians robbing each other's hunting camps near the Missouri River, but those camped across the line near Fort Walsh found they could go into Montana and steal with impunity, racing back to the Queen's territory with their loot. As Magistrate Macleod had predicted, little or nothing was done unless they stole white men's horses. When that happened, an American rancher sometimes went to the Mounted Police to lay charges against Canadian Indians.

Living as they were among the ranchers and the buffalo, Big Bear and his camp often had to take the blame for raids conducted by Indians in the north. And their relationship with the ranchers was tenuous at best, for each time a cow went missing, the loss was blamed on them. Although scores of animals were killed by prairie wolves, drowned in sloughs or simply wandered away, each missing creature added to the anger of the ranchmen. They could see some excuse for United States Indians being in the area, and they could be sent back to their reservations, but the Canadian Cree and Blackfoot were beyond the jurisdiction of the local Indian bureau authorities.

During the winter, the Assiniboine Indians, whose agency was farther east near Fort Belknap, complained the Canadian Indians were trespassing on their reservation and killing cattle. One day a grim-looking group of Assiniboine leaders accompanied by American troops showed up at the villages of Big Bear and Crowfoot. "In peace I come to see you, Big Bear," said the Assiniboine chief. "All of you from Canada — Crees, Blackfoot, Sarcees — I count you as one. I blame you for the loss of our cattle and I want you to give us ten of your best horses as payment. I am not short of horses myself but that is the only way you can pay." There were murmurs of unrest among the Cree warriors. The Assiniboine chief looked at them disdainfully and added: "If you don't do this, I will know what I will do to you."

Big Bear was upset by the demand from these people whom he considered to be allies. He knew that the Crees were on lands set aside for the Assiniboine and Gros Ventre who, if they wished, could force the northerners to be removed. "Haw!" Big Bear said as he turned to the crowd. "You Crees and Blackfoot have heard what has been said. We must give the Assiniboines ten horses if we wish to stay on their reservation. I will start; my family will give two." One by one the Crees came forward, until there were nine horses in front of the Assiniboine chief. The Blackfoot had remained aloof from the proceedings, but at last a man brought forward a wild, unbroken bronco to fill the quota.

"For you chiefs," said the Assiniboine, "it is not hard to do this." Then, as an insult to the Blackfoot, he added: "It is only those who can't get their own horses that are afraid to give. I'll take these, Big Bear, but the next time I lose any cattle I'll find another way to punish you."[55]

In spite of this incident and ongoing problems with alcohol, horse thieves and ranchers, Big Bear enjoyed himself on the Missouri. There were plenty of buffalo, and he was looked upon by everyone as the leading Cree chief in the region. He called meetings of the council, met with fretful ranchers and tried to maintain peace with the Blood and Blackfoot. Whenever his warriors would listen, he tried to discourage them from raiding the Peigan, even though that tribe had turned down the suggestion of a peace pact.

"The Crees have a very good chief," commented Louis Riel. "It is the Big Bear. He is a man of good sense. Whenever the young men of his camp bring any horses branded and showing signs that they were stolen from white people, he invariably will go to a responsible man, put the stolen property into his hands, asking him to advertize and find the owners if possible. His first soldiers are helping him as much as they can in that pursuit."[56]

Big Bear's oldest sons, Twin Wolverine and *Imasees,* and his son-in-law, Lone Man, were a regular part of the chief's inner family circle, where decisions for the camp often were made. Wandering Spirit, the leading warrior, was a good friend of *Imasees* but was never part of this family group and resented it. A hotheaded man with a quick temper, he particularly disliked Lone Man's inclusion since he was left out.

From his lodge Big Bear followed with concern the events taking place back in Canada, hoping Indian farmers would get all the help they needed to settle down to their new life. But as he listened to visitors and had the *Saskatchewan Herald* read to him, he knew this was not the case. The Indians on reserves near Battleford had suffered because of crop failures, complained about the nonfulfillment of treaty promises and chafed under the inadequacy of the treaty itself. Poundmaker, officially appointed a chief that summer, became the leading spokesman for the disillusioned Indians, picking up the fight where Big Bear had left off in 1878. Messengers were sent to other reserves to enlist support, and officials complained that "the Chiefs all over the Country are to join those B/ford [Battleford] rascals next summer in asking for better terms."[57]

Then, when the snows disappeared and the prairie grass began to turn green, the desperate chiefs decided to abandon their reserves and return to the buffalo. Before leaving, Poundmaker declared that they "justify their conduct on the ground of non-fulfillment of promises made both by the Commissioner [Dewdney] and by the retiring agent [Orde]. They saw, amongst other things, that the treaty must be revised, and that a great council will be held at the payment time to bring that about."[58] By May, thirteen hundred Indians had deserted their reserves and headed south, congregating on the prairies at Fort Walsh; within a few weeks the numbers had risen to three thousand. The northerners had planned to go out from Fort Walsh to hunt but found that the buffalo were far off and were obliged to accept rations from the Mounted Police.

Poundmaker reigned as leading chief of the protesters and was accused of "exciting sedition" for continuing to press for better terms.[59] Instead of listening to him, government officials merely refused to pay the northern people at the time of treaty and told them they had to go home if they wanted their money. Relations became so strained that a general attack on Fort Walsh was feared by the police, and when a patrol went to the Cree camps, it "found the Indians all riding around and firing off their guns."[60]

Yet without buffalo, the Indians had no power, and they knew it. In a matter of days, the entire protest movement collapsed, and the broken and dispirited Indians trailed sadly away. Poundmaker, after receiving assurances that his people would not be punished by having their rations taken away, returned crestfallen to Battleford.

Big Bear was also having difficulties with officials in the spring of 1881. A number of Montana ranchers petitioned the secretary of the interior in Washington, asking him to force the Canadian Indians back across the line. "These Indians," said the petition, "ostensibly here for the purpose of hunting buffalo, have killed and eaten many of our cattle, and this, too, in instances where there was an abundance of buffalo within ten miles of their camps."[61] The local newspapers, Washington Delegate Martin Maginnis and businessmen took up the cry, demanding that action be taken. When Washington had done nothing by midsummer, the Choteau and Meagher Counties Stock Protective Association was formed "to protect their property by force of arms if other measures fail."[62]

Although not prepared to move Big Bear's camp, the army did consider his village to be a problem. One day, a hunting party from the camp had just killed sixty buffalo and were butchering them when suddenly they were surrounded by American soldiers armed with cannon. The bluecoats confiscated their horses and ordered the Crees back to their village. Two of them who tried to protest the military action were beaten and left lying on the ground. Taking what little meat they could carry, the hunters returned to the big camp; when the warriors heard what had happened, they were ready to attack the soldiers before they got back to their fort. Instead, four hunters went as a delegation to Big Bear and his council, while the infuriated warriors waited outside the chief's lodge, singing their war songs, impatient to leave. The council itself was divided on the issue: some wanted to fight, others were opposed.

"Aha, this is what I think," one of the councillors said to the chief, "it wasn't the fault of the Grandfather in Washington but his men."

Wandering Spirit was angry and outspoken, ready for war.

"Some want to fight," said another councillor, "but our strength is nothing. But perhaps we deserve this punishment, after all, we are strangers here."

"He has truth," commented another, "we should do what is right."

After persuading the majority of the council to favour a peaceful solution, Big Bear offered to go to Fort Assiniboine to try to get their horses back. Next morning, all the leading chiefs and the members of the soldiers' lodge set out for the fort, and there they gathered in front of a large, impressive house. A half-breed interpreter was summoned, and when all was in readiness, the commanding officer came out on the verandah. Big Bear arose and shook hands with him, a tall, thin soldier who looked unsmilingly at the throng of Crees.

"In peace I come and would speak," said Big Bear.

"Yes, I'm listening."

"I have done no wrong. My people get blamed for everything that happens but we have done nothing. We have come to this land to make our livelihood, to support ourselves."

"Yes?"

"I come to you today with a good heart, thinking that you will have a touch of sympathy for us, that you will pity us. We are poor and in a bad way. I have come to ask you to give us back our horses."

The officer listened, but he was neither sympathetic nor impressed. "Obviously you do not understand our laws here," he said sharply, "so I'll tell you the situation. Plenty of cattle are missing in our country and we blame you people from Canada. We know that our Indians are not at fault because the cattle did not begin to disappear until you came. If I carried out my orders to the letter of the law I would take everything you have, not just your horses, but your guns, your lodges, and your clothes, until you would have nothing left."

"But we have little or nothing now," protested Big Bear.

"You are thieves from another land," shouted the officer angrily, "and you should be shot like dogs! If you had behaved yourselves in the first place you would have been treated well and this wouldn't have happened. You will not get your horses back."[63]

In spite of military campaigns, Big Bear's camp itself was not molested, and by the time it was reinforced by the treaty bands that returned from Canada, it had grown to more than two hundred lodges. Before winter set in, they moved north of the Missouri to camp in the Little Rockies, where there was wood, shelter and plenty of buffalo. With the onset of cold weather, complaints from ranchers and trouble from army patrols ceased, as everyone turned his attention to surviving the winter.

★ ★ ★

Three years had passed since Big Bear vowed he would watch what happened to those who had accepted treaty. He had prayed for honesty and fair play from the government, but he had obviously been expecting too much. He had no wish to go back to a land where men spoke with forked tongues and the Queen would not listen to her subjects. But what choice did he have?

At about this time, Big Bear discovered that someone from his nation had signed a treaty with the Americans in 1855. This chief, named Eyes in the Front and Back, had even travelled to Washington to see the Great Father and to receive presents from him. Big Bear also learned that Maj. John Young, the officer currently in charge of the huge Indian reservation that occupied most of northern Montana, was sympathetic to his people. He considered the eastern part of the reservation to belong to the "Gros Ventres, Assiniboines, Crees, River Crows and Sioux."[64]

In the autumn of 1881, Big Bear received a visitor whom he claimed offered him a reservation in the United States. A scoffing Dewdney believed that "this has been done by some designing trader, in order that he might be induced to remain during the winter at that point where the buffalo are pretty thick."[65] Yet Big Bear was not so foolish that he did not know the difference between a trader and a government man.

According to family tradition, the offer came from a military officer who visited the chief's camp:

> A steamboat came up the river and on board was a captain who said he had orders from the President of the United States to find Big Bear. When he was taken to the camp, he produced a piece of paper.
>
> "Big Bear," he said, "I came to look for you. I have a document here and if you want to sign it, then I'll sign it too. The buffalo are being depleted; soon there will be no more meat. The government sent me with this document for you to sign. If you sign, you can have this country, any part of it. Just pick out your reservation and we'll take care of you."
>
> Most of the people were in favour of signing and Big Bear thought it was better than the deal they were being offered by the Queen. But then Little Poplar got up and spoke against it. He was opposed to signing any treaty with the American government and at last he talked Big Bear out of signing.[66]

As the rumours persisted, the Canadian government worried that there might be some truth in them. It referred the matter to the Canadian representative in Washington, who responded: "I have the honor to inform Your Excellency that I learn from Mr. Frelinghuysen that he has received a letter from the Secretary of the Interior stating that 'His Department has no knowledge of any such transaction.' "[67]

There is no question that late in 1881 somebody did speak to Big Bear and led him to believe he could have an American reservation. Perhaps it was Major Young, who coincidentally passed Big Bear's camp in a steamboat in October on his return from a trip to Washington. Young may not have offered him a reservation, but if Big Bear had enquired about one and had not received an unequivocal rejection, he might have assumed that his request had been approved. Whatever happened, Big Bear was convinced that he could settle in Montana and proceeded immediately to visit the other camps to give them the news.

To Big Bear, the information had two advantages: he could actually take a reservation or he could use it as a bargaining point with the Queen's men. Either way, it looked like a positive breakthrough.

Imasees, Twin Wolverine and Wandering Spirit — who had come to hate the Queen's men and all they stood for — urged Big Bear to accept the American offer immediately. When he did not, they became extremely angry with him and with Little Poplar for taking his side. It was, according to family tradition, the first major rift between Big Bear and his sons. They were becoming tired of discussions with the Canadians that never seemed to lead anywhere, tired of a chief who was getting too old and tired of his waiting. Significantly, of course, the following year would see the end of his four-year vow.

Although the winter was a bitter one, there was plenty of buffalo and lots of whiskey. One traveller saw forty Indians drunk near Rocky Point, and another reported a trader was killed by a Cree while ladling whiskey out of a keg. By now, the Canadian Indians tended to be a painfully visible part of the Montana landscape, as most of the American tribes had been forced back to their reservations. A few bands were scattered around the prairie hills, but they were insignificant when compared to Big Bear's huge village or to the several hundred Canadian half-breeds camped in log cabins farther east on Milk River.

The foreign invaders had become a political embarrassment to the authorities, so in the spring of 1882, the military mounted the Milk River Expedition to drive the Canadian Indians and half-breeds back across the line. A combination of cavalry and infantry groups, equipped with cannon and gatling guns under the command of Major Klein, planned to make a sweep of the Milk River and then strike Big Bear's camp in the Little Rockies. One man predicted that when they were finished, "considerable expense will be spared the Canadian government as they will have several Indians less to feed."[68]

The half-breeds, with their semipermanent log cabins, were the easiest to find, and so on 15 March, the first settlement was attacked near Medicine Lodge. There was no resistance, and the next two days were spent burning 150 cabins along the river, while the half-breeds fled north to Wood Mountain on the Canadian side. Next the Milk River Expedition pushed westward to Little Pine's camp near the Big Bend of Milk River and "had them running for the Queen's Possessions in an hour."[69] In the meantime, four men were sent ahead to find Big Bear's camp.

Messengers from Little Pine managed to warn Big Bear of the impending attack, and quickly the authority of the camp shifted from Big Bear to Wandering Spirit. Now that they were in a state of war, the soldiers' lodge became the centre of activity, and the war chief its strategist. During the days of peril, Big Bear was just another member of the tribal council, taking his orders from the mercurial war chief.

Wandering Spirit was now in his late thirties, a tall, lithe man with a quick, nervous temperament. His eyes had a "burning intensity, flashing here and there, seeing everything. . . . His nose was long and straight, his mouth wide and lips thin and cruel. He had a prominent chin, deep sunken cheeks and features darkly bronzed and seamed about the eyes and mouth with sharply-cut lines. His voice was usually soft and intriguing; when he spoke in council it rose gradually until it rang through the camp."[70]

The war chief ordered the camp struck and dispatched scouts to watch for army patrols. Then, covering their trail by travelling in places where the horses' tracks and travois marks could not be seen, they moved from the Little Rockies out into the badlands.

Major Klein became concerned when his scouting party failed to return, fearing that they had been set upon by Big Bear's warriors. Instead, he learned that their delay had been caused by their failure to find the enemy camp: Big Bear and his 150 lodges had disappeared. Klein could not keep his troops in the field indefinitely, so after further searches failed to reveal the missing Indians, the campaign was abandoned.

The success of the Crees in avoiding a conflict was due to the swift and decisive action of Wandering Spirit, but since white people did not understand the Indian military and political structure, all the credit went to Big Bear. A journalist sarcastically suggested that the army "present Big Bear . . . the Freedom of Milk river on a silver salver, and acknowledge gracefully that the Crees . . . are too much for them. The expedition never even saw one of Big Bear's tracks, so successfully did he play his part in the game of hide and seek on Milk River."[71]

Once the threat of attack passed, the Crees moved to a new camp on Beaver Creek, and Big Bear resumed his role as chief. They had avoided a conflict, but everyone in the camp knew it was only a matter of time before the soldiers returned. Big Bear's camp was the last group of refugees on the American side; next time there probably would be no warning. And with excitable men like Wandering Spirit and *Imasees,* a conflict might be hard to avoid. The council agreed with Big Bear that they should return to Canada, at least temporarily. They would have their spring hunt first, and with the scouts constantly patrolling the area, they would put up all the dried meat they could carry. Realizing that they soon would be out of the reach of American soldiers and marshals, some of the young men also took advantage of the respite to go out on raiding parties. After months of being held back by Big Bear and the camp soldiers, the young warriors left Montana in a blaze of glory, recovering some of the herds plundered from them over the previous two years.

Late in April 1882, still undisturbed by the military and with their travois loaded with meat, Big Bear and his camp set off for Fort Walsh. This was his first trip to Canada in two years. He had vowed to wait four years to see how the Crees fared under the Queen's government, and now he would find out for himself.

No More Choices

B IG BEAR HAD WAITED four long years, two of them in self-imposed
exile from his homeland. The Canadian government had had
enough time to help the Indians find a new life, to relieve their suffering
and their worries about the future. There had been enough time for
officials to appreciate the viewpoints of the Indians and to become more
compassionate and understanding.

Yet when Big Bear arrived at the Indian camp near Fort Walsh in the
spring of 1882, he had visible evidence of what the extermination of the
buffalo and the failure of government policies had meant to the Crees.
Two thousand treaty Indians were camped near Cypress Lake, their skin
tepees rotting and falling apart; families were living in makeshift shelters
of cotton cloth and tree branches. Many people were emaciated and in
rags, their moccasins worn out, their horses sold and even their dogs
gone to make stew. If they were lucky, they got enough rations from the
Mounted Police to keep them alive: three-quarters of a pound of flour
and one-third pound of dried meat one day, a half-pound of flour and a
pound of fresh meat another; sometimes a few potatoes were added to
the fare.

Farther north, on their reserves, other Indians were also utterly destitute. Although they were trying to farm, they usually had insufficient
implements and found themselves completely dominated by agents or
farming instructors, some of whom seemed to be getting fatter while the
Indians got thinner. In that year, Poundmaker complained that the farm
instructor would not let his people use the band oxen and that a
promised grist mill never arrived, nor was there enough seed to plant
their crops of potatoes and wheat.

With sadness, Big Bear learned what was happening to his fellow
chiefs. *Piapot,* still camped in the Cypress Hills, refused to move to
Indian Head to a reserve that had been set aside but which he had not
chosen. He complained of broken promises and starvation among his

people. Farther west, old friend Bobtail had taken a reserve in the Peace Hills, south of Edmonton. He told of his band's dire poverty "with little or no help, and apparently less sympathy from those placed to watch over us. . . . If no attention is paid to our case now, we shall conclude that the treaty made with us six years ago was a meaningless matter of forms and that the white man has indirectly doomed us to annihilation little by little."[1]

But perhaps the most poignant plea came from Foremost Man, as he spoke to a white man about his new life. "We are hungry," he began simply. "The Great Mother does not know it. Her agents tell her we are happy, but we are not. Where are the buffalo? Where are our horses? They are gone, and we must soon follow them. Your people have our lands. These prairies were ours once, and the buffalo were given us by the Great Spirit. They kept us warm; they kept us from being hungry; they kept us in fuel. But they are all gone. Look at me; look at those round me, and say we look happy. Are these blankets warm enough for the winter; are they like the buffalo robes we used to have? Let them send the buffalo back, and take their own people to the reserve where they came from. Give us the prairies again and we won't ask for food. But it is too late. It is too late. It is too late."[2]

Big Bear may have been reluctant to join the destitute Crees at Fort Walsh, realizing that he could not bargain from a position of strength while his followers were starving. Yet he had no choice, for Montana was out of bounds to him, until the political pressures eased among the military, ranchers and settlers. Besides, his four years of waiting would expire in the summer, and he would have had to return anyway to keep his promise to the Indian commissioner and to the Great Spirit.

Big Bear's reputation preceded him to Fort Walsh, where the Mounted Police were busily confiscating all ammunition from local traders, moving the rations of meat and flour into the fort, mounting a seven-pound cannon in the front bastion and putting all men on the alert. However, when this chief — described by Dewdney as the leader of "the most worthless and troublesome Indians we have" — arrived at the fort, he was alone.[3] He had come in ahead of his three hundred followers to let the Queen's soldiers know he was back. He was told curtly that because he was nontreaty, his camp would get no food but should move to Cypress Lake, thirty miles (48 km) away, where they could try to survive by fishing.

From *Piapot* and others, Big Bear learned the government had ordered all Indians to leave the district, the Treaty Four people for Qu'Appelle and the rest for Battleford or Fort Pitt. Little Pine's request for a reserve in the Cypress Hills was rejected, and he too was told to go north to Battleford, even though his hunting area had been west on the Alberta plains. Fort Walsh was going to be closed, and anyone left behind, treaty or nontreaty, would receive no help. In addition, Big Bear was informed none of his people would get any help until he surrendered his freedom and signed the treaty. By these actions, the delicate international problem created by Indians raiding back and forth across the border would be resolved; the government would force the Crees onto reserves, where they would be under the direct control of Indian agents. The policy was dispassionately clear: move north or starve.

Within days after Big Bear had reached the Cypress Hills, hungry and dejected Indians began going north. The first to leave were the Assiniboines from Treaty Four. Their fellow tribesmen from Battleford under Mosquito and Bear's Head were the next to return north, followed by Thunder Child and Young Chipewyan. Along the way, the Assiniboines were raided by Bloods, who took thirty-one of their horses, leaving them in a more pitiful condition than when they had started. Before they finally staggered onto their reserve, one old woman had died along the trail.

When summer came, Big Bear was still at Cypress Lake with about 260 lodges, including those of Lucky Man and Little Pine. The treaty Indians continued to receive meagre rations, including bacon (which they hated) instead of dried meat. From time to time the chief met with Mounted Police officers who spoke to him about the treaty, but he would not tell them whether he had made up his mind to accept.

Meanwhile, Big Bear was concerned about the bad image that he had been given in reports by Dewdney and other government officials, so when an article appeared in the *Saskatchewan Herald,* blaming him for the problems around Fort Walsh, he had a rebuttal forwarded to that Battleford newspaper. He felt that "he is being made a scapegoat of, by being charged with being anxious to create trouble by refusing to give in his adhesion to the treaty. He has so far refused to take his annuity because he wanted to see whether the white man would keep faith with his people, and the term of probation expires this year. He says that the Commissioner promised him at Sounding Lake that if, when he was satisfied that the Government intended to keep its promises and would take his money this year he would himself pay over the money."[4]

During the summer, the poverty in Big Bear's camp became acute, as hunting in the area virtually ceased. Going back to Montana was out of the question, so Big Bear was forced to stay on the Canadian side, his people slowly and deliberately being starved. Pressures from his own followers to sign the treaty increased; they could see no benefit in waiting while everyone went hungry. The broader issues of the value of their surrendered land, the honesty of the government and the treatment of those on reserves was now less important to them than food in their stomachs and clothing on their backs. In his own way, Big Bear was forced to agree. He had promised to wait for four years; from the government, he had looked for honesty and compassion, which did not exist; from the Great Spirit he had looked for help, which had not come. Now, he was the last major chief to resist signing; the buffalo were out of reach, and the suffering of his people was increasing day by day.

In mid-October, Frederick White, comptroller of the North-West Mounted Police, and physician Augustus Jukes visited the camps of Big Bear and the treaty Indians who had refused to go north. Both men were appalled and told Dewdney what his strategy was doing to the people. Doctor Jukes wrote:

> They are literally in a starving condition and destitute of the commonest necessaries of life. The disappearance of the Buffalo has left them not only without food, but also without Robes, mocassins [sic] and adequate Tents or 'Teppees' to shield them from the inclemency of the impending winter. Few of their lodges are of Buffalo hide, the majority being of cotton only, many of these in the most rotten and dilapidated condition. . . . Their clothing for the most part was miserable and scanty in the extreme. I saw little children at this inclement season, snow having fallen, who had scarcely rags to cover them. Of food they possessed little or none; some were represented to me as absolutely starving and their appearance confirmed the report made of their condition. . . . It would indeed be difficult to exaggerate their extreme wretchedness and need, or the urgent necessity which exists from some prompt and sufficient provision being made for them by the Government.[5]

Dewdney, however, interpreted the report as evidence that his scheme was working and was opposed to offering any assistance, particularly to Big Bear and his refractory band. When the prime minister intervened, Dewdney downplayed the evidence of starvation, telling Sir John, "It must be recollected that Dr. Jukes has not had much experience with Indians."[6] Appeals from Little Pine and other treaty chiefs to be given reserves near Fort Walsh were turned down, but in spite of Dewdney's objections, the Indians were told that their annuity money would be given to them so they could buy food and clothing. They previously had been informed by the unyielding commissioner that no one would be given money until the bands went north.

As for Big Bear, the one remaining nontreaty chief, nothing was done, and his people continued to freeze and to starve. Daily, the pressures against him increased; his sons, who had been angry when he had declined to pursue an American reservation, now had fears of losing a Canadian one as well. He was being perceived increasingly as a stubborn old man who could not make up his mind and who was causing needless suffering among his followers. Twin Wolverine, *Imasees* and even Lone Man wanted him to sign the treaty.

When word spread through the camp that the treaty Indians would be paid, the criticism of Big Bear became open defiance. Amid their poverty and destitution, people saw a chance to get food and clothing if their chief would sign. Each person would receive the twelve-dollar bonus promised in 1876, plus their regular treaty money — twenty-five dollars for chiefs, fifteen for head men and five dollars for everyone else.

Big Bear's family knew that the money would come from a bank in Fort Benton and that if they waited too long, nothing would be left in the cash box for them. As they talked, their anger and impatience increased, until one of Big Bear's daughters, the wife of French Eater, stormed over to the chief, insisting that he take treaty. Look at his own family: his youngest son, Horse Child, only nine years old, was slowly starving to death, and his youngest daughter, Earth Woman, not old enough to know what was happening, was hungry all the time. Over in the nearby tents, *Imasees'* two sons and two tiny daughters, as well as Twin Wolverine's five children, were suffering from malnutrition. Her sister, who was married to Lone Man, had three small boys and two girls, all of them weak from hunger. And what about her own lodge? Were her ten children to starve or freeze to death while the treaty Indians spent their annuities? If Big Bear would not take treaty, then she would be the first of his children to break with him; she would take it on her own. Her mind was made up: hungry babies came before politics.

News that French Eater's wife was going to accept treaty spread swiftly through the camp. With that bold move, resistance crumbled, and by the time the pay table was cleared to receive her, almost all of Big Bear's family and many members of his band were also there. *Imasees* defiantly stalked forward first to claim sixty dollars in back annuities. Then came Twin Wolverine, who collected $208 for the large group around him, followed by French Eater's wife, who picked up $109.

Big Bear's defeat was not complete, for Lone Man and his wife refused to leave his side, and French Eater himself rejected the payments, even though his wife had gone forward. Men like *Anekoos,* Stone Quill and Animal Child also let their wives and children take treaty, though they chose to stay with their chief. His twenty-two-year-old son King Bird did not accept treaty, nor did his adopted children, Small Magpie and Thunder.

At the end of the payment session, 133 members of Big Bear's band had left their chief and taken treaty. It must have been a bitter experience to see his people leave him one by one. They did not share his political dream, and he knew they had hungry families to feed, but it made the event no less humiliating. Proudly aloof, he could only watch rigidly as the control of his followers and the hopes for a better treaty seemed to be slipping from his fingers.

A couple of weeks after the treaty payment, Big Bear spoke to Mounted Police Commissioner Irvine in a last attempt to improve the terms of the treaty. He spent hours each day with the officer, and sometimes their sessions stretched far into the night. Over and over, the chief pointed out the shortcomings of the treaty; the rights of his people to the land; the forked tongue of the Indian commissioner and his agents; the fact that when the Queen had taken the land that belonged to the Great Spirit, she had taken the responsibility for looking after her children of the plains. Irvine listened to it all, but could not negotiate any changes. The Cree chief came to believe that somewhere far downriver lived a man named Government who had taken Big Bear's land but would not meet him face to face. Instead, he sent his servants who had no authority. Whenever Big Bear reached out to shake hands with Government, he was not there, just a Mounted Policeman or an Indian department official. How could he negotiate with a man he could not see?

In the end, Big Bear had no choice but to accept the treaty as it stood: otherwise, the 114 faithful ones who had stayed with him would starve to death over the winter.

On 8 December 1882 Big Bear led a solemn procession of chiefs and head men into the office of Allan McDonald, the Indian agent who had come to Fort Walsh to pay treaty. With the chief were *Piapot,* Lucky Man, Lone Man and other members of his family. Big Bear spoke for four solid hours, repeating all the problems, demands and needs that had become so familiar to those around him. At last, the chief's son and Lone Man, "fearing no more back pay would be allowed Indians who did not take the Treaty this year," interrupted the fifty-seven-year-old chief and urged him to sign.[7] Resignedly, Big Bear took the pen and put his mark on two copies of the adhesion document.

He had signed.

For his head men, he selected neither Twin Wolverine nor *Imasees,* nor, for that matter, anyone who had deserted him two weeks earlier. His choices were Wandering Spirit (who had taken treaty in 1879 with Lucky Man) and Four Sky Thunder and The Singer, both of whom had been receiving their money with *Piapot's* band.

Big Bear had been badly hurt both personally and politically by the repudiation of his two eldest sons, who had become imbued with a hatred for the Queen, which, combined with the impetuousness of youth, made them hard to control. Twin Wolverine emerged from the treaty affair as a family leader, and as he proudly told officials, "My father's people . . . never move anywhere or do anything without coming to me for advice. The young people always follow me & take my advice."[8] Openly defied by his sons, the chief's stature was diminished and his authority reduced. Men began to turn to *Imasees* or to Twin Wolverine, who were part of the warrior element in the band, and as soon as the weather moderated, hunters and war parties began slipping away, in spite of Big Bear's objections. In the spring of 1883, *Imasees* himself defied his father and left for central Montana with a following of fifty people. They wanted to taste real buffalo meat again and would risk the ire of Montana ranchers and the United States army to get there. The hunting party had just reached the Musselshell River when suddenly they were surrounded by an American army patrol from Fort Maginnis. Most of the Crees surrendered quietly, but *Imasees* and a dozen other young men dashed away into the trees. "Lieut. Steele, of Maginnis," reported the *Benton Weekly Record,* "while out scouting in company with a corporal, ran on to them in the thick bush, but finding themselves covered by the Indians' guns had to retreat. After getting reinforcements, however, they returned and captured the whole outfit."[9] All the guns in the camp were seized, and none too gently after *Imasees'* demonstration; then the group was escorted to Fort Assiniboine and from there to the border. At the boundary, all horses were taken from the Indians and the Red River carts and contents piled high and burned. The officer then warned *Imasees* "that on no pretext whatsoever must any Cree Indians re-cross to this side of the line, that if found in Montana hereafter, they would be considered enemies and horse thieves and be severely punished."[10]

Canadian officials were still trying to get *Piapot* to leave for Qu'Appelle, and Big Bear, Lucky Man and Little Pine to go to Battleford, but they all refused to move. Finally, the Mounted Police dealt a double blow to the Cree camps. First, they brought to trial several Indians charged with stealing horses in Montana. Such charges in the past had resulted in mild reprimands, but in this instance some of the raiders were sentenced to five years and others to two years in Stony Mountain Penitentiary. The action was taken "with a view to get the Indians to move Northward," even though those who had to serve long sentences were prone to contract tuberculosis in the dark cells of the penitentiary and die of the disease.[11]

The second step, taken late in May, was to abandon Fort Walsh, tear down the buildings and move the NWMP detachment to the railway line at Maple Creek. If the chiefs insisted on staying in the south, they would do so with the knowledge that they would get no rations.

Although Big Bear's control over the young warriors and his own sons had been weakened during the previous few months, the head men and older members were solidly behind him. Even Twin Wolverine and

Imasees, impatient and outspoken as they were, realized that their father was the only one whom many people in the band would heed, and more important, he was the only one who could speak to the government. One of his conditions on signing the treaty was that the payment come directly from the hands of Indian Commissioner Dewdney, and now he refused to leave until he had seen the Queen's representative.

Big Bear had waited four years before signing the treaty, and during that time, he had refrained from political campaigning. Instead, he had watched and prayed to the Great Spirit. Conditions now were worse than before, and he had accepted treaty because he had been pressured to, not because he had wanted to. But, with his period of waiting over, he intended to attack the obnoxious treaty and, with the help of other bands, to change it. He knew that the government had revised other treaties after they had been in effect for a few years, so there was no reason they could not do the same with Treaty Six.

Early in July the Cypress Hills chiefs met with Commissioner Dewdney at the nearby village of Maple Creek. They wanted to talk about rations for their Thirst Dance, but he was there to break up their camp and move them out. *Piapot,* Big Bear, Lucky Man and Little Pine all asked that any decisions about moving to reserves be postponed until after their religious festival. When the commissioner demurred, *Piapot* repeated his criticisms about unfulfilled promises and his desire for a reserve in the Cypress Hills. Then, realizing that the dialogue was leading him nowhere, the chief angrily tore down his treaty flag, took the medal from around his neck, passed them both to the interpreter and stalked out of the council.

On the following day Big Bear had a private session with the commissioner and demanded certain concessions before he would agree to leave the area. These were not treaty negotiations, but efforts to pave the way for him and his tribe to travel to a reserve once a site had been selected. They talked about many possible ways for the government to assist the band to leave, but in the end a short shopping list was approved: a chest of rice, fifty pounds (22.5 kg) of sugar, twenty-five pounds (12.3 kg) of tobacco, six Red River carts, two ponies with harness and shotguns with ammunition for hunting along the way. Big Bear himself would get a buckboard, horse and harness and a chief's suit, all promised under the treaty, as well as a three-room house on his reserve.

The chief knew those who entered treaty after 1876 had received their annual annuities back to the date of the original treaty. This was normally done by paying one year's back annuity each year until the total amount had been paid. When Big Bear had signed at Fort Walsh, he had asked for two years' back annuities, and these had been granted. Now he asked for this payment system to remain in effect until he had received all of his back annuities, so that they would be paid off in two years instead of four. This, too, was approved.

By the end of June 1883, Big Bear and his followers were at last ready to go north and to leave forever the prairies that so recently had been thick with buffalo. They would travel to the woodlands near the North Saskatchewan River, to the place where they had formerly gone only for winter.

"The trek back to our former home was a hard one to live through," recalled Big Bear's granddaughter, "because of the lack of food and the scarcity of game. We travelled forever northwards and ran into severe storms. Deaths were numerous. We stopped only briefly to bury our dead; amongst the victims were my mother and sister. My father [*Imasees*] performed many feats of bravery which contributed greatly to some of us reaching our destination."[12]

The band was twenty-one days on the trail, and though a few people had horses and carts, many were obliged to walk. There were about 550 people in the caravan: twenty-five lodges under Big Bear, fifteen under Lucky Man, plus another twenty-five whose chiefs were not with them. The government did the best it could to assure a safe passage for the ragged group of wanderers: an Indian department employee and fifteen Mounted Police accompanied them, bringing two wagons loaded with supplies and a herd of cattle, which were slaughtered along the way. But even with food to sustain them, the trip was hard on everyone, particularly the elderly.

Big Bear was supposed to travel to Fort Pitt, but once on the trail, he decided to visit Poundmaker and his other friends on reserves in the Eagle Hills district. Big Bear knew that of all the chiefs, Poundmaker was the one who had tried the hardest to co-operate, throwing himself into farming with great enthusiasm and counselling his people to fend for themselves and not to depend on the government. But, in the end, he had been treated no better than the most recalcitrant chief; he complained bitterly that while "he has fulfilled his share of the compact entered into when he agreed to leave the plains and settle down, he has not received all that he understands he was to get."[13]

The day after Big Bear's arrival at the tiny village of Battleford, a council was held at the office of Indian Agent J. M. Rae. The warriors from the newly arrived bands formed a large semicircle in front of the building, kneeling with their rifles prominently displayed before them. Standing behind them were the Eagle Hills people, and at the centre stood Big Bear, Lucky Man and Poundmaker. Facing them was Indian Agent Rae, reclining in an armchair, "a florid and portly-looking personage, with red face, short thick neck, reddish hair and beard, and resolute-looking eyes."[14] He was flanked by his secretary and an interpreter. In contrast, Big Bear was a short, slight man wearing a broadcloth suit, Balmoral boots and a large bearskin cap. "As his unwieldly body bends backward and forward," commented a witness to the event, "and his dirty paws dart up and down, while he shows his white teeth to the self-possessed looking agent, his looks certainly are very suggestive of his name."[15]

Big Bear opened the meeting by announcing that he had seen the great chief Big Tomorrow (Dewdney), who had made a number of promises to him. There was a long pause, the agent sitting silently.

"You do not answer me," said the chief.

"I am here to listen. Go on."

" 'Tis well. I note, however, that I am not a welcome visitor?"

The Indian agent told him he had not been expected and "since you do not belong to my agency, I have not the means to make your people rejoice and be happy. We are poor, I am sorry you should have come two hundred miles out of your way. Why is it so?"

"Long before the advent of the palefaces this vast land was the hunting ground of my people," said Big Bear passionately. "This land was then the hunting ground of the Plains and the Wood Crees, my fathers. It was then teeming with buffalo and we were happy. This fair land from the Cumberland Hills to the Rockies and northward to Great Green Lake, the River of the Beavers, and the shores of Lac la Biche, and south and westward toward the setting sun," he said, gesturing, "is now the land of the white man — the land of the stranger. Our big game is no more. You now own our millions of acres — according to treaty papers — as long as grass grows on the prairies or water runs in our big rivers (commotions and grunts). We have no food. We live not like the white man, nor are we like the Indians who live on fowl and fish. True, we are promised great things but they seem far off and we cannot live and wait."

Rae listened unemotionally to the chief's words, then offered to give him some food if his people would work for it.

"Alas," replied Big Bear, "we cannot work. We are tired. Feed us until we recoup our wasted bodies and then speak of labor. We are hungry."

"Why did you not go direct to Fort Pitt?"

"We came here to see our old friends (points to Poundmaker and band) before they too die of starvation." Then Big Bear's tone hardened, as he added: "We have heard of you; your name is not respected. You are not reported to act as a gentleman. This is the opinion prevailing in the south."

"This does not matter to me at all," replied the Indian agent with a shrug. "I don't care whether I am considered a gentleman or not. But I wish you to understand that I keep my word and when I say no, I mean it. I never break my promise, and carry out instructions to the letter. What I say I mean."

"We shall see."

Agent Rae told Big Bear that he would issue enough rations for his people to go to Fort Pitt and would send an armed escort along with them. If he refused, they would get no food.

"Then we are going to remain right here!" the chief exclaimed defiantly, and there was vigorous applause among the Indians.[16]

His reluctance to go to Fort Pitt was based upon word he had received that their promised agricultural implements were not waiting for them. Also, he had been told that "the reservation set apart for the Bear" was located six miles (10 km) east of Frog Lake, even though he had not yet chosen a site.[17] He did not intend to be forced onto a reserve he had not selected.

Big Bear, suspicious about any statements made by Rae, requested him to send for William McKay, the Hudson's Bay Company factor at Fort Pitt. The chief was prepared to believe his trader friend. Offended, Agent Rae terminated the session.

If Big Bear was looking for evidence that Rae did not always keep his word, he found it a few days later. After first refusing to give them food and telling them "when I say no, I mean it," the Indian agent began issuing bacon and flour to the indigent band. Not only that, but Fort Pitt turned out to be a subagency of Battleford, so in spite of Rae's contention that "you do not belong to my agency," in fact, Big Bear did.[18]

After the meeting, an Anglican minister and a photographer visited Big Bear and found that he had lost none of his biting sense of humour. The missionary, Thomas Clarke, was just out from London and wanted to talk religion to the chief, but Big Bear laughingly turned him down. 'You wish to speak to us of the Great Spirit," he scoffed. "No, no; not now. We have not received the Black Robes only as we do the traders. At present, our ideal religion is flour and pork, and pork and flour. Let us discuss nothing more serious." Then he added, significantly, "I am the Black Bear and the Black Robe of this band." When the missionary suggested that the chief see Charles Quinney, the Anglican clergyman near Fort Pitt, who could give him good advice, Big Bear commented with a twinkle in his eye: "That is well. I trust he also keeps a good supply of pork and flour to season his wise counsel."[19]

The photographer, Walpole Roland, fared no better than the preacher. He wanted to take Big Bear's picture but was astounded when the chief demanded fifty dollars worth of tea, bacon, sugar and tobacco for the privilege. "After giving him some presents," commented Roland, "I said I could not afford so much; that he was reversing the order of things seriously, and further that I would try and find, if possible, a more repulsive-looking Indian between here and the Rockies and call him Big Bear. At this he laughed very heartily and, wishing me good day, gave me a parting shot by adding that I would probably have to go beyond the Rockies to find his rival in ugliness." Somewhat admiringly, the photographer concluded that Big Bear "is altogether the most obstinate and influential chief in the Northwest."[20]

While Big Bear waited at Battleford for McKay to arrive, he learned more about the current administration of Indian affairs and about the people who would be supervising him at Frog Lake. The farm instructor, John Delaney, had been at Frog Lake for three years and was heartily disliked by many Indians. He was considered to be one of those employees who "prostituted their authority to the debauchery of young Indian women."[21] In particular, he was accused of having stolen the wife of a man named Sand Fly; when the Indian protested, Delaney had him charged with assault. This failed to have him jailed, so a further charge of theft was levied against the Indian, and he was sentenced to two and a half years in prison. The feeling was general that "Mr. Delaney had the man arrested in order to accomplish his designs," and he cohabited with the prisoner's wife all winter.[22] Sand Fly's brother, Dancing Bull, resented the actions of the autocratic farm instructor and may have become a threat, for in 1882 Delaney accused him of witnessing the killing of a government ox and saw him sentenced to four months in jail.

The subagent, Thomas Trueman Quinn, was part Sioux, well educated, fluent in Cree and married to Owl Sitting, who was from Big Bear's band and a niece of Lone Man. Quinn, however, was a pugnacious man who had been fined for beating up another Indian department employee and was considered "hardly up to the mark for his position, which he owed, no doubt, to some political pull at Ottawa."[23]

Charges of corruption within the Indian department were also rampant. The Liberal press complained that Commissioner Dewdney possessed "no knowledge of the Indian character nor spirit enough to keep himself from being cowed, brow-beaten, and laughed at by every Indian with whom he treats."[24] Corruption was implied in his career, not from his Indian administration, but from various land dealings at Regina and the Bell farm. "Mr. Dewdney went out west as poor as a church mouse," commented the *Stratford Beacon*," and he is now reputed to be worth half a million. He is certainly a very wealthy man. He did not save this out of his salary. How did he get it?"[25]

Generally, Indian department officials were painted as insolent and incompetent men, "the most insignificant of whom assumed more arrogant airs than if he owned the country."[26] One of their corrupt practices was "in purchasing from the Indians the implements which they were naturally not anxious to use, for a bagetelle of trinkets, and finding profitable markets for the same among the white settlers."[27] Significantly, when an inventory was taken of Delaney's Frog Lake storeroom just before Big Bear arrived, it was noted that "the mowers and ploughs were not from the makers required in the contracts," implying that a substitution had taken place.[28]

After two or three weeks, William McKay finally arrived. Assured by the trader that all was well in his former wintering grounds and that the government had prepared for his return, Big Bear agreed to leave. Hayter Reed, the assistant Indian commissioner, assumed he would settle on the reserve that the government had set aside for him and had been using as a supply farm. The chief, however, had no intention of taking land chosen by someone else; he knew he had the right to pick his own reserve. As a result, when he reached Fort Pitt and would go no farther, he was accused of breaking a promise where none had been made. Instead, he announced that he would camp at the fort, near his friend McKay, until the treaty payments were made at the beginning of October. Many Indians from the nearby reserves at Frog Lake, Onion Lake and Long Lake immediately abandoned their fields and joined him, excited by the wild new arrivals. Although impoverished and ragged, Big Bear's followers had an air of independence and bravado that the others had not seen since they had given up their freedom.

As soon as government officials learned that Big Bear would not move from Fort Pitt, twenty-four Mounted Police under Insp. Francis Dickens were sent to establish a detachment at the fort. Dickens, the youngest son of the famous novelist Charles Dickens, was a questionable choice, for he had already alienated Blackfoot chief Crowfoot and turned him against the Mounted Police. This had occurred the previous year, when a dispute had arisen between a minor chief and Indian department employees; without proper investigation, Dickens had sided with the whites, even though later evidence pointed to corruption and mismanagement on the part of the government men. This action had broken the promise that the law would be applied equally to Indians and whites.

At Fort Pitt, Big Bear met many old friends, plains people and woods dwellers, who now shared the same fate. Half Blackfoot Chief had stayed on the plains as long as he could, but now he was occupying a reserve with Cut Arm. *Kehiwin,* old and almost blind, stayed at Long Lake most of the time, a sick and dejected man. The Frog Lake Indians were a little better off, having combined hunting with farming before the government had sent them a farm instructor. But, like others, they were hungry most of the time. They chafed under the inadequate food supply and domineering whites, eking out an existence by hunting, fishing and taking the meat and flour doled out to them by the government. They were becoming accustomed to the new life and were making an honest effort to be farmers, but the combination of poor seed, early frosts, unaccustomed physical labour and the temptation to break out of the monotonous routine to go hunting meant they had indifferent success. The rations, plus what they could harvest and find for themselves, kept them from starving, but they fought a grim day-to-day battle with poverty, malnutrition and boredom.

The Struggle Continues

BIG BEAR HAD WAITED four years before deciding to take treaty. Although starvation had forced him to sign, he was determined to continue his fight. It would be, as before, a fight with words and laws, not with bullets and scalping knives. The people needed to be united, for that was the only way the government would listen to them. Big Bear sent a message off to *Piapot* to see how he was faring in the south. "Are you, Pie-a-pot, treated in the same way," he asked, "not getting what was promised you? The Indian is not to blame; the white man made the promises and now does not fulfill them."[1] He also sent a message to Crowfoot and to the other chiefs of the Blackfoot nation, suggesting they meet in 1884 in a grand council to discuss common problems and seek redress from the government. Rumours of these activities reached the assistant Indian commissioner, but he could not be sure what was happening. "I am confident these Indians have some project in view as yet undisclosed," he said, "and it would not be a source of surprise to find that they are making efforts to procure a large gathering from East and West, at Battleford or adjacent thereto in the Spring in order to test their powers with the Authorities once more."[2]

Big Bear's timing in seeking help from the government could not have been worse. After several years of growth and prosperity across Canada, a recession had descended upon the country late in 1882: businesses had failed, prices for stocks and commodities had tumbled and exports had fallen drastically, leaving the government and the whole country strapped financially. The Indian department, like other branches of government, was required to cut costs wherever possible, so just before submitting his 1884 budget, Lawrence Vankoughnet, deputy minister of Indian affairs, toured western Canada to observe conditions for himself. A martinet, he firmly believed that those in the field were wasting money on needless expenditures and that they were vastly overstaffed. So just at the time when Big Bear arrived in Fort Pitt, just when

the Indians of western Canada needed food and assistance during a delicate period of adjustment, just at the time when most Indians thought
the situation could not be worse, Vankoughnet came to the prairies.
When the bureaucrat and the chief met at Fort Pitt, Big Bear tried to put
forward some of his people's problems, but without success. Vankoughnet told the chief that the government already had done more for him
than it had agreed to do and that the treaty terms were binding on both
parties. He was disappointed that the chief had not yet taken a reserve; if
he did not select one and move there by the beginning of November,
rations for the entire band would be cut off. Big Bear protested that the
matter of a reserve already had been discussed; he had seen Indian Agent
Rae and informed him that he would not pick a reserve until the following spring. However, the deputy minister was obdurate.

On his return to Ottawa, Vankoughnet slashed $140,000 from the
funds destined for the West, issuing orders to dismiss clerks, assistants
and other employees and, wherever possible, to reduce rations. He also
centralized all authority and control in his own office in Ottawa, cancel-
ling most discretionary powers of the farm instructors, Indian agents
and even the Indian commissioner. The results over the next couple of
years proved to be disastrous. Many hard-working employees of the
Indian department had not been tainted by corruption and were trying
to help the Indians: some, like Indian Agent Cecil Denny, resigned,
while others saw their earlier efforts crumble in the face of bureaucratic
interference and cost-cutting. There was considerable suffering on the
reserves, particularly as many crops had failed and there were few potatoes, turnips or grain to supplement the people's diets. Vankoughnet
wanted to bring in a regulation to prevent Indians from leaving their
reserves without a permit, but with the rations so low the people had to
go hunting. Long Lodge summed up the problem when he said that
"numbers of his people were dying and that if they stayed there they
would all die."[3] An Indian department employee, who was laid off about
this time, attacked the ration situation. He later complained of "the
small pittance that the Indians used to get of one pound and a half of
flour & half a pound of Bacon every Monday morning, and then the
same again on Thursday morning to do until the next Monday . . . and
then part of the flour was musty with all the colours of the rainbow to
look at. Many a time I had to take a hatchet to cut it to pieces, and then
pulverise it with a piece of wood in a Barrell."[4]

After his meeting with Vankoughnet, Big Bear became stubborn and
defiant on the matter of a reserve, refusing to move away from the Fort
Pitt and Frog Lake area. Accordingly, when the deadline passed, all
rations to his band were stopped, and everyone was obliged to suffer
through the winter, trying to live by hunting and fishing. Considerable

anger in the camp was directed at Big Bear. It was almost a repetition of
the situation at Fort Walsh, when his followers had needed food but
were denied rations because Big Bear would not sign the treaty. Now
they were starving again, this time because he would not choose a
reserve.

"I noticed that my people complained all the time while seated around
their campfires after sundown," recalled Big Bear's granddaughter, who
was about twelve years old at the time. "I, and other children, played at
our various games but could not help hear and see that our friends and
neighbours were unhappy, therefore, we too felt insecure. Our Chief
Big Bear was quite elderly and always tried to tell the other men of our
village to wait and be patient, that someday things would be better. The
younger men of our village, including my father [*Imasees*] forever
bemoaned the fact that we had failed to obtain ourselves a new home in
amongst the Big Knives [Americans]. These remarks would cause my
grandfather to feel very humble because it reflected on his inability to
lead his people."[5]

The camp was divided all winter. Lone Man continued to support
his chief, while Twin Wolverine, *Imasees* and Wandering Spirit were
his most vocal critics. The split within the family was a political one,
but it could not help but affect their personal lives as well. Big Bear
tended to spend more time alone, going off hunting and staying away
for days at a time. Saddened by the ever-widening rift between him
and his sons, he nevertheless remained dedicated to the idea that the
Crees deserved a better deal than they were getting. He, and perhaps
Piapot, were the only ones who could unite the tribes so that they
could bargain with a firm, single voice. He knew that the government
usually listened to Crowfoot and Red Crow, but those two chiefs of
the Blackfoot nation each had all their bands on a huge single reserve.
The Crees needed either a big concentration of reserves, or a grand
council to represent everyone.

During the winter, Chief Factor McKay offered Big Bear the job of
taking freight to Edmonton, and he was glad to accept, both for the
wages and for the chance to visit some of the western Indians. On his
way back, he stopped at Saddle Lake to discuss the political situation
with *Pakan,* the Christian chief. He found the man to be as dissatisfied as
other chiefs about his treatment. In particular, *Pakan* had asked in 1876
for a reserve between Dog Rump Creek and White Earth Creek on the
North Saskatchewan River, but was offered only a fraction of that land.
He proclaimed he "never would have taken the treaty if he had not been
promised this."[6] Like Big Bear, he was denied rations all winter because
he would not go to his reserve, and he too wanted a peaceful solution to
their problems.

Reactions to government policies were not always so peaceful, however, particularly in Big Bear's own camp. Early in January 1884, Big
Bear's father-in-law, *Yayakootyawapos,* returned from a long hunt, hungry and empty-handed. Exasperated, he went to see Delaney to beg a
little food for his family. Because of Vankoughnet's strict orders, the
farm instructor was forced to turn him down and brusquely ordered him
to get out of the ration house. Instead, the tired and frustrated Indian sat
down on a pile of frozen fish and declared he would not move until he
had some food. Delaney's response was to grab him by the arm to
forcibly eject him, but *Yayakootyawapos* reached under his blanket and
drew his knife. Surprised and frightened, Delaney dashed for the door
but had enough presence of mind to lock it on the way out. When the
Mounted Police arrived a few minutes later, *Yayakootyawapos* was taken
into custody and sentenced to two years in the guardhouse at Battleford.
This incident was just one of many that involved hungry Indians that
winter.

In response to the deteriorating conditions, Big Bear sent messengers
to as many reserves as possible, notifying them that he would be spon-
soring a Thirst Dance that summer and would, at the same time, call a
grand council. Traditionally, the Thirst Dance gave people from many
bands an opportunity to gather for religious ceremonies and to reaffirm
their faith in the Sun spirit. During the ritual, a huge lodge of greenery
and poles was built, where the sponsor supervised the dances, prayers
and songs that marked the holy occasion. The Thirst Dance also was a
social occasion: people visited and renewed acquaintanceships, arranged
marriages, changed bands and visited relations. Politically, peace pacts
with enemy tribes were considered, hunting strategies were discussed
and old disputes were negotiated and settled. And so it would be in the
summer of 1884. Instead of buffalo, they would talk about rations;
instead of enemy Blackfoot, they would have the government to consider. But above all, Big Bear wanted a commitment from the other
chiefs of the Saskatchewan district to empower him to speak for them
all. His earlier invitation to the Blackfoot tribes had come to naught, but
he was encouraged to learn that *Piapot* was following a similar course in
the Qu'Appelle region. That chief also had been sending messages to the
local chiefs, telling them of a Thirst Dance on the Pasqua reserve in the
spring to discuss rations, reserves and treaty terms.

Big Bear's plan was to hold meetings at the Thirst Dance, scheduled
for Poundmaker's reserve in June, and then go south to see *Piapot* and
Commissioner Dewdney. From there he would go to Ottawa, the home
of Vankoughnet and the men who were over him. Perhaps there he
would at last meet this man Government, the one who could make all
decisions, change the treaty and feed the starving Crees. "He has seen

and conversed with many of the chief officers of the Department," commented the *Saskatchewan Herald,* "but none of them seems to be 'the head' — there is always some one higher. To settle who this higher power is has now become the one object of his life."[7]

By now, the alienation within Big Bear's family had become so open that Twin Wolverine made plans to leave and take with him the followers who had become tired of the chief's vacillations. Now in his mid-thirties, he decided that he could be a chief in his own right, rather than constantly waiting for his father to make up his mind. He admired the aggressive stance taken by *Piapot,* which was far more confrontational than the methods used by Big Bear. At times, *Piapot* even gave the impression that he was willing to resort to violence if his people's problems were not resolved. Accordingly, early in 1884, Twin Wolverine sent word to Young Sweet Grass, Thunder Child and other chiefs near Battleford, urging them to follow the recommendations of the Qu'Appelle chief to refuse to plant their fields in the spring. Shortly after sending this message, Twin Wolverine moved to the Battleford area with his personal following of five lodges, or about forty persons.

Twin Wolverine's departure left his younger brother *Imasees* as the heir apparent to Big Bear. These two brothers had grown up to become different in nature and temperament. In some ways, Twin Wolverine was like his father, shrewd, determined and the kind of person who inspired confidence. He did not counsel war with the whites, but he had none of the religious feelings of his father and was impatient to get matters settled, even if it meant a confrontation. *Imasees,* on the other hand, was wild and intemperate, in a hurry not so much to settle on a reserve but to get what was promised to him. He fervently supported his father's contention that the government had swindled them out of their lands and was breaking its promises, but this created in him a silent hatred for the Queen's men. He was not a close companion of Wandering Spirit, the leader of the soldiers, but naturally gravitated to him because they shared a desire to resolve their problems by whatever means necessary.

In the late spring, Big Bear, *Imasees* and a few of his followers went to the Battleford reserves, where they met Twin Wolverine; he had not yet moved to another band, and Big Bear urged him to stay with him during the Thirst Dance. So the three men — Big Bear and his two recalcitrant sons — were together again. Support within his own band was eroding steadily, but Big Bear was still accepted by the government as the leading spokesman in the area, and his family knew it. They were infuriated with his slow, deliberate pace, neither realizing nor appreciating that this was part of a deliberate strategy. Big Bear had few weapons with which to fight the government bureaucracy, so he nursed them carefully. Each time he said "wait" — in signing the treaty, in going north, in going to Fort Pitt, in taking a reserve — it was all for a purpose. When the government wanted him to do something, an official had to meet with him, giving Big Bear the opportunity to lay out his grievances. In this way he had confronted David Laird, Edgar Dewdney, Hayter Reed, Lawrence Vankoughnet, A. G. Irvine, Frederick White and a procession of lesser officials. Whenever they had a meeting, he spoke for hours, telling them of the Cree ownership of the land, their relationship with the Great Spirit, their puzzlement at the Hudson's Bay Company being paid £300,000 for the land that belonged to the Cree, their understanding of the treaties and the way in which the government had not kept its promises. If he had done as the government had told him, Big Bear would never have had these chances to air his problems, and while his successes were few, he hoped the day would come when he would meet a Queen's man who would be sympathetic and understanding and who would at last resolve this problem. But the only way Big Bear could accomplish this was to keep seeing officials and repeating his grievances. Now, he was delaying once more, because he wanted the strength of the other bands behind him, hoping that their united front would make a difference.

In the weeks before the Thirst Dance, Big Bear camped with Poundmaker, who had become thoroughly disgusted with the machinations of Indian department officials. He had been served an ultimatum to be more co-operative or to have his chieftainship stripped from him, as had been done with Lucky Man a year earlier. Instead of bowing to government authority, Poundmaker had become sullen and hostile, ready to confront the authorities, by joining Big Bear or *Piapot*.

While he was waiting to put on the Thirst Dance, Big Bear met with Dewdney, who reminded the chief that he had promised to pick out his reserve in the spring, but had not yet done so. Big Bear responded that Vankoughnet's interference and a winter without rations had negated any commitment he might have made; however, he liked the Eagle Hills and asked if he could take a reserve alongside his old friend Poundmaker. This would place seven reserves almost adjacent to each other: those of Little Pine (who had finally come in from the plains), Lucky Man's followers, Poundmaker, Big Bear, Young Sweet Grass, Moosomin and Thunder Child, while a short distance downstream were the Assiniboine reserves of Lean Man, Grizzly Bear's Head and Mosquito.

This area was not part of Big Bear's normal hunting grounds, nor was it for Lucky Man or Little Pine, but as Farm Instructor Robert Jefferson noted, Big Bear's plan "was to get as many people as possible settled close together so that they might act in concert."[8] Another reason was that Twin Wolverine had established a friendship with Woodpecker, a head man in Little Pine's band, and might settle on his reserve. In this way, the family would still be close together. Neither Dewdney nor Indian Agent Rae saw this request as a danger and were prepared to agree to it. Indian Agent Rae, whom Big Bear had offended on his earlier arrival from the plains, told Dewdney why he supported the chief's request: "My own idea is that Big Bear might just as well be allowed to settle near Poundmaker . . . I feel sure that if the proper power is placed in my hands and supplies given me so that I can deal more liberally with these Bands, there will be no more trouble, but I do not think that Big Bear or any of the others are going to submit to be starved out, and there is no doubt that these men are particularly hard up. If, on the other hand, the Department are bound to stick to their present orders, then preparations should be made to fight them, as it will sooner or later come to this if more liberal treatment is not given."[9]

However, Indian Commissioner Dewdney was not allowed to make major decisions since the change in policy; when he wired Vankoughnet, the Ottawa bureaucrat flatly rejected the idea, viewing it as a possible "repetition of the Fort Walsh mismanagement as regards these Indians, namely a big camp composed of all the idle Indians in the country being fed at large expense."[10] Therefore, Dewdney had to instruct Big Bear to find a place near Fort Pitt. He was to let the Indian commissioner know by the end of May, and if proper assurances were given, full rationing would be restored to all the working Indians in his band. Upset at having his choice rejected again, Big Bear ignored the deadline, and his followers continued to starve.

By mid-June the results of Big Bear's messages to the reserves were beginning to bear fruit, as Indians began to arrive for the Thirst Dance and the grand council. There were people from Carlton House and Prince Albert districts, and even a few from Qu'Appelle, Peace Hills and the Fort Pitt region. All were experiencing the same problems of malnutrition, inadequate farming implements and a loss of faith in the government. They listened to the harangues of Big Bear and Poundmaker, then made long speeches of their own. The basic message was the same: more food. The treaty had promised them help in times of famine or pestilence, and in their minds, a disappearance of the buffalo and their lack of experience in farming had resulted in famine. As a priest observed at Poundmaker's reserve, the previous winter, "I saw the gaunt children, dying of hunger, come to my place. . . . Although it was thirty to forty degrees below zero their bodies were scarcely covered with torn rags. It was a pity to see them."[11]

The councils agreed that Big Bear should speak for all the Indians of the region, as their problems were the same. After the Thirst Dance he would go to Regina to once again visit the Indian commissioner, and from there he would travel to Ottawa, perhaps to see the man Government himself.

As the Crees gathered for the ritual, rumours began to circulate that trouble was brewing. Battleford residents, always uneasy about the large Indian population at their back doorstep, heard that Big Bear and Poundmaker were organizing the people and holding meetings, so they assumed the Indians were planning an uprising. This was a recurring problem in Big Bear's career: in order to unite the Crees in a common peaceful cause, he had to bring them together; but whenever he did this, the government assumed he was planning war, and his reputation as an untrustworthy troublemaker grew. Then, to complete the circle, young warriors within Big Bear's following saw that they were viewed with fear and apprehension, so they assumed the white man was afraid of them and that warfare might indeed be the best solution. The white people were creating their own problem by not acting upon Big Bear's reasonable demands, and their fear was giving his unruly warriors cause to think they could succeed in battle.

The Thirst Dance was a time of great excitement, for many of its customs and practices were associated with the wild and free days of buffalo hunting and war. Old men recounted their battles with the Blackfoot and Sioux; young men painted their faces according to their societies or spirit helpers and paraded about in their war paraphernalia. One man might be seen with the skinned head of a coyote drawn over his own head, while in his hand he carried a whip decorated with brass studs. Another might wear a bearskin cap and carry a Winchester carbine, while still another rode a horse with huge symbols painted on its front. All were evidence that the Crees quite recently had been warriors. The recollection of stealthy raids into an enemy village or a revenge attack on a lonely camp brought a light into the eyes of the storyteller, and let everyone forget for a while the poverty and hunger that gripped their ragged camps. The young men, drawn together from various reserves, had a chance to extol their own accomplishments and to regret the passing of the glorious days. The arrival of Lone Man from the south with a captured horse herd further excited this feeling and reminded them all that perhaps those times were not entirely gone.

The actual Thirst Dance normally lasted for only three days and was the climax of all the other activities. Soon after it was over, people would drift off to their own reserves.

On the day before the ceremonies were to start, an incident occurred that had far-reaching effects. It was the kind of situation Big Bear had been trying to avoid, but with scores of Indians prowling the reserves, there was no way that he or the soldiers could control them all.

On 18 June two sons of Lucky Man, who had been receiving rations because they were ill, showed up for more food. These were Man Who Speaks Our Language, or *Kaweechatwaymat*, and The Clothes; both were young and caught up in the excitement of the festivities. John Craig, the farm instructor, could speak practically no Cree but communicated to the two men that The Clothes would get rations but the other would not, as his injury had healed. This led to a heated dispute, and according to another farm instructor, Robert Jefferson, "Craig seems to have lost his head, since the controversy culminated in his pushing the men out. One of the intruders then took an axe-handle that was near the door and struck Craig on the arm with it. This was an unpleasantness which at such a juncture should have been avoided. Craig's arm was not injured, but his feelings were, so he took his case to the police."[12] A detachment of Mounted Police had been assigned to keep an eye on the Thirst Dance camp, but their numbers were too few to attempt an arrest, so reinforcements were sought from Battleford. In the meantime, Man Who Speaks Our Language went to the main camp to tell everyone what had happened. The commotion became so great that the dance was almost forgotten, particularly when the warrior and his brother announced that "they would not allow themselves to be taken, even though they had to shed blood preventing it."[13]

This was the same day that Big Bear had withdrawn to pray and prepare for the Thirst Dance, so he could not do anything to allay the furor created by the incident. His whole concentration was focussed upon the forthcoming ritual, cleansing his mind and body so that the Great Spirit would hear their supplications. A member of Strike Him on the Back's band remembered that fateful day and the Thirst Dance itself. "I was there and took part in the preparations and dance. The day before the dance, all gathered around Big Bear, who naked, except for the clay which covered his body, prayed that the dance might be successful, and that all prayers would be answered, especially the prayer for water. Big Bear did not eat or sleep that night." Next morning, the warriors went out to get the centre pole for the Thirst Dance lodge and when a suitable one had been found, the chief joined them. "Big Bear prayed, facing east, north, west, south, in turn," continued the informant. "The Tree was chopped down, falling to the south. The moment it fell the guns were fired and then all rushed to get a branch as a trophy from the battlefield. The young warriors dragged the tree to the spot. A nest was prepared at the top which contained some precious articles from the Indians to please the Great Spirit." After the lodge was built, Big Bear went inside and sanctified it by smoking and praying. Afterwards, he gave the pipe to others taking part in the ritual. "The pipe was passed from warrior to warrior gathered round the square. When it had gone round the bowl of the pipe was placed over the centre hole and the stem was thrown away. Incense was made with sweet grass. Big Bear uttered another prayer before the drum commenced, which was the signal for the dance. These men and women dancers thirsted in preparation, as their prayers demanded more or less sacrifice [half a day to a day]. The great deeds of each were recounted as he danced and made his promise."[14]

The day after the ration house incident, Inspector Crozier arrived with a detachment of Mounted Police to search for the two brothers. Unmindful of the religious ceremonies, the police forced their way into the medicine lodge itself, peering at the sun-gazing dancers who performed their hopping step as they blew repeatedly with bone whistles. Because the dancers were so heavily painted for the ritual, the police were unable to recognize the men, so they had to withdraw. Outside, they were met by an excited crowd, some on foot, some on horseback, all angry at the invasion of the sacred lodge. Crozier pushed through the mob until he reached Big Bear, who had stepped outside to see him. The chief refused to help the police during the Thirst Dance but promised when it was over he would go to Poundmaker's ration house with the whole camp, so that Crozier could try to pick out and arrest the wanted men. Big Bear did not want a confrontation at the holy lodge, but neither did he believe it was his responsibility to apprehend people wanted by the police.

Crozier had no choice but to accede to the chief's plan, so the police spent the remainder of the day and most of the night moving all the bacon and flour from the Little Pine reserve's ration house to Poundmaker's. To do so, they had to pass near the big camp, and again there were tense moments when mounted warriors dashed towards the wagons, firing shots into the air. "But the Indians were only trying to frighten us," said Jefferson, "since the bullets that flew overhead might just as easily have dropped in our midst. We hurried on with as little confusion as possible, passed the camp and got out of the range of the shooting."[15] By next morning, two crude bastions had been built onto the ration house, and the police, reinforced with volunteers from Battleford, waited for the Indians to show up.

The confrontation placed Big Bear in a tense and politically complex situation, for there were many young warriors in camp who were just waiting for an excuse to attack the police. All that held them back was the fact that the police had not opened fire on them, even in the face of provocation. "An Indian is despised who commits murder without being attacked," said Fine Day, so the hothead Crees could only taunt, shoot into the air and hope that the Queen's men would attack first.[16]

On one hand, Big Bear was as angry as the others for the violation of the Thirst Dance lodge, particularly when Lucky Man assured him that Craig had pushed Man Who Speaks Our Language first, thus instigating the incident. On the other hand, Big Bear had just succeeded in gaining a consensus from a large group of Indians, so that he could speak for them in Regina and Ottawa. Violence at this stage could seriously impair or destroy any chance for reasonable discussions. The government would have great difficulty in meeting in council with a chief who permitted the Queen's soldiers to be attacked. To further complicate matters, though Big Bear was the religious leader and political spokesman in the camp, he had ceased to be in full control as soon as the Mounted Police arrived. Just as in the buffalo days, head soldiers like Fine Day and Wandering Spirit took over the camp; though they might listen to Big Bear and Poundmaker, they had full authority to direct the camp soldiers and to protect the women and children from danger. *Imasees*, Miserable Man and other dissidents from Big Bear's camp were among those urging direct confrontation, while Twin Wolverine and Lucky Man counselled peace.

By noon on 20 June, Big Bear and Poundmaker had convinced the camp to move towards the ration house, but when they were still a half mile (800 m) off they stopped. Then an argument broke out between the chiefs and the head soldiers, the latter refusing to take the wanted men any closer. "As you will not give up this man," Poundmaker angrily told the head soldiers, "I will go down and surrender myself sooner than blood be shed."[17] Big Bear agreed, so the two chiefs turned their backs to the crowd and went alone towards the ration house, ignoring the police guns pointed directly at them. Once inside, the two men discovered Crozier wanted Man Who Speaks Our Language and his brother, no one else. As they went back to the hill, they saw the police and volunteers line up in a defensive position, facing the Indians, while Crozier, Craig and a small troop of men rode out to apprehend the wanted men.

William McKay, son of Big Bear's old fur-trading friend, was there interpreting and trying to calm down both sides. As he stood watching the two armed groups facing each other on the slope of the prairie hill, Twin Wolverine walked over to him. "You take one side or the other," advised the Indian, who had noticed the young man moving freely between both groups.

"I'm going to see what happens."

"There will be much blood shed today," Twin Wolverine said sadly. He pointed to the warriors on the hill — Wandering Spirit, *Imasees*, Miserable Man, Fine Day — and concluded grimly, "You talk to the Indians."[18] Like his father, Twin Wolverine saw the futility of this confrontation, but was powerless to intercede. He would not join the warriors, but neither would he leave the scene.

"The Indians by this time, were intensely excited," reported Crozier, "and making the most threatening and indescribable noises, some of the older ones, including Big Bear, shouting 'Peace! Peace!' Craig in the meantime could not see the prisoner; he had hidden himself. I shouted to the Indians, 'Bring me the prisoner or I shall arrest you all if we have to fight for it.' "[19]

At this point, Lucky Man convinced his son, Man Who Speaks Our Language, to go forward to talk to the police, but his claims that Craig had attacked him first made no impression on Crozier. He told the Indian that he would have a fair trial, and that there was no danger of his being hanged. When the Indian still refused to surrender, Crozier had him surrounded by policemen and forcibly took him, struggling all the time, towards the ration house.

"When the Indians realized just what had happened without a shot being fired," said McKay, "the painted mob flew around the police, yelling like madmen as they dashed their ponies hither and thither, hoping to terrify the police to fire. . . . Here and there a policeman was disarmed and even Poundmaker secured a fine rifle. Everything was done except firing a gun."[20] Fine Day said in later years that if the police had fired a shot, "the Indians would have killed them all. There were many armed Indians and few police, and we would have rushed down to Battleford to attack and massacre. We yelled, pushed against their horses, tried to frighten them, to get their things, to make them fire. Our old men said, 'Do not shoot first.' "[21]

It was almost a miracle that someone, Indian or white, did not panic during those few tumultuous minutes: *Imasees* snatched a revolver away from a Mounted Policeman but did not use it; Fine Day also got a gun but kept it silent; an interpreter was taken prisoner but was given up to McKay. During the whole period of shouting, war whooping, pushing and threatening, neither the mob on the hill nor the policemen, waiting anxiously at the ration house, fired a shot. And throughout the demonstration Big Bear rode among the warriors, shouting at them not to shoot and to keep away from the police.

On the way to the ration house, the police picked up the second wanted man, and soon were safe inside the barricade. At this point, Crozier hit upon the ideal solution for defusing the explosive situation. Vankoughnet or no Vankoughnet, he told the men to begin issuing flour and bacon to anyone who promised not to cause further trouble. Soon there were two long lines from the doorway of the ration house, as the promise of food quelled the crowd's anger.

A few days later, *Imasees* went to Battleford on behalf of his father to invite Crozier, Indian Agent Rae and McKay to their camp. Rae was afraid to go at first, but finally all three rode out to find everything quiet. Now that peace was restored, control of the camp had reverted to Big

Bear. He apologized for the trouble, explaining that his people did not understand the white man's laws. They did not believe Man Who Speaks Our Language should have been arrested, because the trouble had been started by the farm instructor. At the end of the session everyone shook hands, and a gift of tobacco was given to the chief. A short time later, at the trials in Battleford, the charges against The Clothes were dropped, and when testimony had been given in the other case, the magistrate came down hard on Craig. "From the evidence before me," he said, "I believe that Craig was in a great measure to blame in this matter. But if Craig pushed or struck an Indian, it was the Indian's duty to complain to his agent or to a magistrate, and then he would be punished . . . Craig in this instance acted indiscreetly and might easily have tided over the difficulty."[22] In the end, Man Who Speaks Our Language was found guilty and sentenced to seven days in the guardhouse.

Everyone in the West — the Mounted Police, Indian department employees and the newspapers — recognized that the real culprit of this incident was Vankoughnet. By stripping farm instructors of any discretionary powers, he had forced Craig into a situation in which he had to turn away the Indian, or risk being dismissed. In official reports and in newspapers, everyone railed against the narrow-minded edict, until the Ottawa bureaucrat was obliged to retreat. "If you concur in Crozier's recommendation," Vankoughnet wired the Indian commissioner, "that the Agent have more discretionary power as regards these [Big Bear's] and other new arrivals, [you] may authorize it, provided no loss of prestige by [giving] too many concessions."[23]

The result of the whole confrontation was disastrous to Big Bear. He realized as soon as the melee occurred on the hill that his hopes for meeting the authorities had been dashed. If he saw Dewdney, all they would talk about would be the troubles at Poundmaker's; and if he went to Ottawa, everyone would point to him as the man who had nearly caused an Indian war on the frontier. Not only that, but the incident had made some chiefs withdraw their support; Young Sweet Grass had left the camp even before the trouble with Crozier.

Each time Big Bear believed he was accomplishing something for his people, the ultimate goal seemed to elude him. At Cypress Hills he had hoped to hold out for better terms, but he had failed. Now, he had planned all winter and received good support from the other chiefs, but at the last moment the precipitous actions of one of Lucky Man's sons had caused his whole strategy to collapse. While Big Bear was musing about his future plans, Twin Wolverine came to say good-by. His friend Woodpecker had suggested that the two of them travel west to Buffalo Lake with their respective followers and perhaps get a reserve. They would be only a few miles from Bobtail and the others at Peace Hills, so they would not be alone.

As *Imasees* had become more insolent and overbearing, Big Bear had found himself turning to Twin Wolverine for guidance. He knew that his eldest son did not share his views on outwaiting the government, but they did agree on finding peaceful solutions to their problems. This was proven when Twin Wolverine declined to be drawn into the troubles at Poundmaker's. *Imasees,* on the other hand, was not content just to disagree with his father, but belittled him whenever possible and gave the impression that he now ran the band. When Farm Instructor Jefferson met Big Bear that summer, he observed that "the chief himself was old, and whatever ferocity he may in former times have been distinguished for, had entirely cooled with age. He was a mere figurehead. One of his sons, 'Ah-yim-is-sees,' in person very like Big Bear, had apparently caught the mantle of authority that fell from the ageing chief, but used the old man as spokesman."[24] Now that Twin Wolverine had decided he could wait no longer for his father to settle with the government and was striking out to be on his own, Big Bear would be left to the mercy of *Imasees.* When the chief found that his eldest son could not be dissuaded, he announced that he would follow him and also take up a reserve at Buffalo Lake.

The setback at Poundmaker's reserve and the departure of his eldest son was discouraging for Big Bear, and for the first time in his career, he contemplated giving up the fight. Perhaps he was feeling his age, for he was now almost sixty — which was old for the gruelling kind of life he had experienced on the plains and the starvation of the past two or three years. He had been a chief for almost twenty years, during which time he had seen his followers change from being proud, self-sufficient people to dispirited mendicants or hate-filled dissidents. Perhaps it was time to admit defeat, to cease the constant struggle for a better treaty and to take whatever the government was prepared to give him — rations, a reserve, farming tools and someone to supervise his every move. The noose was there, hanging in front of him; all he had to do was to step forward and it would be around his neck.

"At an interview with Major Crozier and Indian Agent Rae," reported the *Saskatchewan Herald* in mid-July "[Big Bear] announced it as his intention to select his reserve at once and to move on to it. He pleaded in extenuation of his former course that he was laboring under a false impression and did not understand things as they really were." This was the first sign of a graceful surrender by the old chief. "He could now see that the Government had done more for them than they were required to do by the treaty. He was ready to go on to a reserve with such of his people as would follow him. He said they were all very ignorant of farming and the modes of settled life, and begged that the Government would send a man to teach them who would have some patience with their ignorance and not get angry and abuse them because they could not do things at once."[25] It was an abject statement of defeat from a man who had fought long and hard, but who felt that now he was alone. Twin Wolverine had gone, taking some of the band with him; Young Sweet Grass and a few other chiefs no longer supported him, and *Imasees* was trying to wrest the remainder of the band from his hands. To add to his misery, his scheme for a reserve at Buffalo Lake was rejected by the government, so he had no idea when he would see his eldest son again.

When he set out from Battleford about 20 July, Big Bear really did intend to travel to Fort Pitt, but as he and his band were approaching the Little Hills, they were overtaken by a messenger who had ridden all the way from the South Branch to find him. Louis Riel was back in the country, and Big Bear was needed for an important Indian meeting at Duck Lake.

Thunder before the Storm

L OUIS RIEL WAS BACK!
The Métis leader had spent the past five years in Montana, where Big Bear had first met him in 1879. While living there, Riel had become increasingly obsessed with the idea that he was receiving direct messages from God to save the people of the North-West, so when a delegation from Batoche came for him, he believed that his holy mission was about to commence.

The half-breeds at Batoche and other areas along the river near Prince Albert had been suffering as much as the Indians since the disappearance of the buffalo. There was no one to give them rations, so they had eked out a living by trapping in the woods and by farming their small river lots along the North Saskatchewan. Then the recession that had struck Canada late in 1882 had depressed the prices of raw furs, so that the Hudson's Bay Company was paying only a dollar for a mink skin or twenty-five cents for three muskrats. The white farmers near Prince Albert were having problems as well; though some of their grievances were directed against the railway, many were similar to those of the half-breeds. As a result, some of them joined Riel's movement in an attempt to get some action from the moribund government in Ottawa. Riel, who had been responsible for the formation of the Province of Manitoba in 1870, was still a hero to many half-breeds and was regarded as the only spokesman whose message would be listened to by the government.

Within days of his arrival at Batoche, Riel was in conference with Beardy and other chiefs near Duck Lake. "The Carlton Indians are so hard up that they sympathise with the movement," commented Agent Rae, who wanted to offset the half-breed influence by giving the Indians more rations.[1] The session created great excitement, as Beardy decided to take up the Indian cause. He had been active a few years earlier but had given up in the face of apathy on the part of other Carlton chiefs.

Now, even the peaceful Big Child and Star Blanket were dissatisfied with their treatment. Riel gave Beardy the encouragement he needed to call a council of chiefs to petition the government for better treaty terms. Soon messengers were riding out to leaders far afield: one to the Eagle Hills to Poundmaker and the other chiefs, another to *Piapot* and a third to seek out Big Bear.

When the old chief stopped on the trail to listen to the words of the messenger, his heart lifted and his eyes brightened. He found hope rising from the ashes of his recent defeat. He was needed! Beardy and the other Carlton chiefs were finally conceding that action must be taken, and they wanted him to be with them. When his father turned back, *Imasees* must have been both disgusted and angry. He thought that the time for playing games was past and that they were finally going to select a reserve. Instead, Big Bear was off to another meeting. As the chief set out for Battleford, *Imasees* decided there was no point in returning to Frog Lake, so he turned south to hunt along the Battle River.

The news that Big Bear was going to Duck Lake created a mild sensation among the white population. The *Saskatchewan Herald* called him "a fraud and a liar" for taking rations to go in search of a reserve, then turning back.[2] Crozier was convinced that "Big Bear & his followers could have been upon their reserve but for the emissaries of Riel who it is said invited him to meet that person at Duck Lake."[3] And Agent Rae, with memories of the debacle at Poundmaker's reserve still fresh in his mind, was worried about where it would all lead. "I have been dealing with Indians for the past 14 years," he said, "& never saw the Indians mean business before. The thing has to be looked at seriously & precautions taken ere it is too late."[4] Big Bear's motives for travelling to Duck Lake were, however, beyond reproach. He was going neither to see Riel not to talk treason; his whole life had been dedicated to finding a peaceful way of wresting better treaty terms from the government. Now that the Carlton Indians were involved and the government was in a panic over the presence of Riel in the region, officials were likely to listen to anything the conference had to say.

When the meeting assembled on Beardy's reserve on 6 August 1884, twelve leading chiefs were there, including Big Child, Star Blanket, James Smith, *Okemasis,* One Arrow, *Petequaquay,* John Smith, Joseph Badger and Lucky Man. Some of them had long-standing reputations as responsible men who had completely accepted their new way of life and who had never given the government trouble. To find them meeting with dissidents like Beardy and Big Bear was a surprise to everyone. In fact, their complaints were similar to those often repeated to government officials, but they had been reluctant to take part in any action that might have had unfavourable repercussions: they knew that Big Bear's

followers had been denied rations and that Poundmaker had been threatened with having his chieftainship removed. But now, encouraged by
the unsettled conditions in the district and Beardy's re-emergence as a
spokesman, they had thrown caution to the winds and gathered at his
reserve.

Initially, the government denied rations to the assembly, but after two
days officials became curious and worried that the chiefs might be considering throwing their lot in with Riel's followers. So, to monitor
them, the local agent offered to feed the delegations if they would move
to Carlton House, where they would be free to discuss their problems
with government officials. So they went to the fort on 9 August, and
two days later they presented a list of grievances to J. A. Macrae, the
subagent for the region. For the first time since 1876, Big Bear was
attending an official meeting in which a full and accurate list of
grievances was being recorded for transmittal to the Indian commissioner, and from him to the prime minister. By this time, Vankoughnet
had fallen out of favour for his mishandling of the Big Bear and Poundmaker trouble, so Dewdney had resumed direct control over Indian
affairs in the West. But it had taken the fear of Louis Riel for the government to even listen to what the Indians had to say.

This meeting was a realization of Big Bear's hope. If he spoke long
enough and often enough, he prayed that someday he would be heard by
the people who made the decisions. During the sessions, and later at the
meeting with Macrae, he made his general position clear. "A year ago, I
stood alone in making these demands," he said. "Now the whole of the
Indians are with me." He praised the Mounted Police for the way they
had handled themselves on the Poundmaker reserve but said that they
had avoided "any serious results at that place by his efforts as a
peacemaker."[5] When discussing the problems of the Carlton bands, Big
Bear could relate to his own experiences at Battleford and Fort Pitt, and
he was willing to share them with anyone who would listen.

"Yes," he said, "I am willing to speak. Since the leaves have begun to
come, it is why I have been [talking, talking], trying to make myself
understood. It is why I have come to Duck Lake to show you why I
have been so anxious. It is because I have been trying to seize the promises which they made to me; I have been grasping but I cannot find
them. What they have promised me straightway I have not yet seen the
half of it."

"We have all been deceived in the same way," he continued. "It is the
cause of our meeting at Duck Lake. They offered me a spot as a reserve.
As I see that they are not going to be honest I am afraid to take a reserve.
They have given me to choose between several small reserves but I feel
sad to abandon the liberty of my own land when they come to me and

offer me small plots to stay there and in return, not to get half of what
they have promised me."

"When will you have a big meeting?" he asked the other delegates. "It
has come to me as through the bushes that you are not yet all united.
Take time and become united, and I will speak. The Government sent to
us those who think themselves men. They bring everything crooked.
They take our lands, they sell them and they buy themselves fine
clothes. Then they clap their hands on their hips and call themselves
men. They are not men. They have no honesty. They are an unsightly
beast. Their faces are twisted from the appearance of honest men."[6]

The chiefs discussed many grievances, including a criticism of the
Hudson's Bay Company for selling Indian land to Canada for £300,000.
Relations between the native peoples and the trading company had been
good, but the recent depressed fur prices had caused anger and conster-
nation. They demanded that the chief factor give the £300,000 to the
Indians, and this would provide "a basis on which to build new treaties."[7]

When the delegates met Subagent Macrae, they presented him with
eighteen grievances, which were common to most reserves in the district. Most of these dealt with the nonfulfillment of promises made in
the treaty or the inadequacy of the terms themselves. The medicine chest
for each reserve had not materialized; schools had not been provided on
all reserves; oxen were too wild and either died or were killed; cattle
were so wild they could not be stabled in winter and died of exposure;
wagons were so poorly made that they broke down, and horses to pull
them were unbroken broncos. The chiefs also said that Lieutenant-Governor Morris had promised "that they should not be short of clothing,
yet they never received any and it is feared that this winter some of them
will be unable to leave their houses without freezing to death." They
requested that all inferior implements and stock previously issued to
them be replaced with better quality items and that more threshing
mills, mowers, reapers and rakes be provided so they could farm like the
white man. Maps showing the boundaries of reserves were requested to
be sure they were not being robbed. On the subject of food, they said
that "the promises made to them at the time of their Treaty was that
when they were destitute, liberal assistance would be given to them.
That the crops are now poor, [musk]rats are scarce, and other game is
likely to be so, and they look forward with the greatest fear to the
approaching winter." They claimed, "in view of the above mentioned
promise . . . that the Government should give them liberal treatment
during that season for, having disposed of all the property that they
owned before the treaty in order to tide over times of distress since, are
now reduced to absolute and complete dependence upon what relief is

extended to them. With the present amount of assistance, they cannot work effectively on their reserves, and it should be increased." They also requested beef instead of bacon as their rations, as was being done with the Blackfoot tribes.

The chiefs were unanimous in the belief that "at the time of making the treaty they were comparatively well off; they were deceived by the sweet promises of the Commissioners and now are 'full of fear' for they believe that the Government which pretended to be friendly is going to cheat them. They blame not the Queen, but the Government at Ottawa." Stressing that their protest was peaceful, the delegation said that "they are glad that the young men have not resorted to violent measures." They concluded that they would wait until the following summer, 1885, to see if their problems were resolved; if nothing had been done, they would call another council of all the bands from the entire Treaty Six area, and perhaps the surrounding areas as well. If the government had kept its promises in the first place, they said, everything would have been fine "instead of the present feeling existing."[8]

When the grievances had all been laid before the subagent, Big Bear rose to speak. "The chiefs should be given what they asked for," he said simply, "all treaty promises should be fulfilled."[9]

Endorsed by men as well regarded as Big Child and Star Blanket, the document was a condemnation of the whole Indian department policy and revealed the extent of their disillusionment with and loss of trust in the government. Many items they sought were not provided for in the treaty, such as clothing and farming implements for each individual; but as the discontent had grown, so had the demands for assistance, until the chiefs now believed they had been promised more than was in the treaty document itself. But the primary source of concern was the government's failure to provide adequate food to a starving people. The Indians did not view more aid as a permanent commitment but as a source of help while they were learning how to farm. As Big Bear had always said, it was a small price to pay for the land the Crees had given away.

The government's reaction to the petition was predictable. Indian Commissioner Dewdney and his assistant, Hayter Reed, admitted some of the charges were valid but clouded the whole issue by attacking the men who had raised them. They claimed that Big Bear had been the instigator of the conference and that he had received moral support from Riel and the half-breed community. However, the political climate was such that the petition could not be entirely ignored and would be investigated.

Big Bear did not leave the northern district immediately. A couple of weeks before the session started, Riel's supporters had issued a manifesto in Prince Albert, and among its objectives was a statement on Indians:

"Our local press is not to be relied on. It is in the hands of a few government favorites who inspire its editorials which are anonymous. It is, accordingly, circulating wild reports about impending rebellion and Indian troubles, seeking a pretext for placing the country under martial law and so goad the people into a false step. Riel will do more toward pacifying Big Bear than could be accomplished by twenty agents in a month of Sundays."[10] In order to fulfill this claim, a message was sent to Big Bear, inviting him to meet the half-breed leader in Prince Albert. Well aware of Riel's reputation and influence, the chief decided to hear what he had to say and to expound again the problems of his own followers.

Big Bear arrived in Prince Albert on 15 August and waited in camp for almost a week, driving about with his entourage in two buckboards and declaring "his intentions are peaceful and affirms that no man loves a state of quiet in all things more than himself."[11] Finally, Riel came in from the half-breed settlements and, accompanied by Ambroise Lepine, held a meeting with the Cree chief in a suite above Jackson's drug store. According to the druggist, "Big Bear complained that the conditions of the treaty had been violated by the Dominion Government and asked that when the whites and half-breeds had secured their rights they would assist the Indians to win theirs."[12]

In Indian accounts of the meeting, Big Bear was ushered into a luxurious apartment and marvelled at the splendour of his surroundings. He was then taken to a table that was groaning under the weight of food piled upon it. After eating and saying he felt good, Big Bear expressed his surprise at the lavish treatment he was receiving. "Yes, my brother," said Riel. "This is a nice house, these are nice things, but if you do as I tell you, you will have a grander house, better things and plenty to eat. I am poor, but you will be rich. They call you chief now, but it is for nothing; by and by you will be a chief in reality and what I say to you I say to all my brother chiefs, and I want you to tell them my words when you go back."[13] Then, Big Bear was said to have been asked to sign a document, to which Riel also affixed his name, and to promise "to obey all future orders Riel should give."[14] A copy of it was given to the chief for him to show to other leaders so that they could sign it as well. According to Rev. Charles Quinney, who circulated this story after the rebellion and was strongly opposed to Big Bear, the document was a guarantee to support Riel in his "contemplated fight with the white man."[15] In fact, however, the meeting and the document (if one existed) appear to have been for peaceful purposes; Riel at this point was not counselling war, but was sounding out the feelings of Indians, whites and half-breeds in his quest for political support. After his meeting with Big Bear, he added a plank to his party's platform that "the Indians' rights should be protected as well as their own."[16] As for Big Bear, he simply hoped that Riel and his followers could help him to achieve some of the goals sought by the chiefs at the Duck Lake meeting. However, the *Saskatchewan Herald* noted that "the old man does not seem to have been favourably impressed with the prospects held out to him by Riel," and this was true.[17] Still, he was not the broken, dispirited man who had set out on the trail a few week earlier, but a man with a renewed enthusiasm to carry on his work. And it was the Duck Lake conference, not Riel, that had accomplished this. With the Carlton reserves drawn into the fold and the addition of such creditable chiefs as Big Child and Star Blanket, he believed his mission might finally succeed.

When Big Bear set out for home, the worried government instructed Subagent Quinn to handle the old chief with deference. He was told to issue full rations to the band and to give "a small qty. of clothing" to them at the time of treaty payments. He was not to press the issue of a reserve immediately upon Big Bear's return but to wait until after the payments were over. If they did choose a reserve, Quinn was to issue their oxen and harness to them, even if he had "to borrow from one of the farms or some of the [Indians'] oxen being replaced by others." He was then to arrange that the full quota of implements and cattle be ready for distribution to Big Bear's band in the spring. "It is of not a little importance," added the directive, "that Inds. shd. be located permanently on some spot selected by them as a Reserve." And, in an order reflecting the concern felt by authorities over Big Bear's visit with Riel, the subagent was told to "be extremely watchful of their every movement noting everything & reporting same, bearing in mind that every round of [ammunition] obtained by them must be known to you."[18]

Big Bear realized that this would be the wrong time to take a reserve, for it was his last negotiating point. As long as he held out, officials would have to come to him; he would be at liberty to roam, and he would continue to be a symbol of freedom to the other chiefs. Moreover, his band had been so fractionalized that he feared his reserve would not be large enough for his people to make a living from it. Over the past few years, Thunder Child and Lucky Man had left him, and now Twin Wolverine had gone recently with more of his people. And within the remaining camp, some supported *Imasees,* some followed Four Sky Thunder and a few of the young single men were with Wandering Spirit. If any of them should reject his choice of a reserve, his following would shrink even more.

A few leaves along the Saskatchewan Valley were beginning to turn to their bright autumn colours of orange, red and yellow as Big Bear passed the places well known to him since childhood. The Eagle Hills were a bluish-grey in the distance but took on their mantle of green and brown as he came closer and passed them by; across the valley, Jackfish Lake lay to the north, cool and still amid the trees. Farther along, the Little Hills, the Two Big Hills and Frenchman's Butte all stood out prominently from the bluffs and meadows that huddled around their base. As he left the broad, dry prairies and directed his team down the trail into the valley of the North Saskatchewan, Big Bear could see the familiar outlines of Fort Pitt across the river. It had become old and decrepit over the years, just like the chief himself. The palisades had long since rotted and been torn down, and nestled there on the broad flat, the buildings looked lonely and forlorn.

On the near side of the river, Big Bear was pleased to see about twenty familiar lodges, the smoke from their campfires curling lazily upwards in the afternoon air. His two youngest boys, King Bird and Horse Child, came out to greet him, but he noted that *Imasees* was nowhere to be seen. Only later did he learn that his son was camped several miles south with another seventeen lodges. It was good to be back in his own country, among his friends and relatives, and to tell them about his travels. Lucky Man, of course, had been at the Duck Lake conference, but knew nothing about the chief's meeting with Riel. Many hours passed while Big Bear told his family and the head men about his renewed campaign to press for a better deal from the government. "He does not think the Government pays him anything for his Lands," reported a government spy who heard Big Bear's orations after his return. "He also states if the Government would pay him for the Lands in the same way as it is sold to the White settlers he would be well satisfied."[19]

Imasees, upon his return a few days later, was angry that his father had been attending meetings with other old men instead of picking out his reserve. When he realized that Big Bear had engineered another postponement and would not make a choice until sometime after the annuity payment, he took this as further evidence that the chief would continue his delaying tactics as long as possible. *Imasees* feared a complete breakup of the band if his father did not soon choose a reserve, and in order to avoid having councillors Four Sky Thunder or Two & Two leave with their own followings, as Twin Wolverine had done, he became increasingly aggressive in his self-imposed leadership role. "My father quite unofficially became our leader," recalled Isabella, "although Chief Big Bear was still our chief."[20]

The hostility of *Imasees,* Wandering Spirit and other outspoken men were directed as much at Big Bear for his stubbornness as they were against the government. Increasingly, the chief was perceived as an old fool who was more interested in politicking than he was in looking after his immediate followers; he was like present-day politicians who are concerned with national issues but neglect the problems of constituents at home. There was considerable truth in their allegations. Age and extended privation had reduced Big Bear to a shadow of the dynamic leader who had rejected the treaty in 1876. Hayter Reed, the assistant Indian commissioner, noticed this decline in Big Bear. "I managed to meet him at Fort Pitt after the meeting at Carlton," he said, "and had two or three long talks with him, and although he laughed when I asked him in what way the government was not carrying out its promises with the Indians and what he meant when stating it was at fault in so many particulars, he could not enumerate them. I demanded that he give me a few instances and one case in which he had a just claim, which could not have been settled at an earlier date, I settled on the spot. After this he admitted to the Interpreter that the government was carrying out all its promises."[21]

With the presence of Louis Riel causing near-panic among government officials, Big Bear was in a position to get down to hard bargaining, but all he could do was to speak in nebulous terms about the Hudson's Bay Company sale of lands, the fact that the treaty was inadequate and that government promises were not being kept. Now, when the government wanted him to be specific and might have considered taking action, he was so wrapped up in his own oratory that he could not get down to individual issues. A few years earlier, he would have demanded that the provision of five people per square mile (2.6 km²) for reserves be altered, the annual annuities be increased, the provision for giving food in times of starvation be liberalized and the issuing of machinery and cattle to bands be extended to individual families. No doubt the government would have turned him down on most issues, but it might have conceded some points; for example, a few months later the Indian commissioner authorized the agent at Peace Hills to give pairs of oxen to individual farmers who had proven themselves and to increase the numbers of plows and harrows on the reserve. Also, the issuing of rations had become a common practice, rather than being limited to times of general famine.

As for the Duck Lake demands, they were receiving more consideration than any submitted earlier. The prime minister went to the trouble of consulting the official transcripts of the treaty to see if he could find evidence of legal nonfulfillment of any provisions and seemed honestly puzzled when he commented, "I cannot find that any of the promises claimed . . . were made to the Indians."[22] However, he directed Hayter Reed to visit as many chiefs as possible to determine which treaty obligations had not been met. This was when Reed had seen Big Bear, and had the chief been capable of elucidating specific problems, his complaints would have gone directly to Prime Minister Macdonald.

Imasees and other family members were undoubtedly aware of Big Bear's deteriorating condition and resented the fact that his obstructive-ness was preventing them from getting a reserve and assistance being provided to other bands. They were restive, fretful and increasingly disturbed, as another long and dismal winter lay before the homeless band.

Into this unhappy situation bounded an unlikely catalyst from the southern plains. When Big Bear and his followers had moved north from Fort Walsh the previous year, Little Poplar had been with them; finding the confinement of their new life not to his liking, he had dashed away to Montana to visit the relatives of one of his wives on the Crow reservation. Now the handsome, irrepressible warrior was back. Proud of his reputation as a fighter, quick tempered and temperamental, he was unwilling to give up his nomadic life and believed that warfare should still be the main preoccupation of the Cree. He did not consider himself inferior to the white man and was not cowed by Indian agents, Mounted Policemen or other officials.

When he had heard about Big Bear's troubles at the Thirst Dance, he had thought there was going to be war; he claimed that he had organized a war party of eighty Montana Indians and ridden with them as far as the Canadian Pacific Railway line before discovering that peace had returned to the north. At that point the warriors had turned back, but he had decided to go on to Fort Pitt to collect his annuities. On his way, he stopped at the Mounted Police detachment at Maple Creek to ask for food; when he was turned down, "he was exceedingly impertinent and said when he came back, he would have enough men to take provisions if they were refused him."[23]

Little Poplar spoke constantly about standing up to the government if it did not give the Indians what they sought. He was a lively, inspiring man, who created excitement and enthusiasm whenever he spoke. As a son-in-law of Lucky Man and a brother-in-law of *Imasees'* wife, he was closely identified with the hierarchy of the two bands, and his words were taken seriously by all the Indians, particularly the warriors. After all the months of starving and waiting for something to happen, Little Poplar was telling them to take matters into their own hands. He did not directly counsel them to resort to arms, but he implied that war might be the inevitable result. His harangues made a deep impression on the group of disgruntled and impatient people. Little Poplar was advocating a solution that many had secretly considered, but few had vocalized: perhaps the best way to resolve the problem of the white man was to get rid of him.

Imasees was particularly vulnerable to Little Poplar's fanciful outpour-ings, for he was a frustrated man trying to face two problems at the same time: his father and the government. Another sympathetic listener was Wandering Spirit, the mercurial head soldier, whose mind had never left the war trail. As a result, the Indians were in an extremely unsettled state when treaty payment time arrived, and as Inspector Dickens noted, Little Poplar "appeared to have more influence with the Indians than was possessed by any of the Chiefs."[24] Before the payments began, the outspoken warrior demanded they be given rations of beef instead of bacon. When Subagent Quinn refused, Little Poplar challenged him. "You are the man sent here by the Government to say no to everything the Indians ask," he said sneeringly. "Are you going to give us beef?"

I have no authority to do so," replied Quinn.[25]

Three times Little Poplar asked the question; when he received the final refusal, he drove all of the Indians, including Big Bear, out of the room," as a dog does a flock of sheep."[26]

On the following day, Big Bear made a speech in support of Little Poplar's demands, adding his own list of now-familiar grievances. "He said that the Indians did not get enough money, land, or rations, and had sold their country too cheaply, that they had always had beef at previous payments and would wait until the Agent gave them beef, that the Government had promised to feed them but that they were starving."[27] The impasse lasted for another two days, during which the Indians danced and held ceremonies in their camp but would not accept annuities. At last, seeing that Quinn would not change his mind, their resistance was weakened by those who were eager to get their money. They wanted to buy clothing and supplies from the Hudson's Bay Company and the free traders, who were waiting with their goods. The camps of Big Bear and Lucky Man finally received their annuities together; 135 women, 162 boys, 149 girls — and 58 men who, according to inquiries by the Mounted Police, possessed fifteen Winchesters and twenty muskets. In total 504 persons were paid, which was almost equal to the combined populations of the nearby reserve Indians at Onion Lake, Frog Lake and Long Lake.

After the payments Big Bear was true to his promise — in his own way — about choosing a reserve. He went to Subagent Quinn and said he would move his band to a reserve opposite the mouth of Vermilion Creek if they were given additional food to enable them to make the trip and become settled. When Quinn refused, Big Bear announced that the weather was too severe for them to go without food and that they would wait until spring. By that time, he hoped to have Twin Wolverine back so that the reserve would be surveyed on the basis of a larger population.

Big Bear had managed to delay again.

The subagent was not inclined to dispute Big Bear's delay; the proposed reserve would be directly south of Frog Lake, and he wanted time for the Mounted Police to abandon Fort Pitt and move to his agency. Dewdney also favoured the delay, because his officials could then determine if the reserve had good agricultural land and build a farm instructor's house. When the Indians learned they were not going to get the extra rations and would be without a reserve all winter, the full fury of *Imasees* and his supporters turned entirely on the old chief. He was their enemy; he was the one who stood between them and their reserve.

As it turned out, the winter of 1884–85 was a long and bitter one for Big Bear's band, which moved over to Frog Lake to be near the ration house. Big Bear camped along the west edge of the lake with his young wife and children; whenever he went out hunting, he received ten days' rations from the farm instructor and headed north into the bush. His favourite son-in-law, Lone Man, also was away much of the winter, hauling freight for the Hudson's Bay Company between Fort Pitt and Cold Lake. According to a man who was at the settlement, the rest of Big Bear's followers "preferred lying in their tents or shanties and trusting to Providence, the Government, or the Hudson's Bay Company, and their miserable begging powers to feed them."[28] However, a Mounted Policeman stated that "Big Bear had his band cut some 600 cords of wood for the Indian Department. They receive a certain amount of food according to the work they do. Those who work will receive quite enough to eat."[29] In spite of work and rations, the winter with its extremely cold spells and deep snow was hard on everyone. The area near Frog Lake was almost entirely devoid of big game, so that hunters had to either travel far afield or be satisfied with their occasional success in killing rabbits or spruce hens.

At Frog Lake, Big Bear was friendly with most white people, but he had few long-standing relationships with them. Some were popular with the Indians, but others had given cause for personal grievances. For example, Little Bear's daughter had wanted to marry a Catholic boy,[30] but the local priest, Father Leon Adelard Fafard, would not perform the ceremony unless both father and daughter were converted. Little Bear "got quite peeved and was never friendly with the man of prayer after that."[31] Also, there was considerable animosity shown by Wandering Spirit towards Subagent Quinn. This may have stemmed from the fact that Lone Man, whom the head soldier detested, was an uncle of the agent's wife. With the band splitting into cliques, Wandering Spirit would have regarded Quinn as part of the Lone Man–Big Bear faction; he himself was associated through politics and marriage with the Little Poplar–*Imasees* group. A major loss felt by Big Bear at this time was the absence of his old friend William McKay from Fort Pitt, who after years in the service had retired to Edmonton and died. Big Bear had completely trusted the chief factor and would have listened to his counsels in any emergency. Now, an Ojibwa-speaking trader William McLean had taken his place.

There also was a rumour that the Indians' laborious work of cutting logs was being done for the personal benefit of the subagent and farm instructor. "Tom Quinn and George [sic] Delaney knew from experience," said Louis Goulet, a Métis who spent the winter in the district, "that as soon as the land had been cleared it would be much in demand for homesteads, once the Indians had been removed to their reserve. They were cooking up a plan to clear land before it was opened for settlement."[32] Certainly, there was a deep suspicion on the part of many Indians that they were being exploited and misused: for example, some could not understand why at times they were given rations but more often were refused. After the Riel Rebellion one former Indian agent commented that such questionable practices had been common: "An Indian having accepted treaty goes into the Indian agent's storeroom. He had run out of grub. He wants, say, some tea and bacon, some sugar, and tobacco, and a sack of flour, possibly some dried apples and ammunition as well. He may get what he asks for; he may get half of it; he may get kicked or bundled out of the place." Even when an Indian did not get supplies, a corrupt agent might "have them 'charged' to him;" in other words, the agency accounts would show the Indian had been given supplies though he had not received all or any of the items listed.[33]

It may have been only a coincidence, but when an inventory was made of the stores under Instructor Delaney's care, the flour supply was found to be short by thirteen hundred pounds, and there were discrepancies between the books at the subagency and those at the storehouse. In any case, the issuing of rations had always the basis for hard feelings, and with Delaney's reputation as a stern man, any rumours about him would have gained immediate acceptance. On the positive side, Delaney had brought a wife from the East, so he was presumably leaving the Indian girls alone.

The anger and discontent that had arisen with Little Poplar's orations were fed by Big Bear's refusal to take a reserve in the fall and continued to mount during the winter. Yet Big Bear, perhaps because he had become so alienated from the other leaders in his camp, appeared to be unaware of the situation, or else chose to ignore it. In February he created another furor when he recanted on the choice of a Vermilion Creek reserve and would not name an alternate site. In fury, Four Sky Thunder demanded permission to leave and join another band, while other individual Indians came to Subagent Quinn with the same request.

Confronted with the possibility that his band might be broken up, Big Bear was distraught and upset. Almost pathetically, he took Quinn's hand in his own and said plaintively, "Believe me, I am going to take my Reserve this spring. Do not doubt me. I cannot see anything else to make a living, only to go to a Reserve."[34] Two weeks later a public meeting was called to make the final choice of a reserve. Two people who were determined to see it succeed were the subagent, who was feeling the pressure from Regina, and *Imasees*, who did not want to see his father's delaying tactics break up the band whose leadership he would someday inherit.

The first choice for a reserve was on Spotted Creek, near Buffalo Lake; this was Big Bear's idea, for it was the place where his eldest son Twin Wolverine was wintering. However, the majority favoured a location closer to their own wintering grounds and agreed on the mouth of Dog Rump (now Atimoswe) Creek. This was directly south of *Kehiwin*'s reserve and mid-way between Frog Lake and Saddle Lake. "I must not omit to mention Big Bear's son I-am-e-sies," said Quinn, 'who stood by me to impress upon his father the importance of selecting a reserve; in fact, seeing his father hesitating, he called all the young men of the Band together and they informed their chief that if he did not take his Reserve he and most of the young men would leave the Band as they were tired of waiting and starving. I think this made the chief give in at last."[35]

But Big Bear's decision came too late to heal the split camp and, in fact, actually caused the breach to widen because of Wandering Spirit's opposition to the site, or perhaps to the idea of accepting a reserve. In any case, the decision had left the Indians divided and angry, with much of the hostility directed to Big Bear himself. But the chief, who had been away hunting when the selection meeting was called and had to be brought in from the bush, paid no heed to the unrest and returned again to the hunt. At this point, Big Bear was chief in name only: to all intents and purposes, *Imasees* had taken over the leadership of the band. As the chief's grandnephew, Joe Dion, wrote in later years: "It may truthfully be said that Big Bear's chieftainship had more or less ended. He was getting old and wanted nothing better than to be left alone while he tried to adopt the new mode of making a living."[36]

Over the winter, the poverty of Big Bear's camp had been appalling. Many horses had died, and people had been so hard up for dwellings that two or three families had occupied each lodge. "Many of these proud people spent a miserable existence throughout the cold winter," commented Dion, "in tepees long-since fit for the discard, for they had not been able to renew their tents since the total disappearance of the buffalo. When the pangs of hunger could not be relieved they would speak of the events of the past few years, the whole-hearted agreement with the white man as voiced by their leaders in the signing of the treaty. The promise 'You will never again suffer for want of food,' so recently given them, was still ringing in their ears."[37]

The combination of cold weather, destitution, hunger, Little Poplar's provocative harangues and impatience with Big Bear created a seething undercurrent of unrest. On the surface all seemed calm, as men chopped wood, women cooked bannock and bacon, and a few people ventured out to hunt; but, in fact, the camp was like a hungry, sleeping grizzly, needing only a small provocation to send it raging through the countryside.

Rebellion!

IN THE SPRING of 1885, there were only four centres of white habitation within a thirty-mile (48-km) radius of Frog Lake. The largest of these was the village of Frog Lake itself; the farm headquarters at Onion Lake was twenty miles (32 km) southeast, and the Hudson's Bay Company post at Fort Pitt was ten miles (16 km) beyond that. To the northwest, the farm headquarters and mission at Long Lake were twenty-five miles (40 km) away. Frog Lake was isolated from the rest of the world, particularly in winter when no boats could operate along the river. However, from messengers, passing freighters and issues of the *Saskatchewan Herald,* the white populace learned the latest news; the Indians, with their own means of communication, seemed to get their own versions almost as quickly.

In the Batoche–Prince Albert region, matters had remained relatively calm during the winter, as Louis Riel had carried out his organizing activities in a peaceful manner. Concerned and suspicious, the government kept abreast of all the rumours, fearing a repetition of events that had occurred at Red River in 1869 and placing themselves in readiness for any eventuality. Early in February, the prime minister responded to the half-breed demands in a way that was neither decisive nor satisfactory to Riel and his followers, and though some of his more vitriolic followers wanted to rebel, Riel sought a forty-day devotion in prayer and supplication. More and more, he saw himself as a messianic leader awaiting direction from Above before restoring the land to the true and faithful children of God. Finally, on 3 March, Riel began to follow the pattern of his Manitoba uprising when he formed a provisional government and claimed he would receive support from thousands of people from the United States. He announced his government would administer the West as part of Canada and that the land would be divided equally among the half-breeds, Indians, French Canadians, Irish, French, Italians, Poles, Bavarians, Scandinavians and Belgians.

The half-breeds at Batoche then began openly to carry arms, but no overt action was taken until a hundred North-West Mounted Police were ordered to travel from Regina to Carlton House. By the time rumours of this move reached Riel, there were said to be five hundred police coming to destroy the new provisional government. To prepare for possible attack, Riel ordered his followers to take over the stores in Batoche, confiscate arms and ammunition and to place the local traders in custody. With that action on 18 March, the Riel Rebellion had begun.

★   ★   ★

On the following day Hudson's Bay Company clerk Henry R. Halpin was on his way back to Cold Lake from Frog Lake when he met Big Bear near Beaver River, about thirty miles (48 km) north of the agency. The chief, who had been hunting and trapping alone, had not had contact with his people since the meeting to select a reserve on 10 March, and was eager for the latest news. "I told him," reported Halpin, "I had seen in the Battleford *Herald,* at Frog Lake, that there was trouble in Batoche, and that Riel had stopped the mails there. I told him I thought there was likely to be trouble." The chief was surprised and found the information to be puzzling. However, he took no immediate steps to return home, even though he must have realized how men like Wandering Spirit and *Imasees* would have reacted to news of possible violence. Instead, Big Bear went to the Hudson's Bay Company post at Cold Lake two days later to visit Halpin. On the afternoon of 22 March the chief announced that "he thought he would start home this evening and go around in the bush, and he might get a chance, it was blowing so hard, to kill a moose in the bush."[1]

Big Bear was still in the forest, wending his circuitous way back to Frog Lake, when the tense situation at Batoche exploded into violence. On 26 March a mixed party of Mounted Police and volunteers from the town of Prince Albert fought Riel's forces in a bloody engagement that became known as the Battle of Duck Lake. When it was over, the police had been forced to retreat and had suffered ten dead, two near death and eleven wounded. They would have been completely annihilated had not Riel, armed only with a crucifix, stopped the half-breeds and Indians from pursuing the fleeing soldiers. Two days later, the police abandoned Carlton House and withdrew to Prince Albert.

News of the battle reached Big Bear's camp before any of the neighbouring whites heard about it. *Imasees* was on the Eagle Hills reserves seeing Little Poplar when he heard a rumour of the fight, but he had no specific information other than that the Mounted Police in Battleford were being mobilized to move north because of trouble with the half-breeds. *Imasees* left with Little Poplar's son and reached Frog Lake with the news on 28 March. The Indians in Big Bear's camp were interested in the agitations of Riel, though they did not necessarily identify with the problems of half-breed land entitlement and political rights. However, they recognized that both groups, though separate and distinct, had a common enemy: the Canadian government.

Information about the bloody engagement at Duck Lake did not reach Inspector Dickens at Fort Pitt until 30 March, when he immediately dispatched a message to Subagent Quinn, suggesting that all the white residents of Frog Lake move to the fort for protection. Quinn called a meeting of local white residents, who at first felt they should comply with Dickens's order but in the end decided to stay at Frog Lake. "Mr. Quinn said that he would remain at his post; the Farm Instructor Mr. Delaney said the same; Mrs. Delaney then said she would stay with her husband. All the others then said they would stop but insisted that the Police should leave as their presence only tended to exasperate the Indians. . . . Mr. Quinn again stated that all was quiet and that he did not fear any disturbance."[2] Dutifully, Cpl. R. B. Sleigh and his two-man detachment returned to Fort Pitt, leaving the small village to carry on as though nothing was happening. Quinn and Delaney believed that their own continued presence and the issuing of rations would have a settling effect on the community.

The following day, the first of April, was one of merriment in the village, as people played practical jokes on each other. This was April Fools' Day, or as the Crees called it, Big Lying Day. An HBC clerk, William Cameron, was the butt of one of the good-natured jokes by Wandering Spirit and Miserable Man, who sent a messenger telling him to go immediately to Delaney's house, as Subagent Quinn wanted to see him. "As soon as I opened the door," said Cameron, "Wandering Spirit commenced to laugh and said it was 'big-lie-day,' and that Quinn had not sent for me. Everybody seemed full of good humour, and there were no signs of danger."[3]

A similar joke was played on Little Bear, who was camped on Moose Creek, a few miles west of Frog Lake, where he was hunting and selling game to some half-breed woodcutters. As his grandson recalled: "On April 1st, one of these fellows whose name was Gladu, he went up to my grandfather and says, 'Uncle, they're already starting to kill everybody at Frog Lake. They want all the people to come there, so you have to come.' 'All right,' said my grandfather, 'I have some traps set so I have to go and pick them up first.'

"My grandfather told his wife to get packed. They had four children, my aunt who was 17, my mother 15, and two younger ones. My grandfather went to pick up his traps — there were only two or three so it didn't take long. When he got back, his wife was all ready so they went towards the settlement. When they crossed Frog Creek they saw the people just walking around at the place where they were going to build the mill. Someone then said to my grandfather, 'My gosh, I guess you didn't know it was April Fools' Day.' 'My nephew told me a big lie,' said my grandfather, 'so I'm not going back to the creek.' "[4]

Some Métis woodcutters at nearby Moose Lake heard on April the first about the Duck Lake fight and decided to go to Frog Lake that day for more news. Among them were André Nault, nephew of Louis Riel; Adolphus Nolin, son of the former minister of agriculture for Manitoba, and Louis Goulet, who was both anti-Riel and anti-British. They arrived at the village in the afternoon and met *Imasees,* who had stolen a letter from Quinn to Dickens from the subagent's office, hoping it would tell him their plans. *Imasees* was looking for someone to read the letter for him, but the three Métis, not wishing to get involved, said they could read only French.

Later that same day Big Bear finally returned to the village to discover just how much news of the rebellion had excited his people. *Imasees* had managed to learn the contents of the stolen letter, and over at Onion Lake there had been a wild demonstration and shooting into the air around the farm instructor's house. Big Bear spoke earnestly to Wandering Spirit, Four Sky Thunder and the others, but it was obvious that he had no power or authority. When he suggested that the council meet with Subagent Quinn, only *Imasees* agreed to go, probably more to reaffirm his leadership of the band than to support his discredited father. At the meeting, *Imasees* revealed he knew all about the Duck Lake affair but promised that he would be loyal to the government. His father was pleased that his words of conciliation to his son seemed to have taken effect. "They say Big Bear is going to rise to war," the chief told Quinn, "and I am going to let them know and see that I am not going to rise."[5] He did not explain whether "they" were the white people, as his listeners assumed, or "they" were his own followers.

That night, Big Bear's warriors slipped away from their lodges and assembled along the west side of the lake, where Wandering Spirit and Little Bear had pitched their tepees. "Pretty soon other people started to come across," recalled Little Bear's grandson, "and camped all around them. Then they started to build a place for a war dance and when it was finished they started to dance. While the dance was going on, Wandering Spirit got up and said, 'Quiet! Tomorrow I am going to eat two-legged meat [i.e., kill someone]. So what do you think?' No one answered him and pretty soon they started dancing again. Then Wandering Spirit stopped the dance again. 'Hey, listen to what I'm going to do,' he called out. 'Tomorrow I'm going to eat two-legged meat. If you don't want to join me, then go home and put on your wives' dresses!' So they started to agree, saying, 'Okay,' 'Okay,' 'Okay.' They started to dance again until it was almost daylight. Then Wandering Spirit stopped the dance again. 'Look here,' he laughed at the ones who were leaving, 'I just made some of our brothers like women.' "[6]

Meanwhile, the residents of Frog Lake slept. The focal point of the scattered village was the Indian agency, under the supervision of Subagent Thomas Quinn, who lived there along with Farm Instructor John Delaney and his wife Theresa, Interpreter John Pritchard, a Métis carpenter, Charles Gouin, and their families. The Hudson's Bay Company was represented by its trader, James K. Simpson, with his half-breed wife, Catharine, and a clerk, William B. Cameron. There was also a blacksmith shop run by the subagent's nephew, Henry Quinn, and a free trader's store owned by George Dill. Near the creek was a mill under construction; its employees were John C. Gowanlock and his new bride, Mary; William C. Gilchrist, and John Williscraft. At the Oblate mission were Father Leon Adelard Fafard and his assistant, Father Felix Marchand.

Before daybreak on 2 April, Wandering Spirit and his followers returned to the settlement; all were fully painted for war. The head soldier had taken command, as was the custom in time of war, and led his warriors to the subagent's house. Lone Man, fearing violence, pushed his way past the war party and dashed upstairs to awaken Quinn. "Man-Speaking-Sioux, come down!" Wandering Spirit called from the main floor. Lone Man urged Quinn to stay where he was, but the subagent thought the "Indians had been blustering a good deal" and meant no harm.[7] However, as soon as he came downstairs he was taken prisoner, and so were his wife and frightened child.

While this was going on, two Indians went to Delaney's house and told him that half-breeds had stolen the government horses and that the Indians were afraid of an attack by Riel's men. Before the farm instructor could become suspicious, they took his weapons; Delaney and his wife became captives, together with the Gowanlocks, who had spent the night there. Over at the Hudson's Bay Company store, trader James Simpson had gone to Fort Pitt on business a few days earlier, but William Cameron was taken into custody, and all the arms and ammunition were removed from the store.

Big Bear did not hear about the raid until it already was underway. He got to the village just as some warriors were helping themselves to goods in the HBC store. Excitedly, Big Bear entered the building, waving his arms around and saying, "Don't touch anything here in the company's place. If there is anything you need, ask Cameron for it."[8] In the face of the old man's anger, the Indians silently filed out.

The work of rounding up the settlers continued at all the houses. The three Métis woodcutters, Goulet, Nault and Nolin, had spent the night with William Gilchrist at the Gowanlocks' house, but Nolin had left before dawn to visit a friend at the neighbouring Woods Cree camps. There he learned about the impending attack and rushed back to warn his friends. However, just as the four men were preparing to flee, they were detained by three warriors, "armed to the teeth and looking like they meant business. . . . They had black stripes under their eyes and their faces painted red."[9] A few minutes later, *Imasees,* with about twenty men, came through the door and told Gilchrist to open the storehouse. After this had been looted, the four men, and two Métis employees — Pierre Blondin and Gregoire Daunais — were herded over to the village. Once there, the half-breeds were left unattended, and Gilchrist was taken to the group of people at Delaney's house. By this time, just after sunrise, the prisoners included Quinn, his Indian wife, daughter and nephew Henry, Interpreter John Pritchard, the two priests, the Gowanlocks, the Delaneys, Gilchrist, Dill, Williscraft and Cameron.

Most of the prisoners believed the worst that could happen would be the killing of cattle and oxen, the looting of stores and the stealing of horses. No one had any reason to fear violence, and perhaps they were right. A day earlier, some people in Half Blackfoot Chief's band at Onion Lake had demonstrated at the farm instructor's house, but the man who had threatened to kill Instructor George Mann had lost his nerve.

At Frog Lake, however, a new and dangerous element was introduced to the tense situation. "The Indians had become more or less frenzied by drink of some kind," Mary Gowanlock noted, "possibly pain-killer got from the stores that had been plundered, though I did hear afterwards that they had drunk of the wine and spirits found at the house of the priest."[10] Cameron admitted that there were two cases of Perry Davis's Pain Killer in his store, and Dill's place also would have had a supply. It was about ninety per cent alcohol and a potent drink.

When all the white persons in the village were assembled, Wandering Spirit gave permission for the prisoners to attend church as it was a holy day, and everyone went, Catholic and Protestant alike. Charles Gouin and Louis Goulet, sitting outside the agency building, decided to go along as well. "Father Fafard said a few words of encouragement to us," said Goulet. "He advised us to pray devoutly and commend our souls to God. And then, in commemoration of the first Holy Thursday, he put on his vestments and began to say mass." Big Bear accompanied the prisoners, staying near the back of the church, as the war chief and Miserable Man kept watch over them. According to Cameron, Wandering Spirit "remained half kneeling in the center of the little church, with his rifle in his hand. He had a war hat on and his face was daubed with yellow paint."[11] During the service, Goulet could hear the effect that alcohol was having on some of the Indians outside. "While looting the stores," he said. "the Indians had helped themselves liberally to liquor and spirit. The Indians came in and out of the church, singing, shouting, howling and beating drums, storming around and strutting in under-clothes and suits they'd taken from the stores and the prisoners. Father Marchand closed the door at one time, but Wandering Spirit opened it five minutes later."[12] Inhibited by the noise and the presence of the warriors, Father Fafard cut the services short and warned the Indians "against committing excesses."[13] After the prisoners had left and the priest was closing the door, Little Bear ordered him to hurry and catch up with the others. When the priest hesitated, the Indian struck him in the face, blackening his eye. The earlier grudge against the missionary obviously had not been forgotten.

Big Bear realized that the combination of excitement and alcohol was producing a dangerous situation. Although he possessed no authority, he could still use his powers of persuasion to keep the Indians peaceful — but he knew that once they started drinking, they would not listen to him. Hurriedly, he sent a young girl to *Kehiwin*'s reserve to urge the Woods Cree to come to Frog Lake to help keep the peace. Eventually, the entire band came, but by then it was too late.

For the next hour or so, the prisoners remained at Delaney's, and Goulet and Gouin returned to their comrades who were sitting idly outside the abandoned police barracks chatting with Henry Quinn. Dill's trading post had been completely gutted by this time, and other buildings were being searched for liquor, guns or other items the Indians wanted. "It was getting hard to be optimistic," said Goulet. "The Indi-ans were getting drunker and drunker, more and more provoking."[14]

Realizing that the warriors were out of control, Big Bear sought out Delaney and, according to the farm instructor's wife, told him that "he was frightened some of his young braves intended shooting the whites but that he, my husband, would be safe any way."[15] Big Bear then went over to warn the wife of trader Simpson about the new dangers that had arisen. Sitting down glumly at her table, he said, "Pack up your things, I think there is going to be trouble. I can't be everywhere to look over my young men."[16] Mrs. Simpson tried to calm him down, gave him break-fast and tried to reassure him. While they sat chatting, Subagent Quinn and Pritchard came in with the news that Wandering Spirit had ordered the prisoners to go to the Indian camp. Quinn had argued with the war chief, then had marched over to see Big Bear to secure permission for the prisoners to stay at Delaney's. Obviously, he had no appreciation of the political structure of the band, believing that Big Bear was in control, when, in fact, Wandering Spirit was now in charge. Big Bear said wearily they could remain at Delaney's house, even though he knew his words had no authority.

After Quinn and Pritchard left, the chief watched Mrs. Simpson as she gathered a few things in her shawl and prepared to leave. Suddenly, three shots rang out, and moments later Man Who Speaks Our Language — the one who had struck Instructor Craig a year earlier — burst through the door to announce excitedly that the white people were being killed. Big Bear jumped to his feet and rushed outside, shouting, "Stop! Stop! Don't do it! Don't do it!"[17] But his words fell upon deaf ears, for the slaughter had already begun.

Although Big Bear had given permission for the prisoners to stay at Delaney's, Wandering Spirit had paid no attention to the chief's wishes and ordered them to go to the Indian camp. However, as far as Quinn was concerned, he had received permission from Big Bear, and though the other prisoners began to walk away, he refused to move. "You have a hard head," Wandering Spirit told him. "When you say no, you mean no, and stick to it. Now, if you love your life you will do as I say. Go to your camp!"

"Why should I go there?"

"Go!"

"Never mind," Quinn said, quietly, "I will stay here."

Wandering Spirit then levelled his gun at Quinn's head, saying "I tell you go!" and shot him.[18]

Big Bear's young granddaughter witnessed this incident as though it were a dream. "We saw Wandering Spirit raise the gun," she recalled, "and fire at the Agent who was at the time standing in front of the Agency. Mr. Quinn, who was wearing a Scottish beret, suddenly fell forward and his cap tumbled to within a few feet from where I stood. Immediately Wandering Spirit and his friend Memekoeso [Man of Little People] yelled 'Let's all go and get something to eat now [i.e., let's kill someone].' All I remember is that I was then very frightened and ran away back to our house."[19]

For a few moments, the prisoners who were walking ahead thought the Indians were simply firing shots into the air; but Gilchrist and Dill, who saw what had happened, began to run away in terror. As the two men separated, Man Who Speaks Our Language was leaving the Simpson house and immediately went in pursuit of Gilchrist, bringing him down with a single shot.

Little Bear was sitting on his pinto pony near the root house when Dill went running past. "See that man running?" shouted one of Little Bear's companions. "I dare you to shoot him."[20] A dare was a serious matter with Indians in time of war; it was a challenge that implied cowardice if the man failed to act. As Little Bear galloped off in pursuit of Dill, he heard Wandering Spirit urging the warriors to kill all the whites. The rider was quickly joined by Iron Body, Man of Little People and *Paskowkwiwin,* and though Little Bear shot five times, the prisoner kept running. Dill had just reached some bushes when Iron Body fired and hit the trader in the back of his neck. He fell into the bushes, dead.

Gouin, Goulet and Henry Quinn, who had been sitting and watching the Indians, scattered when the subagent was shot. Quinn jumped between two houses and raced away to the nearby bushes without being seen; Gouin and Goulet ran towards Pritchard's house, where Nolin and Nault had gone earlier. As Goulet grabbed for the door latch, Gouin tried to duck under his arm but was fired upon by Miserable Man. As Goulet dived for safety, Bad Arrow shot Gouin in the chest and he fell dead on the steps.

The first intimation of trouble came to the Gowanlocks and the Delaneys when they saw Williscraft run past them. As he went by the Gowanlocks, an Indian shot at him and knocked his hat off. Seeing that escape was impossible, Williscraft turned momentarily to plead, "Oh, don't shoot! Don't shoot!"[21] By this time Man Who Speaks Our Language was also bearing down on the helpless old man. As Williscraft ran off screaming, the warrior shot him and watched with satisfaction as he fell dead into some bushes.

"As soon as I saw Mr. Williscraft fall in front of us," said Mary Gowanlock, "I then knew all were being killed and I became greatly alarmed. I saw an Indian aiming at my husband by my side. In a moment he fell, reaching out his arms towards me. I caught him, and we fell together. I laid upon him, resting my face upon his and his breath was scarcely gone when I was forced away by an Indian. It was not the Indian who fired that dragged me from my husband. I did not seem to know what it all meant, and I went through it dazed and stunned, with only the power of my limbs left to me to follow after the Indian, as he dragged me after him."[22] No Indian was ever charged with Gowanlock's murder, but Cameron claimed that Bad Arrow had performed the deed. As Pritchard later recalled of the whole incident, "there were too many around us, too many Indians."[23]

The Delaneys watched in horror as their friends the Gowanlocks fell to the ground; they thought that both of them had been shot. "When I saw Mrs. Gowanlock fall," recalled Theresa Delaney, "I saw also some hideous object, an Indian got up in a frightful costume, take aim at my husband." Before she could utter a cry, John Delaney staggered away from her, then came back and moaned, "I am shot!" When he fell to the ground, his wife cradled his head in her arms and called Father Fafard to help her. The priest knelt beside them and was praying with a Bible in his hand when the same Indian, Bare Neck, fired again. "I thought his shot was meant for me," said Mrs. Delaney, "and I laid my head down upon my husband and waited. It seemed an age, but it was for my poor husband and he never spoke afterwards. Almost immediately another Indian ran up and ordered me away. I wanted to stay, but he dragged me off, pulling me along by the arms through the brush and briar and through the creek, where the water reached to my waist."[24]

As soon as Theresa Delaney was taken away, Wandering Spirit shot the priest in the back and left him for dead, then urged the others on to the slaughter. A few moments later some warriors came up and found that the clergyman was still alive. Bad Arrow shouted, "Shoot, he is still breathing! Shoot him in the head!"[25] Obligingly, Round the Sky stepped forward and finished Fafard off with a single shot. Father Marchand, who had been looking on the scene in terror, sank to his knees in prayer, crossed his arms and raised his eyes to heaven, just as an Indian shot him in the neck. The killer probably was the youngest son of Man Who Wins, chief of the Frog Lake Crees.

There were a number of Indians who were mere spectators, those who had come to share in the looting or to watch the excitement before it suddenly was transformed into a blood bath. One of these was a seventeen-year-old Woods Cree named *Mesunekwepan,* who came upon the dying Marchand. "I found on the hill," he recalled, "one of the Fathers lying helpless on the ground with blood streaming from his throat. He was still alive, breathing slowly. I said to him: 'I am very sorry but it must be God's will.' I took some grass to try and wipe away the blood which was coming from a gash in his throat. This was not very satisfactory, so I took my black silk handkerchief and tied it around his neck. He had his eyes closed but was still breathing as the blood trickled away from his throat at intervals. I stayed with him till the last."[26]

The killing was all over in a matter of a few minutes. Big Bear had cried aloud again and again for the men to stop, but they had listened to Wandering Spirit instead. In those brief minutes of violence, Big Bear's last dreams were shattered, destroyed forever in the hail of bullets that had left nine bodies scattered amid the chaos of what had been a peaceful village.[27]

Big Bear had already lost his fight to stay out of treaty; lost his fight to avoid taking a reserve; lost the leadership of his band; now, he had lost his chance for the Crees to negotiate for a better treaty and a better deal from the Canadian government — all because of Wandering Spirit's hatred of the white man, of *Imasees'* desire to be chief, of alcohol in the form of painkiller and sacramental wine, of the disappearance of the buffalo and starvation, of anger and frustration at being ground under the heel of an unfeeling government. There seemed to be truth in the bleak statement made by one of Big Bear's people: "We are doomed, and will be killed one after another by the whites. But before we die, or disappear altogether, we must enjoy ourselves as much as we possibly can, and therefore we must plunder stores and kill as many white people as we can."[28]

Not all the villagers of Frog Lake were killed. Mrs. Delaney and Mrs. Gowanlock were taken captive by men who considered them to be war booty, just as in the old days. William Cameron was saved by Catharine Simpson and Horse's wife, a Woods Cree, who covered him with a shawl and led him to her people's camp. The half-breed Goulet was protected by his brother-in-law, *Wechan,* who fended off an attack by Bare Neck to get him safely to the Woods Cree. Henry Quinn's escape went unnoticed, and he reached Fort Pitt with news of the outbreak. Pritchard, Blondin, Nault and the other half-breeds in the village were not molested and also made their way to the Woods Cree camp. Like the others, they knew that most of the woodland people were opposed to violence and had resented the presence of Big Bear's turbulent followers who had come in from the plains.

That very afternoon, trader James Simpson arrived back in Frog Lake, unaware of the tragedy that had taken place only hours before. He found the village abandoned, both his store and his house pillaged, and his wife gone. Worried, he drove his buckboard up to Big Bear's camp and there found the council sitting in a circle on the grass. He went directly to the chief, but soon realized that a shift had taken place in the power structure of the band and that if Big Bear "had anything to say, the others would not hear it." Although taken prisoner, Simpson was shown the courtesy usually extended to Hudson's Bay Company men — as opposed to government men, whom they hated — and he was permitted to go to his wife's tent in the Woods Cree camp. After hearing details about the tragedy from her, he went back to see Big Bear, who was alone in his lodge.

"I'm sorry to see what you have done here," he told the chief.

"Well, it is not my doings."

"This affair will all be in your name," the trader prophesied, "not your young men. It will be all on you, carried on your back."

Big Bear knew this, and in a mixture of anger and desperation he shot back, "It's not my doings! The young men won't listen and I am very sorry for what has been done. They have been always trying to take my name from me. I have always tried to stop the young men. [But] they have done it this time and taken my name away from me."[29]

There were other incidents of pillaging in the West during the first few days of the rebellion, particularly by Bobtail's followers at Peace Hills, as well as at Green Lake, Waterhen Lake, Lac la Biche and Beaver Lake. After the Battle of Duck Lake, the people around Battleford had fled to the fort for protection, and the Indians in the Eagle Hills had followed them there, seeking an interview with Agent Rae. When they failed, they pillaged the town and for four weeks the Mounted Police fort was in a state of virtual siege. During the excitement, old grievances were settled when the much-despised farm instructor among the Assiniboine, James Payne, was shot; two other white men also were killed by an Assiniboine.

The incident at Frog Lake, however, was the only one to turn into a such a bloody debacle. Why did it happen there and not at the other places? There were at least four plausible reasons, or more likely, a combination of all four. First, Big Bear's followers were still fresh from the plains and had not yet accepted the routine of reservation life. As such, they were hungry, depressed and angry, both at the government for their poor treatment and at Big Bear for his delaying tactics.

Second, the division within the band left them without a strong, effective political leader: the young people rejected Big Bear, but his son had not shown the wise and steadying influence expected of a chief. In fact, he seemed to be more a war chief, like Wandering Spirit. In spite of the fact that the head soldier automatically took over the band in times of danger, a political chief should still be a strong voice of reason in council. In Big Bear's camp, this was missing. Both *Imasees* and Wandering Spirit may even have had a tendency to do the opposite of what Bear Bear advised, in order to prove their independence.

Third, some of Big Bear's people had specific grievances against individual residents of the village. Edward Ahenakew, a Cree minister, was convinced that the primary cause "was the dislike that some of the Indians had for certain of the white men at Frog Lake. They had kept this to themselves, because a personal quarrel was always a dangerous thing in Indian life, meaning death to one or the other involved."[30] Certainly, Wandering Spirit hated Quinn, though the precise reason is not known; it could have been anything from the subagent's friendship with Lone Man to a rumour of jealousy over a woman. Delaney was disliked because of his harshness and his treatment of Sand Fly (who had escaped custody and was in the village at the time of the killings). Little Bear was known to harbour a grudge against Father Fafard, as did a young man from the Frog Lake Crees who had once worked for the priest. In addition several of the white villagers were married into Indian families and could have been subject to the jealousies and quarrels common in every camp.

The fourth element was alcohol, which could have acted on all the other forces, changing the mix of excitement and exultation to one of anger, hatred, revenge and violence. Of all the demonstrations that took place during the 1885 rebellion, this incident at Frog Lake appears to have been the only one in which the Indians had the opportunity to drink while holding a group of helpless captives. With reason clouded by alcohol, all that was needed was a single spark to ignite the whole powder keg of frustrations. And that spark was provided by Subagent Quinn, or indirectly, by Big Bear himself. In telling Quinn he could remain in the village, the chief gave a permission that was not within his power to sustain. But the subagent, thinking he had approval from the leading chief of the camp, openly and foolishly defied the war chief. The result was tragic.

Attack on Fort Pitt

C ANADA WAS SOON deeply involved in the Riel Rebellion. The militia was being organized in Ontario, Quebec, the Maritimes and Manitoba; hundreds of volunteers were preparing to depart for the scene of conflict on the western plains. At the time of the Frog Lake affair, the Winnipeg battalion already was in the field, waiting at the railway point at Qu'Appelle for orders to march. Farther west, home guards were being established in Edmonton, Calgary, Macleod and other centres, while Prince Albert was fortified against an expected attack from Riel. Once the government was fully mobilized, more than five thousand troops and five hundred Mounted Police were ready for combat.

On learning about the uprising at Frog Lake, the military commanders divided their forces into three columns. One, under Col. W. D. Otter, was to rush to the relief of Battleford; another under Gen. Frederick Middleton was to attack the Métis stronghold at Batoche, and a third, under Gen. T. B. Strange, was to strike at Wandering Spirit's camp by travelling down the North Saskatchewan River from Edmonton.

Several weeks would elapse, however, before the troops could be effectively in the field. The Canadian Pacific Railway was still under construction, so there was not yet a continuous line of steel through the Great Lakes region, resulting in considerable delay while troops and equipment were ferried from one link of the line to the next. In addition, the bombastic commander, Middleton, revealed a hesitancy to take direct and decisive action. Those factors, plus the spring breakup of rivers, meant that even the Winnipeg troops could not start for the north until mid-April, and Strange's force left Calgary a week later.

Meanwhile, the Indians around Frog Lake were unaware of events unfolding outside their isolated domain, or of the forces of retribution heading their way. In the days immediately following the killings, so many things happened that there was little time to think of anything else. The day after the uprising, Wandering Spirit called a meeting of the council to resolve some of the problems of governing the camp. From the outset, it was obvious that the war chief was in command, and though *Imasees* was present, he had hardly more authority than did his father. As for Big Bear, he dutifully attended but said little.

The Woods Cree were upset by the domination of the Plains Cree, but they were fearful about speaking their minds. However, the meeting was just underway when Cut Arm, leader of the Onion Lake Woods Cree, strode into camp. He chided the war chief for killing the whites and said his people had taken Instructor Mann and the Reverend Charles Quinney to safety at Fort Pitt. "Let this be a finish to your work," he told Wandering Spirit. This precipitated a violent argument between the two men, the war chief threatening to blow Cut Arm's brains out, and the Onion Lake chief offering to use his one good arm to cut the warrior to pieces. "I am not afraid of you," he told Wandering Spirit. "I used to be in the front when we fought the Blackfoot Indians. You were behind them."[1]

As soon as tempers cooled, Wandering Spirit called the white prisoners to the council and cross-examined them about their support for the government. Big Bear, fearing a confrontation, "wanted us to state whether we would support him or follow the White man," said Louis Goulet. "Nobody was stupid enough to risk saying he was on the government's side. We were all for Big Bear, scared we'd get killed if we said otherwise."[2]

At this point, an old man named Bald Head came forward and began to tease Wandering Spirit for his timidity in not killing more whites. "Why are you keeping these people here so long for nothing, talking to them?" he chided. "Don't you know that you have work to do somewhere else [i.e., an attack on Fort Pitt]?"[3]

Already stung by Cut Arm's rebuke, Wandering Spirit exploded in rage; he pumped a shell into his Winchester and pointed the gun at HBC trader James Simpson. Before he could shoot, the trader's stepson, Louis Patenaude, and a Woods Cree, Alexis Crossarms, knocked the gun in the air and also took the war chief's knife. Moments later, *Imasees* snatched the knife away and cried, "This is not the right way to do! It will make trouble between us [Woods and Plains Crees]. We want to be friends."[4]

Wandering Spirit then apologized, saying that the old man had made him angry. Throughout the entire incident, Big Bear had remained silent, watching the first steps in the disintegration of an uneasy alliance between Wandering Spirit's warriors and the more peaceful elements in both the Woods and Plains Cree camps.

While Wandering Spirit's soldiers maintained a semblance of order in the camp, people rounded up four hundred head of cattle in the area and slaughtered them as needed, feasting on fresh beef, flour and other foods, which now seemed available in a limitless supply. There was singing every night, and at some place in the camp a dance was usually underway. The warriors sported every imaginable kind of costume, from priests' robes to parts of Mounted Police uniforms from the abandoned detachment.

Other changes, more subtle and ominous, revealed much about the new role of the Plains Cree in the camp. When old *Kehiwin* had arrived with his band of Woods Cree, too late to try to stop the killing, he had pitched his lodge close to the other Woods Cree camps of Standing Man, Man Who Wins and *Makaoo*. Then, quietly, Wandering Spirit had the Plains Cree move their lodges so that they virtually encircled their woodland brothers. They were not prisoners, exactly, nor were they free to decamp whenever they wished. Most of the whites and half-breeds from the village were staying with the Woods Cree and, like them, had considerable freedom of the camp and the region. Some even carried guns when they went hunting with Plains Crees.

The role of the half-breeds was never clear-cut. Some, like André Nault, clearly sympathized with the Indians and regarded their campaign as part of Riel's bigger fight, but others, like Pritchard and Goulet, were opposed both to Riel and to the warlike actions of Wandering Spirit's followers. However, the Indians did consider the half-breeds to be different from the whites, more like cousins than enemies.

Because of Wandering Spirit and *Imasees,* Big Bear had virtually no power, but he was not prepared to forfeit entirely his leadership role. He still had his abilities of persuasion, so he set out new goals in view of the changed conditions. First, he wanted to protect his own people in any way he could, and if it came to a showdown, he would be with them to the bitter end. But if their lives were not immediately threatened, then he wanted to achieve some measure of security for everyone in the camp and the region. This meant protecting the white and half-breed prisoners and avoiding any unnecessary conflicts among Indians themselves.

His first concern was for the neighbouring Indians, half-breeds and whites who were not yet a part of the camp. He was afraid that if Wandering Spirit sent raiding parties out to Cold Lake, Onion Lake and other nearby settlements, they might carry on the killing. To avoid this, he got approval to dispatch his own messengers to bring the others into the camp, where at least he would have a chance to protect them.

Lone Man agreed to take on the task, so shortly after the outbreak he left with some companions for Cold Lake. There he took HBC clerk Henry Halpin and Farm Instructor John Fitzpatrick into custody, pillaging their places, and proceeded to the Catholic mission, where trader Abraham Montour, a Métis, welcomed the news about the uprising and

encouraged the local Chipewyans to join the Crees at Frog Lake. However, Lone Man was worried about the local priest, Father Legoff, and
warned him that "he was no friend of the Crees, and that they would kill
him" if he went to Frog Lake. Lone Man said "he would get into trouble
when he returned to Frog Lake" for not bringing in the priest, but in the
end, only a couple of Chipewyans and the local half-breed traders
decided to go south.[5] When they got back to Frog Lake, Big Bear
greeted Halpin and Fitzpatrick and assured them that they would be safe;
Halpin was a Hudson's Bay Company man and Fitzpatrick an American, so neither would be molested.

Big Bear also sent a letter to *Pakan,* the Christian chief at Whitefish
Lake, telling him about the troubles. According to *Pakan,* the letter said
"he and his Band had dropped work and intended to help themselves to
the Government property and telling me to do the Same, to drive all our
Stock down to Frog Lake and join him."[6] When this failed to get a
positive response, Big Bear sent a further missive. Clearly, he feared that
the Whitefish Lake group could antagonize Wandering Spirit if they did
not join his cause, so when *Pakan* remained firm, Big Bear suggested
that he "buy a swift horse and clear the country."[7] As it was, a supporter
of Wandering Spirit did go to *Pakan*'s camp, and during a heated discussion as to whether they would join the insurgents, one of *Pakan*'s men
shot and killed the emissary. After that, *Pakan*'s followers, fearing
revenge, remained hidden until the military reached the area.

At council meetings Big Bear usually said nothing; only once did he
speak his mind. Turning to Wandering Spirit, he said, "Long ago I used
to be recognized by all you Indians as a chief." He paused, gazing at
Imasees, then at Four Sky Thunder and the others who had rejected him.
"There was not a bigger chief among you than I was, and all these
southern Indians knew it, the [Bloods] and Piegans, and the Sioux and
the Blackfeet, and all the rest of those southern Indians knew it." Big
Bear's councillors listened but there was no respect in their eyes. "When
I said a thing at that time, there was some attention paid to it and it was
acted upon, but now," and he turned to glare at Wandering Spirit, ". . .
now I say one thing and you do another!"[8]

For a moment the two men stared at each other, then the old chief
crumpled down and hung his head, looking at no one. Big Bear, the
proud and determined visionary who had once inspired confidence
among his followers, now brought forth hatred and disdain. This skillful
politician, who had been shrewd and unyielding when dealing with
government officials, was humbled and treated with contempt in his
own council.

Outside of the council, however, many people were still willing to
listen. Lone Man and Two & Two both had stayed faithful to Big Bear,

and a number of families in the camp abhorred what had happened at Frog Lake. Secretly, they looked to Big Bear to give them wise advice, though publicly they deferred to Wandering Spirit and *Imasees*. Big Bear spent his days moving quietly through the camp, checking on the prisoners, speaking with the Woods Crees and trying to plan ahead for the eventual confrontation with the white soldiers that he knew would come. Like a lion without teeth, he plodded through the camp, no longer feared but still respected by some.

In his lodge, there was often just Big Bear, his young wife and their son Horse Child. Even King Bird, now that he was of warrior age, preferred to be with *Imasees*. Behind Big Bear's sleeping place, his bear bundle and medicine pipe still took their place of honour, and the altar remained by the fireplace. He prayed, as he always did, wondering what he had done wrong to bring such bad luck upon himself; perhaps someone with even greater spiritual powers than his was conjuring an evil spell upon him. His luck had been so bad for so long that it could not have been a mere coincidence. Everyone knew that these things did not just happen; they were ordained by some evil spirit, or by an evil man in league with such a spirit. Even his most powerful war medicine seemed incapable of counteracting the forces that were threatening him.

After ten days of feasting and revelry, the new leaders decided to attack Fort Pitt, though some, like Cut Arm who had reluctantly decided to join *Imasees'* camp, believed it was foolish to continue their aggressions. But Wandering Spirit, *Imasees,* Lucky Man and other participants in the Frog Lake affair regarded the next step as inevitable. If the fort remained in the hands of the traders and the Mounted Police, it would pose a threat to Wandering Spirit's camp. Moreover, rebel sympathizers like Abraham Montour and André Nault had been talking about the successes of Riel. Wandering Spirit believed that the Indians and Métis had captured Calgary, Edmonton and Qu'Appelle, burned Carlton House, torn up the railroad, destroyed the telegraph line and that ten thousand Americans with twenty ox-trains of guns and ammunition were on their way north. The capture of Fort Pitt by Wandering spirit would be a further step in driving the government men out of the area. Once this had been accomplished, he believed that the American government would come in and buy the land from the Indians, paying a fair price and thus alleviating forever the hunger and suffering in their camps.

When the decision was made to attack Fort Pitt, Big Bear did not try to dissuade them, but argued that the Hudson's Bay Company people should be evacuated first. Many of them were half-breeds with relatives in the Woods Cree camp, and others were old-time traders who were still their friends. He told the council that he would go with them and speak to the traders to give them a chance to get out.

The caravan that set out from Frog Lake on 13 April was made up of a varied assortment of riders, carts and people on foot. Some of the women and children stayed behind with the prisoners; Pritchard and Halpin were the only prisoners taken along, one to interpret and the other to write letters. A few of the half-breeds went to see the fun. Wandering Spirit and *Imasees,* side by side, led the procession, while Big Bear, alone and ignored, followed near the end. They had not asked him to come, but he had told the council he would be there.

Meanwhile, alerted by Henry Quinn and the Onion Lake settlers about the troubles at Frog Lake, the police and traders had readied Fort Pitt for a siege, as neither traders nor police had enough horses or wagons to flee. The ramshackle fort had no palisades, no bastions, no cannon and no source of fresh water closer than the river. Defensively, it was an impossible place, built for the fur trade, not for war. The occupants of the fort piled sacks of flour, cut loopholes, destroyed outlying buildings, waited and got on each other's nerves. To add to the defenders' problems, Little Poplar and his followers had arrived from Battleford on 7 April and instead of going on to Frog Lake, they seemed content to camp across the river from the fort, where they received rations. They professed friendship, but likely were keeping the occupants of the fort under surveillance until the others came.

On the thirteenth, the same day that Wandering Spirit and his followers set out from Frog Lake, Quinney convinced Inspector Dickens to send out a patrol to see what was happening in the district. In spite of objections from trader William McLean, Cst. David Cowan and Cst. Clarence Loasby were dispatched, accompanied by Henry Quinn as guide. Four hours later, Wandering Spirit's warriors "fully two hundred and fifty strong and all mounted, made their appearance on the ridge north of and about two thousand yards back from the fort."[9]

The weather had turned cold, and Big Bear, without proper clothes, decided that his first message to the fort would be one that considered his own comfort: he asked Sgt. John A. Martin for a blanket and HBC trader McLean for tea and tobacco. When he was successful, Miserable Man also had Halpin write a letter, this one seeking a shirt, trousers and tea kettle. These items were dispatched via a half-breed courier, together with a note asking Big Bear to keep the warriors in camp so they could parley on the following day.

In the meantime, Little Poplar crossed the river to the main camp to provide his comrade-in-arms, Wandering Spirit, with details of the fort and its complement of men. The war chief was excited and, like *Imasees,* he favoured attacking the fort immediately. Big Bear learned what they were doing and called out to them, reminding them of their promise made at Frog Lake. He was determined "to try and save the families that were there, and the police that were there, let them go," recalled Pritc-hard.[10] Reluctantly, the others agreed to try it the old man's way.

Next morning, McLean walked up the hill to meet with the council and soon learned to his surprise that Wandering Spirit was in charge. Big Bear did go through the formality of circulating his medicine pipe, hopefully as a symbol of peace, but otherwise he took no part in the proceedings. After a few opening comments by *Imasees,* McLean was invited to state his viewpoints on the uprising and Indian problems with the government. He told them frankly that any effort to drive the white men out of the country would result in failure, that the Queen's soldiers were more numerous than the hairs on a buffalo. Assuring them of the friendship of the Hudson's Bay Company and his own honesty in speak-ing to them, he advised them to go back to their reserves and to hope that their punishment would not be too severe.

An uneasy murmur ran through the council, with Cut Arm agreeing with the trader but saying it was too late now to turn back. Then Wandering Spirit arose, put a cartridge in the chamber of his Winchester and cradled the weapon in the crook of his arm. "You have spoken enough," he said curtly. "We are in a hurry. We believe that you have said of the Hudson's Bay Company and of yourself; . . . But you have said too much about the Government; we do not want to hear anything about him. We are tired of him and of all his people, and we are now going to drive them out of our country."

"Why do you want us to believe that the Government has plenty of soldiers?" the war chief continued. "Look at the few Red Coats that you are keeping down there at the fort; is that plenty? That is all the Govern-ment can send; he had been trying to send more men out here for the past two years to frighten us, we are not afraid of them. . . . We do not know why you keep the Red Coats in your Fort. That is the only thing we have against you. That Fort was built for us many years ago and not for Red Coats." He concluded with a warning: "They will not be long there; we will make short work of them and kill them as if they were young ducks, but we want you to get your wife and children out of the way of danger."[11]

Suddenly, the council was interrupted by screams from some women, "Red Coats! Red Coats! They are going to shoot us!"[12] The three police scouts, riding back from their patrol, had stumbled into the middle of the Cree camp and were racing forward to the safety of the fort. The Indians, believing the men were the vanguard of a larger force, thought the camp had been flanked and was under attack. At the moment, even the ones who had counselled peace and had stayed out of the Frog Lake affair were spurred into action. This was war! Their women and chil-dren, their families, were in danger.

Quickly, the Indians opened fire on the trio and, as they did so, Quinn's horse veered to one side, and the scout dashed into the bushes. With all attention directed on the two redcoats, he successfully made his escape, only to be captured and made prisoner two days later. Meanwhile, Loasby was ahead of his companion and thought he was clear of danger until his horse was shot and began to stumble; then a bullet struck the policeman in the left side, as both horse and rider tumbled to the ground. Loasby was being hotly pursued by Lone Man and Thunder Spirit; they were so close that they were taken by surprise when his horse stumbled, and the Indians fell right on the top of him. According to Loasby, "Before he had time to rise, a blood-thirsty brave named Thunder Spirit, who had previously been frequently befriended by the mounted police, overtook him at a bound and thinking him dead, cut off his side arms [i.e., his revolver and belt]."[13] However, in later testimony, he claimed that Lone Man had done this deed. A short time later, the wounded Loasby managed to struggle to his feet and stagger to the fort.

Cowan was not so fortunate. Being the last in the group, most of the fire was directed at him. The first man to shoot the policeman was *Koosehat,* or *Peesiwoocas,* who brought down both man and horse. Then Louison Mongrain, part Woods Cree and part Iroquois, shot Cowan as he begged for mercy, and Dressy Man finished him off with a blow of his war club. It was significant that two of the men prominently implicated in the shooting of the policemen — Lone Man and Mongrain — had otherwise staunchly defended whites, particularly the prisoners. However, they had perceived the police as a threat to their camp and acted accordingly.

Big Bear remained at McLean's side, in case the fury of the warriors should turn on the HBC man. And there is no question of the hatred and anger that boiled to the surface. The Mounted Police were the symbols of the government that had starved and mistreated them for years. Later on, an army medical officer, viewing Cowan's body where it had fallen, found it had "two bullet holes in the head, another bullet wound in the thigh, the body ripped open at the chest and the thigh, slashed down to the bone, the head scalped & his heart torn out of his chest."[14]

After the Indians had divided up the war booty, Wandering Spirit made McLean swear that he would stay with the Crees; in exchange, all the Hudson's Bay Company employees would be protected. Still excited, some of the warriors wanted to attack the fort, but with Big Bear's help an agreement was made whereby the police would be permitted to leave in a scow if everyone else would turn themselves over to Wandering Spirit's custody. McLean believed this would be the safest course of action and sent a message to his wife, urging her to accept the arrangement and to convince Dickens to do likewise. "If the police force in the fort cannot get off," he wrote, "the Indians are sure to attack it to-night — so they say — and will burn it down."[15]

At the same time, Big Bear dictated a letter to Sergeant Martin:

Since I have met you long ago we have always been good friends, and you have from time to time given me things, and that is the reason that I want to speak kindly to you; so please try and get off from Pitt as soon as you can. And tell your Captain that I remember him well, for since the Canadian Government had left me to starve in this country, he sometimes gave me food, and I don't forget the blankets he gave me, and that is the reason I want you all to get off without bloodshed.

We had a talk, I and my men, before we left our camp, and we thought the way we are doing now the best — that is, to let you off if you would go. So try and get away before the afternoon, as the young men are wild and hard to keep in hand.

BIG BEAR

P. S. you asked me to keep the men in camp last night, and I did so; so I want you to go off to-day.

BIG BEAR[16]

Over the objections of Inspector Dickens, Mrs. McLean announced that she and her family were going to surrender to Big Bear. In the end, the police had no choice but to accept the terms and to withdraw from the post. That evening, just as heavy snow began to fall and ice was drifting in the river, Dickens set out with his men to float downstream to Battleford. Mrs. McLean sent the HBC people up the hill, where they were taken in hand by various Woods Cree families, but she waited with her daughters until the police had pushed away from shore, knowing that the warriors would not attack them while she was still there.

Forty-four prisoners were now added to Wandering Spirit's camp. These included the eleven members of the McLean family; HBC employees Stanley Simpson, Robert Hodson, Malcolm Macdonald and Alfred Schmidt; the Manns; the Quinneys, and several half-breed families. McLean and his family were taken in by Little Poplar, and for the first night, the Manns were also kept in his lodge, in case the hatred for government men might result in an attack on the farm instructor.

That night the fort was pillaged, and soon happy Crees were hauling away loads of food, furs, clothing and any other goods that took their fancy. There was much celebrating in the camp, in spite of the bad weather, but none of the prisoners was molested.

Big Bear did not try to stop the pillaging, but he did continue to keep a benevolent eye on the prisoners, making sure they had satisfactory accommodations and doing his best to keep them from coming to harm. It was the least, and perhaps the most, that he could do.

Battle of Frenchman's Butte

T HROUGHOUT THE FROG LAKE TROUBLES, Big Bear had fully shared the feelings his people had towards the government. He too believed that many of its employees were evil men who had caused the Crees unnecessary suffering and had led the unsuspecting Indians into a one-sided treaty. Where he did disagree with Wandering Spirit and the others was in the measure of their enemy. He knew that for every farm instructor they killed, another would take his place; and for every policeman they killed, a hundred would revenge him.

Big Bear had believed that the only war he might win was one of words. They were a favourite tool of the white man, and Big Bear, orator and politician, wanted to turn them to his advantage. His only problem was that he had never been able to find the right government man to talk to. But as long as he had kept trying, he had kept alive the hope that eventually he would succeed.

Now, he feared that Wandering Spirit had unleashed a whirlwind that would sweep through his camp and destroy many men, women and children. The white soldiers would come in increasing numbers, looking for the ones who had killed their government men and seeking revenge for their deaths. For this reason, Big Bear had protected the prisoners: the more people who were killed, the greater would be the revenge.

If he had thought there would be any chance of success, Big Bear would have supported an all-out war against the whites, but there was no use dreaming about taking the land back from the Canadians. It was too late. In fact, it had been too late ever since the buffalo had been killed off. Big Bear remembered the vision he had had when he was still a boy: the coming of the white man, the purchase of the land and the offer of bounteous presents to the Indians while their very existence was being stolen from them. Then, in later years, he had dreamed of a spring of water, shooting up from the ground and turning to blood as it spurted between his fingers. Both visions seemed to prophesy the evils that had come to pass.

Wandering Spirit's followers, captives and semicaptives slowly made their way back to Frog Lake, the Indians carrying all the loot they wanted to keep. For the next two weeks they feasted, danced, visited and gambled, as though they did not have a care in the world. Most of the buildings at Frog Lake had been burned and some of the bodies buried,[1] but the countryside was as tranquil and lovely as it always had been.

The only disruptions were the messengers who came and went at frequent intervals. On the day after the raiders got back to Frog Lake, four Indians came from Batoche with a message from Riel; he congratulated them on their victory and at the same time cautioned them to take pity on their prisoners and to treat them well. Then some scouts from Saddle Lake reported that Edmonton had not been taken after all but was being besieged by Indians. More disturbing was the news that the Catholic half-breeds at St. Albert were furious about the killing of the two priests at Frog Lake and threatened to take revenge on the Crees as soon as they could organize an army. "Big Bear himself was frightened at this," commented the Reverend Charles Quinney, for the Crees considered the half-breeds to be their allies, and men like André Nault and Abraham Montour had encouraged this feeling.[2]

In order to reassure the Crees, Montour urged that a letter be written to Alexander Hamelin, a half-breed trader at Lac la Biche, asking the Indians and Métis in that area to join them at Frog Lake. Wandering Spirit agreed and summoned Big Bear to his lodge to have the note sent out over the chief's name. When completed, it set out "in glowing terms that Louis Riel had fought and won a great battle with the Mounted Police at Duck Lake, and that Big Bear's followers had done similar at Frog Lake and at Fort Pitt."[3] However, the Indians at Lac la Biche refused to join the insurgents, though they did pillage the trading Hudson's Bay Company post there.

Another important message was one that arrived on 4 May from Poundmaker's camp after the siege of Battleford. Written by a half-breed, Norbert Delorme, it asked Big Bear's followers to join them without delay and promised a hundred carts and horses would be sent to meet them at the crossing of the Saskatchewan River. The letter, supposedly speaking for Poundmaker, said that the chief "was prepared to give them a good reception, as he was retaining sixty fat cattle for that purpose. After they would have a little rest, they would take Battleford, and with all the large stock of provisions there, they would go on and join Riel at Batoche."[4]

There was jubilation among Wandering Spirit's followers at the news, and that night an announcer went through the camp, urging everyone to support the plan. However, at a council meeting on the following day, the Woods Cree were strongly opposed, and Big Bear announced privately that he would not go. To have spoken publicly might have triggered Wandering Spirit and *Imasees* to leave immediately, just to prove their independence. As it was, the council remained stalemated for two days, until *Imasees* volunteered to go see if Delorme's letter told the truth. In the meantime the rest of the camp planned to move to the Fort Pitt area, as the first step in their journey to the Eagle Hills.

During these weeks, the Riel rebellion was rapidly reaching its climax. By the time Delorme's letter reached Big Bear's camp, Colonel Otter's forces had occupied Battleford and were preparing to attack Poundmaker; Riel's men had fought an inconclusive battle at Fish Creek, and Middleton's army was moving on Batoche itself. To the west, General Strange had arrived in Edmonton and was planning to proceed down the North Saskatchewan River towards Frog Lake. No Americans or guns had arrived from south of the border to help the rebellion; the railway was intact, and all of the settlements except Frog Lake, Fort Pitt and Batoche were firmly in the hands of the army or home guards.

When strange white men were reported in large numbers near Edmonton, Wandering Spirit thought they were American allies, particularly as they were not wearing the scarlet coats of the Queen. However, when *Imasees* returned from his scouting expedition and reported that Poundmaker was fighting both soldiers and police, all the war chief's dreams vanished and were replaced by the sickening reality of events happening in the outside world. With Poundmaker being attacked in the east and soldiers coming from the west, it would be only a question of time until government forces reached Frog Lake.

The next morning, Big Bear could not resist going through the camp and, for the first and only time, speaking his mind in a strong, clear voice. "You have heard the report brought to you by the couriers!" he shouted. "It is an alarming one for you! What are you going to do about it? You were in a hurry to commence trouble and now you have it. The soldiers of the Queen have come to fight you and very shortly you will likely have to show how you can fight them!"[5]

Wandering Spirit and *Imasees* moved everyone to the Fort Pitt area on 15 May, camping on Red Deer Creek in the shadow of Frenchman's Butte. Wandering Spirit had become noticeably subdued, and one evening he stopped at the McLean lodge. "We noticed that he was quite different in appearance from the other Indians," commented Elizabeth McLean. "He was a tall thin man with a long face and a long nose. In contrast with the other Indians, who all had small eyes and straight hair, Wandering Spirit had wonderful large black eyes and jet black hair that hung in ringlets." Feeling depressed and full of remorse, the war chief asked Mrs. McLean, "What would your God do to a man who had done what I did?" She found it hard to answer but finally told him that such a person would be punished for his sins. "We began to notice that his hair was turning gray very fast," commented Elizabeth McLean.[6]

Once the Crees were settled in camp, a number of warriors were eager to go directly to join Riel, now that Poundmaker had been defeated. Little Poplar went through the village, calling for warriors to join him, but the division between the Woods Cree and Plains Cree had become so wide that he could find no support outside his own camp. Finally, Half Blackfoot Chief suggested sending messengers to Riel and offered to sponsor a Thirst Dance while everyone waited for the reply. Soon, the frame structure was erected, the leafy walls were in place and the dancing area set aside. However, on the following day, the ceremony was abandoned when scouts reported that a large force of soldiers had arrived at Fort Pitt.

The camp was immediately thrown into a state of great excitement, as lodges were struck and everyone moved off to a new campsite about three miles (5 km) away. During the evening, a warrior named *Maymenook* gathered together a number of young men and announced he was going to raid the soldiers' horse herd. When they got close to Fort Pitt, the warrior "went into a hollow below the trail which was on a hill. It was dark. Then he could see these white men riding on the trail so he shot at them. They shot back at the place where they saw the fire coming from and they killed him."[7] *Maymenook* was the first Indian casualty of the conflict.

The next day was spent in feverish activity getting ready for the attack. Everyone, including the prisoners, was put to work digging shelter pits, both for the warriors near the expected battle lines and farther away for the women and children. A few shots were exchanged with the soldiers that evening, but both sides seemed to be more intent in securing their positions. Against Wandering Spirit were 195 infantry, 29 cavalry and a nine-pounder cannon. Directed by General Strange, the units consisted of the Winnipeg Light Infantry, 65th Mount Royal Rifles, Steele's Scouts, Alberta Light Infantry and the Mounted Police.

On the morning of 28 May 1885 the Battle of Frenchman's Butte commenced, with the Crees opening fire as soon as the militia appeared over the top of a ridge. After crossing a branch of Red Deer Creek, the soldiers discovered there was a deep swamp between them and the warriors. Wandering Spirit had chosen the site well, for as one of the soldiers commented: "We were at every disadvantage as the enemy overlooked us and could plainly see each man as he lay in the valley, while we firing from the ravine could only judge of their position by the smoke of their rifle shots. They were well entrenched in rifle pits."[8]

Then the nine-pounder was brought into action, and a shell struck a trench that held four Indians, three of whom were injured. One was the irrepressible Man Who Speaks Our Language, whose leg was split right up to his thigh. He kept singing his war song, even as they carried him back to the camp, and it was still on his lips when he died.

When a shell struck another trench, injuring a warrior, the Crees realized that the big gun had their range, so they began to withdraw. As they did so, they expected a mass attack from the soldiers, either through the muskeg or from the flanks. But it never came, as General Strange had also decided to withdraw, fearing that the Crees might be planning to outflank him. After about three hours of fighting, Wandering Spirit had four men injured, one of whom died, and Strange had three wounded.

Big Bear did not take part in the fighting but stayed with the prisoners and old people about three miles (5 km) behind the lines. Proud of the way his people fought, he told the prisoners that the Cree warriors had killed a good many soldiers and some officers as well. His people had not retreated in the face of enemy rifle fire but had managed to use their superior position to advantage until the cannon got their range. Then the warriors were forced to retreat, taking only their wounded and their guns with them. As they did so, Big Bear went to the shelter pits where families were hiding and urged them to leave as well. By noon, most of the Crees were travelling north and east into the heavy bush.

During the confusion of battle, the Chipewyans from Cold Lake deserted, taking their priest with them. Several prisoners also used the opportunity to flee, including the Reverend Charles Quinney and his wife, Henry Halpin, William Cameron, Henry Quinn, Mrs. James Simpson, and several Wood Cree and half-breed families. Everyone else moved off, with Wandering Spirit acting as guide, leader and chief warrior. He seemed to be everywhere at once, seeing to the wounded, getting people moving and watching for an enemy attack. That day he was in every sense a true chief, inspiring confidence and courage among all those in the scattered camp. He was solicitous of the white prisoners, guarding them when Man Who Speaks Our Language died so that a relative of the dead warrior would not kill one of them in revenge. In fact, he became the kind of leader that Big Bear had been many years earlier — bold, decisive and inspiring.

The Crees moved away rapidly from the site of the battle. The warriors, pleased because the soldiers had withdrawn, were convinced the fight had been a victory for the Crees. At the same time, they were aware that the soldiers were not travelling with their women and children, so they were more mobile and had no responsibilities other than to fight. It was just as Big Bear had warned them.

When the soldiers later came to the abandoned battleground, they saw all the signs of a hurried departure: "In and around these pits were deserted bedding and pillows, and household utensils. Valuable furs were spoiling in the wet. Clothing and flour, cart harness and bacon, empty cans and steel traps, carpenter's tools and medicine bags, made an indescribable mess. . . . In the flat below, up the coulee and among the bushes, were waggons and carts deserted. In some were sides of bacon, in others flour spilt, with empty trunks, boxes and waggon harness. The hurry of departure was obvious when such things as 'medicines' were left. Several large bags full of small bundles of roots, powders, grasses, herbs, and chrome-yellow and vermillion, with totems and shields, and charms, were left lying about."[9]

The withdrawal turned into an ordeal, as Wandering Spirit led the Crees through dense forest to discourage mounted troops from following with wagons and cannon. They camped the first night in the bush and the next two nights between Horse Lakes. Big Bear no longer had a horse and plodded along with the rest, neither offering help nor being helped by others. Someone had even stolen his blanket. Like the others, he and his small family had only the food they could carry on their backs, or on the few horses and oxen that accompanied the retreating band.

On the first of June, Wandering Spirit's scouts reported the army was on the move again, so the tired Indians set out for Loon Lake in a cold, drenching rain. At this time, André Nault, John Pritchard, Peter Blondin and several half-breed families took Mary Gowanlock and Theresa Delaney away during heavy fog and effected their escape. Each day, too, a few Woods Crees slipped away, and the camp slowly disintegrated.

Big Bear could only watch helplessly as old men and women struggled through the mud and the muskeg. Hunger, exposure and a sinking fear gripped many of them, but he had neither horses nor the means to help them; he could not even help himself. If his people had listened to him, at this very moment they probably would be building cabins on their new reserve, breaking land or perhaps hunting in the bush. Instead, they were cold, wet and expecting to be slaughtered by the white soldiers.

Two days later they reached Loon Lake, while some warriors fought an intermittent rear guard action. In one brisk exchange near the Horse Lakes, two soldiers were wounded, and Steele's Scouts were forced to withdraw to safety. By the morning of 3 June most of the Crees had crossed the narrows at the lake when the soldiers caught up with them again.

"At Loon Lake there were two camps," said Jimmy Chief. "My grandfather Cut Arm was in one and the rest were on the point. They heard shots and went to join the others. My grandfather went with his two boys and that's when he was killed with two others, *O-show-wu'n* and a young fellow from farther east."[10] Until his death, Cut Arm had been an inspiration to the others, fighting alongside *Imasees* and Little Poplar and keeping the younger warriors with him by the demonstration of his own bravery. At one point in the fight, he had shouted, "I have confidence in you young men! You will never run away, but fight while there is a drop of red blood left. We will destroy the white robbers who have taken our country from us."[11]

For about half an hour a rapid exchange of gunfire took place across the still waters of the narrows. During this time, Big Bear took his famous bear medicine from its wrappings and placed it around his neck, the paw with its savage claws hanging down in front. If this battle was to be their last, he knew that the soldiers would come looking for Big Bear, and he would rather die fighting than become a prisoner. He expected they would be like other enemies on the battlefield, harsh and merciless with their prisoners. And so he waited, his face painted, the bear collar in place, a broken old man waiting for the moment when the government's soldiers came riding across the narrows.

But the attack never came. Big Bear did not know that Steele's Scouts were an advance company of only sixty-five men and of these, three had been wounded. A day or two behind him were the combined forces of Strange and Middleton, the latter having come to Fort Pitt after defeating Riel at Batoche.

When the Crees realized that the fight was over, they withdrew, burying the four men who had been killed in the fight — Cut Arm, O-show-wu'n, The Bush and a relative of Little Poplar. With the death of Cut Arm, Louison Mongrain became the new leading chief of the Woods Cree, while Wandering Spirit continued as war chief of the entire camp. However, it was obvious to everyone that the bands were falling apart, and people seemed to be looking to their respective chiefs for their next move. *Imasees,* Little Poplar, Half Blackfoot Chief, *Kehiwin,* Winning Man, Four Sky Thunder — each had his own followers, who knew that a camp of more than two hundred lodges could not remain as a single unit without food in a swamp while being pursued by an enemy that seemed intent on exterminating them. One old woman, Sitting in the Doorway, could not bear the thought of struggling through the muskeg and starving as she tried to keep up with the others; she hanged herself from the limb of a tree.

The first major separation in the camp took place six days after the battle, as they were travelling on the north side of Loon Lake. The Plains Cree were taking the lead, bound for Big Island Lake, when the Woods Cree veered off to the west and headed for Beaver River. Their departure was not noticed until the Plains Cree camped that evening, at which time Wandering Spirit and Dressy Man set out to find them. Instead of trying to entice them back, however, the two men joined them. Wandering Spirit knew they were going to surrender, and he wanted to be with them, for reasons he did not express. He may have felt it would be safer to give himself up with the Woods Cree, or he may have believed that his surrender would appease the angry soldiers. Dressy Man probably came closest to the truth when he opposed turning the last of the prisoners free. "I am afraid to let you go," he told them, "as the soldiers if they came up to us would be sure to shoot us, and if you went away we would have no one to stop the soldiers from killing us."[12]

After the departure of Wandering Spirit, the rest of the Plains Cree decided to head for Batoche. They chose to not believe the rumours of Riel's defeat and hoped to find shelter among the half-breeds. Travelling through wild, unsettled country, they maintained a slow pace so that those without horses could keep up. From time to time, families quietly slipped away, planning to surrender before they starved.

Those who remained had become the last holdouts in the rebellion. Riel and Poundmaker were behind bars, and Wandering Spirit and the woodland people had surrendered at Fort Pitt. There were almost 750 prisoners in the camp, most of them starving and destitute. With the rebellion virtually over, a major four-pronged offensive was now launched to capture the last of the Plains Cree warriors. General Strange went to Cold Lake, in case they were fleeing towards Edmonton; General Middleton tried to pick up their trail at Loon Lake; Colonel Irvine went from Prince Albert north to Green Lake, and Colonel Otter took his force from Battleford to Turtle Lake.

By 25 June the supplies of the Cree rebels were exhausted, so a council was held of those who remained. *Imasees,* now the leader, made it clear he had no intention of surrendering and planned to travel to the United States; Little Poplar, Lucky Man, Four Sky Thunder and Miserable Man agreed to go with him.[13] On the other hand, Big Bear was determined to make for Carlton.

So it was good-by. All of Big Bear's family, except for his wife and youngest son, were leaving him — *Imasees,* King Bird and the others.

Imasees' following of 137 people swung south past Birch Lake and headed for the Thickwood Hills, which took them safely down to the Elbow of the North Saskatchewan at the edge of the plains. At this point Miserable Man and Four Sky Thunder decided they would not go to Montana after all; with about thirty men, women and children, they travelled upstream to Battleford, where they surrendered. But *Imasees* and his band continued south, avoiding patrols and foraging for food along the way. Three weeks later, they reached the South Saskatchewan

River, a short distance downstream from The Forks. By this time they were starving, but they found an ox that may have wandered away from a settler's place and slaughtered it before crossing the river.

While they were camped on the north side, Bull Boy, Lucky Man and some other warriors went out on a scouting expedition and saw a man named George McIvor frying fish on a small island in the river. Beside him was a rowboat, which he evidently was using to cruise down the stream. Thinking to get food and a means of crossing the river, Bull Boy opened fire on the man, wounding him, but not so badly that McIvor could not push his boat into the current and escape downstream. He floated into Saskatchewan Landing two days later, where he died of his wounds. By then, *Imasees,* Little Poplar and the others had crossed the river and had no trouble reaching the safety of Montana.

Meanwhile, scattered families still in the woods began surrendering to anyone who would take them. Forty people walked into Colonel Otter's bivouac near Turtle Lake, seventeen gave themselves up to Colonel Irvine on his way back from Green Lake and five turned themselves over to a group of surveyor scouts. Another fifty starving Indians went directly to the Duck Lake Indian agency, where they surrendered and were issued rations.

By this time, Big Bear was virtually alone. His wife had gone with the other women and children to Duck Lake, leaving her husband with their twelve-year-old son, Horse Child, and his councillor, Two & Two. Hungry, exhausted and on foot, they reached Turtle Lake and almost stumbled into Colonel Otter's camp but managed to pass through his lines without being seen. They then went eastward into the Thickwood Hills, where they again had to go into hiding to avoid a scouting patrol from Colonel Irvine's column. There was no doubt now that the soldiers had conquered the Indians and half-breeds. Big Bear, fearful for his life, decided the safest course of action would be to go to a Hudson's Bay Company post to surrender. He had always trusted the traders and believed they would protect him.

When the trio reached the North Saskatchewan River, they began going downstream towards Carlton, and at nightfall made a raft and floated to a small island where they thought they would be safe. However, no sooner were they camped than they heard the whistle of a steamboat, the *Alberta,* coming downstream from Battleford. To Big Bear's horror, the boat passed too close to his little island and became stuck on a sandbar. For a while he had visions of men swarming over the place, looking for logs to work the boat loose, but then breathed a sigh of relief when it worked itself free and continued its journey.

On 4 July, when they were about five miles (8 km) from Carlton, Big Bear and his companions came to a ferry crossing, where he went to a tent to beg for food. He was surprised to find it occupied by a Hudson's Bay Company trader, who had been living there since Carlton House had been burned to the ground. Instead of waiting to hear what the fugitive had to say, the trader dashed away to get help. "About three o'clock in the morning," reported the *Saskatchewan Herald,* "Mr. Garson shouted across that there were some Indians over on his side of the river. Cons. Warren Kerr of Battleford, A. Sullivan of Carlton detachment, and Nichols, of B Troop, went across to see, and found an Indian and a boy, whom they arrested. Continuing the search, Cons. Kerr found another Indian crouched in hiding behind a tent, and having seen Big Bear at Poundmaker's last summer, immediately recognized him as the much-wanted Indian and arrested him."[14]

On Trial

A T THE BEGINING of April 1885, the first shots fired at Frog Lake had
ended Big Bear's political career. Since that time, the old chief
had been ignored, insulted, humiliated and even robbed by his own
people. He had been a man without power, a chief without a following, whose sole objective had been to prevent the troubles from
becoming worse than they already were. He had saved the occupants
of Fort Pitt, protected the prisoners taken by Wandering Spirit and
helped to prevent a union with Poundmaker. But now, with his capture, he was Big Bear again, the notorious and feared chief whose
name was on everybody's lips. He was the savage creature who had
slaughtered innocent people, cut out policemen's hearts and led the
army into a morass of muskeg and wilderness. He was a rebel who
should be tried with the other arch-criminals like Louis Riel and
Poundmaker. He was described by a journalist as "a sixty-year-old
coward, a black Indian with an enormous head, his face being as long
as a flour barrel and about as expressive. His glances were furtive, his
mien humble to servility."[1]

Big Bear was resigned to the fate that the spirits had planned for him.

After a preliminary examination in Prince Albert, Big Bear, Horse
Child and Two & Two were transferred to Regina, where the boy shared
a cell with his father until he could find his mother. There were no
charges outstanding against Two & Two, so he was later sent to join
friends at Fort Pitt. At Regina, Big Bear was fitted out with handcuffs,
chains and guardroom clothes, then taken over to see his friend Poundmaker. The two prisoners sat quietly, Big Bear puffing on an old pipe
and interrupting his conversation from time to time to receive a hug
from Horse Child.

As Big Bear rested and was fed, he regained some of his old spirit
during those first few days in jail. He had lost his medicine pipe and his
bear medicine, but he still had his powers; they had not deserted him.

Alphonse Little Poplar, a respected historian on the Sweetgrass Reserve, told of one adventure Big Bear had in jail when he used his powers:

These people who had lived outside all their lives found it hard to stay indoors all day long, day after day, although they were taken outside for a few minutes' exercise once in a while. One day when there was no one around, Big Bear told his son to go to sleep. Then Big Bear went outside and walked around for a while, then he sat down on the grass to enjoy the sunshine.

After sitting there for some time, Big Bear saw a man running, shouting at the top of his voice. Soon the place was full of soldiers and policemen. Big Bear spoke no English. An interpreter was brought in.

"The soldiers say you are to go back to your cell," the interpreter said to Big Bear. The soldiers searched Big Bear on the spot and finding nothing, allowed him to return to his cell. Many soldiers followed Big Bear as he walked back to his cell. All of them carried guns. When they entered the building, for a moment no one saw Big Bear. The next they saw of him, he was standing inside his cell.

He asked the interpreter to come over. "Tell the policeman and the soldiers," he said to the interpreter, "I am very sorry that I frightened them and I will not do it again. You may also remind them that when the Great Spirit gave us sunshine and fresh air, he intended that it was for all to enjoy."

After this, Big Bear and his son were given more freedom.[2]

In the weeks spent waiting in Regina for his trial, Big Bear learned that Indians from his old camp had surrendered and that some were being charged with crimes ranging from murder to possession of stolen property. Wandering Spirit was camped at Fort Pitt with the others when the soldiers came around with wagons to collect all the Indians' firearms. After that, an announcer called out the names of the men who were wanted for their crimes. When the war chief's name was called, the women in his camp started to wail, "They're going to take him!"[3] Wandering Spirit knew it, too, so he took a woman's knife and tried to kill himself, but the doctors bound his wound and sent him to Battleford with the other prisoners.

The trials, mostly conducted without jury by Judge Charles Rouleau, were held in September and October of 1885 and resulted in death sentences for nine Indians: Wandering Spirit, Round the Sky, Bad Arrow, Miserable Man, Iron Body and Little Bear — all for their roles in the Frog Lake affair; Louison Mongrain for the killing of Constable Cowan at Fort Pitt, and Dressy Man and Charles Ducharme for killing a cannibal woman during their march. The latter three terms later were commuted to life imprisonment, and in 1887 Dressy Man was charged with Cowan's murder but was acquitted.

Most of the other penalties were also harsh: Little Wolf, ten years for burning a stable at Frog Lake; Four Sky Thunder, fourteen years for burning the church; Toussaint Calling Bull, ten years for burning a house at Frog Lake; God's Otter, charged by the Reverend Charles Quinney with horse stealing, four years; Old Man, charged by Quinney with horse stealing, six years; The Idol, possession of a stolen horse, six years; Little Runner, charged by Dufresne with possession of a stolen horse, four years; Erect Man, possession of a stolen horse, two years, and Mountain Man, possession of a cow and calf, six months. A few of the accused, like Half Blackfoot Chief, Yellow Plume and Sitting Horse, were found not guilty of cattle or horse theft, while others, like Thunder and Jean Baptiste, were investigated but never charged.

Some wanted men, of course, could not be arrested. Man Who Speaks Our Language had died at Frenchman's Butte; Bare Neck, One of the Little People, *Imasees,* Lucky Man and Little Poplar all were across the border. Lone Man had gone to the Peace Hills and managed to stay in hiding until a year later, when he was caught selling horses in Edmonton. By that time the hysteria of the rebellion had passed, and he received five years for wounding Constable Loasby.

Most of the chiefs who had accompanied Wandering Spirit on his travels were not charged but were thrown out of office. Even old *Kehiwin* was not exempted. Described as "a short, ugly chief, blind in both eyes, and considerably deaf in both ears," he was bitter when his medal was taken from him and "had the gall and impudence to say that it was hunger and starvation only which drove him to the white chief's camp and compelled him to lay down his rifle."[4]

As for Louis Riel, he had been tried for treason late in July and been sentenced to death; Cree chief Poundmaker had been tried on the lesser charge of treason-felony. In spite of evidence that he had not been in control of his camp and had saved the soldiers at Cutknife Hill, he still had been sentenced to three years in penitentiary. Only the intercession of Crowfoot had prevented him from having his hair cut short, as had been done with the other prisoners.

Big Bear's trial started on 11 September before Judge Hugh Richardson. F. B. Robertson, who had defended Poundmaker, acted in his defence, and chose a jury trial, impanelling six townspeople from Regina. D. L. Scott handled the prosecution for the crown.

Four charges were levelled against Big Bear, all under the general charge of treason-felony, which was a noncapital offence. Specifically, the old man was charged with the intention "to levy war against our said Lady the Queen" and to "conspire, consult, confederate, assemble and meet together, with divers other evil disposed persons . . . to raise, make and levy insurrection and rebellion" on 2 April, the day of the Frog Lake affair. He also was charged with the same offence on 17 April, the capture of Fort Pitt; on 21 April, in sending a message to Alexander Hamelin, and on 28 May, the Battle of Frenchman's Butte. The charge ended with the statement that the offences were "against the peace of our Lady the Queen, her Crown and dignity."[5]

The long statement was read in English and translated by Peter Hourie, who could find no Cree equivalent for many of the legal phrases. As a result, some words such as "crown" were translated literally. When he had finished, Big Bear was understandably confused. "These people all lie," he said, "they are saying that I tried to steal the Great Mother's Hat, how could I do that? She lives very far across the Great Water, and how could I go there to steal her hat? I don't want her hat and did not know she had one."[6]

The judge then rephrased the charge in simpler terms, telling the chief that he was accused of failing to show his allegiance to the Queen and, with other evilly disposed persons, of compassing to levy war against her. To these charges, Big Bear pleaded not guilty.

Seven main witnesses testified during the one-day trial. Of these, six spoke in Big Bear's favour: John Pritchard, James Simpson, Catharine Simpson, William McLean, Henry Halpin and William Cameron. Only HBC clerk Stanley Simpson, who had been taken prisoner at Fort Pitt, testified against him.

Pritchard admitted that Big Bear had invited *Pakan* to join the Frog Lake Crees and had warned him to leave the country when he refused to come. He also admitted the chief was present when the letter was sent to Hamelin over his signature but emphasized that Abraham Montour had drafted it at Wandering Spirit's urging, and Big Bear had simply agreed with its contents. He said that Big Bear had no authority in the camp, and that *Imasees* and Wandering Spirit were the leaders. Defence lawyer Robertson questioned him.

Q. "Is Big Bear's son a good son to his father?"

A. "No, I don't think so, because when the father said anything the son bucks against it."

Q. "The direct contrary?"

A. "Yes."

Q. "Did he do that through the whole of this trouble?"

A. "Yes."[7]

James Simpson said he had known Big Bear for nearly forty years and believed he had always been a good friend to the white man. When the chief got older, his son had taken away his leadership and constantly acted contrary to his father's wishes. Simpson's wife, Catharine, confirmed that Big Bear had come to warn her about impending trouble on 2 April and had tried to stop the shooting. William McLean testified that the chief had not participated in the looting of Fort Pitt and that *Imasees* treated his father "with utter contempt."[8] He also stated that even after the ordeal at Fort Pitt, Loon Lake and in the wilderness, he considered Big Bear to be a good man.

Henry Halpin said that Big Bear had been surprised to hear about the troubles at Batoche and that the chief had not rushed back to Frog Lake. At the Battle of Frenchman's Butte, he said that the chief had not taken part in the fighting but had helped people to get away as quickly as they could. He was questioned by Robertson, the defence lawyer.

Q. "How did these leading chiefs in his band treat Big Bear while during the time you were a prisoner there?"

A. "They treated him with contempt altogether."

Q. "Had he any control over them?"

A. "I don't think he had."[9]

William Cameron told how Big Bear had tried to stop the killings at Frog Lake and had sent the Indians out of the Hudson's Bay store when they were going to pillage it.

Q. "When you opened the store, they all crowded in?"

A. "Yes."

Q. "Did they commence taking things before Big Bear came in?"

A. "Yes, a few of them did reach over the counter and help themselves."

Q. "And took things without asking for them?"

A. "Yes."

Q. "And the prisoner [Big Bear] came in and ordered them not to take anything without asking for it?"

A. "Yes."[10]

Stanley Simpson, who had been taken prisoner at Fort Pitt, complained that he had been badly treated by Lone Man, his captor. "I was made to work, to cut roads and dig rifle pits, make breastworks, and different work, and work they chose to put me to."[11] He said he had suffered a great deal during his two months of captivity and considered himself to have been a slave. He had become ill because of the exposure and had not fully recovered by the time of the trial. His testimony centred around two major points: that Big Bear had encouraged the Battle of Frenchman's Butte and that the chief was pleased with the results.

On the first point, Simpson swore that during the Thirst Dance at Frenchman's Butte, Big Bear "cut up a piece of tobacco, and he said he wanted his men to cut the head of the white people off the same as he cut this piece of tobacco. He wanted the head. I suppose it is the officer who was commanding the police at that time."[12]

In cross-examination, the defence attorney focussed on Simpson's ability to speak and understand Cree.

Q. "Just tell us in Cree what it was that Big Bear said on that occasion in the camp, at the battle of Frenchman's Butte?"

A. "I can't say it."

Q. "You can't say? Can you say any part of it in Cree?"

A. "Yes, I can say a word here and there through it, but I can't make any sense of it. I can't pronounce the words properly."

Q. "And that was about all you could hear, all you could make out of the sentence?"

A. "I can understand a good deal more than what I can say."

Q. "But you cannot understand perfectly?"

A. "No; I said so."

Q. "And after all it was to some extent a guess of yours, that that was the meaning of what he said?"

A. "No; I could understand that he said this."

Q. "Are you prepared to stick to that, although you cannot tell us, you cannot repeat even the sense of it in Cree?

A. "No, I can't repeat it in Cree."[13]

Simpson's second point had to do with Big Bear's actions behind the lines during the battle itself. Although Simpson contradicted himself as to whether Big Bear was already in the camp or arrived later, he insisted that the chief received news of the battle and came over to tell them. "He said, they have killed twenty soldiers already, my men — he did not say his men, but we have killed twenty soldiers already, and then he made use of an expression which meant very good. (Mr. Hourie, court interpreter, says it means well done.)"[14]

Robertson then called Henry Halpin to the stand and had him admit he knew Stanley Simpson.

Q. "Have you had any conversation on the subject of Big Bear's trial with him?"

A. "Yes, I had a little."

Q. "What did he say to you?"

A. "He seemed — "

Q. "What did he say?"

A. "I told him that I had been called on the defence, and he thought it was strange, very strange, any white man should get on the defence of an Indian. His idea was that Indians should have been hung."[15]

During the trial, much of the testimony was interpreted into Cree, but Big Bear still found the whole proceeding to be confusing. "I had much sympathy for him," commented an onlooker, "as he could not understand English and constantly gazed at the Judge, Jury and Prosecuting Attorney, who was a very large man and very aggressive. Big Bear was

closely guarded by a Mounted Policeman and it was quite noticeable he
regarded the Policeman as his friend and constantly looked to him for
information as to what it was all about, and much to his credit, the
Policeman appeared to be very kind and considerate of the prisoner."[16]

Stanley Simpson was the only witness to appear for the prosecution,
and the press was frankly surprised that most of the evidence appeared to
favour the chief. Predictions were made that Big Bear would be found
not guilty, as the prosecution had not been able to make a case.

Louis Goulet, who had been arrested after his escape and was examined regarding his role in the Battle of Frenchman's Butte, later
claimed that attempts were made to have him commit perjury on the
question of Big Bear's loyalty. He was in Regina awaiting his own trial,
when D. L. Scott, the prosecutor, asked him privately if he would admit
that André Nault, Abraham Montour and Big Bear had had a meeting
the night before the killings. "I answered," said Goulet, "that I didn't
think they were there, and Scott replied, 'You know they were there. If
you'll swear they were there, we'll drop the charges against you and
you'll go free.' " Goulet rejected the offer, saying that Montour had been
in Cold Lake when the trouble started and that Nault had been with him
that night. "I don't give a damn about any of you from the Queen on
down," he said hotly.[17]

During Big Bear's appearance in court, a journalist tried to analyze the
chief, describing him as a man "of medium stature, dark, stern, rather
repulsive features, with fairly small nose, inclined to turn up denoting a
spirit of mischief, wit, and forwardness. His swelling lips denote great
decision of character and philosophical turn of mind, while his impressive
eyes, not infrequently flashing forth a clear, pleasant light, denote a
measure of honesty and sound understanding. His thick, strong nostrils
denote daring and strength of purpose, while a lean wrinkled face indicates the wisdom of declining years with the philosophy of the coward."[18]

When all the evidence had been presented, the two counsels addressed
the jury. Robertson spoke first for the defence. He said he sought justice
for "this poor old man, tottering now almost on the brink of the grave,"
and went through the evidence point by point to show that the prosecution had no case. "What else has my learned friend, Mr. Scott, to rest
upon here in making a case against Big Bear," he said, "except that he
was with his band? The Crown has not only failed to show affirmatively
that the prisoner actually committed one of the overt acts charged in this
indictment, I think it has been conclusively proved to you as to each one
of those charges that the prisoner did not commit them, those overt
acts."[19]

Robertson then described the events of 2 April and asked, "Was that
the act of a man that was ringleader in the rebellion? . . . a shot was fired,

which they heard. What does he do then? He rushes out of door, running up the street, screaming: Stop, stop! Was that the act of a man that was going into rebellion? . . . that old man was no more than a feather in the blast before their influence. He was powerless, utterly powerless. The massacre took place in spite of him. It is all done almost in the flash of an eye, but he tried to stop it."[20]

Robertson went on to say that at Fort Pitt, Big Bear had gone with the others to "try to save the lives of the people that are in the fort. He was powerless, and he knew it, he was powerless to prevent those Indians from going out to pillage that fort but he might help perhaps, not by his influence with the Indians but by friendly dealing with the whites. . . . Is that the conduct of the man that wants to fight the police and kill the police?" On the question of pillaging Fort Pitt, the defence lawyer emphasized that the chief had not taken part in the action, though someone did give Big Bear some tea that had been taken from the fort. "But I don't think my learned friend will seriously contend or ask you to say that he was guilty of a desire to levy war against the Queen because he accepted a cup of tea that another man had stolen," he commented.[21]

Similarly, at Frenchman's Butte, no one had seen the chief on the battlefield, the defence pointed out, and the only testimony against him came from Stanley Simpson. "The suffering that Mr. Stanley Simpson has endured," Robertson said, "has prejudiced him so much against these Indians that he is prepared to go as far as he can to convict any Indian, and particularly the poor old Big Bear, because he is looked upon as sort of chief of the band. . . . He pretends to tell us Big Bear made a bloodthirsty speech, it was not a short speech, gentlemen, it was not a speech that would be said so slowly, it was a speech that was said in the excitement and quickly, and Mr. Stanley Simpson asks you to believe after what he has shown us of what he knows of Cree in that box — he asks you to believe that he is able to swear that that old man used that language."[22] He concluded by drawing attention to the discriminatory remarks Simpson had made to Halpin about serving as a defence witness and suggested that the jury ignore his entire testimony.

Scott, for the prosecution, covered the same territory but drew opposite conclusions. He claimed that *Imasees* "was one of the worst in the crowd from that time till the end of the rebellion. If Imesis [*sic*] on the 1st April had any intention of committing those depredations, Big Bear, the prisoner, would have known it, and it would have been his duty at that time if he had been loyal, a loyal citizen, as my learned friend tries to make him out to be, he would have given warning the night before to these men, in order that they might be prepared for some defence."[23]

The prosecutor then pursued Cameron's testimony about Big Bear having evicted the Indians from the store on the morning of the killings.

"Now, the contention throughout of the defence in this case," he said, "is that the prisoner was wholly without influence in his own camp, and that his influence was for good throughout, and to show you that that influence was not such as my learned friend represents it, but that he had a great deal of influence in his own camp at that time." Scott pointed out that when Big Bear's band had been looting Cameron's store, "the prisoner came in and ordered them not to take goods, but if they wanted anything, if they saw anything they wanted, or wanted anything they saw — I forget which — ask for it. . . . It turned out during the time the prisoner was there they did not take anything, but they asked for it, and as soon as his back was turned, they commenced taking the goods again. Does that show that he was totally without influence in his own band?"[24]

Scott was willing to concede that Big Bear had used his influence to save the lives of prisoners, but again, it was evidence that he did have authority. The fact that most of the prisoners were associated with the Hudson's Bay Company made this task easier because of the reputation it had among the Indians. Yet, he went on, "there is no evidence given for the defence or throughout the whole case here to show that he resisted the efforts or the conduct of the Indians with whom he was associated in levying war or in pillaging Fort Pitt."[25]

On the question of the letter to Alexander Hamelin, the prosecutor reminded the jury that Big Bear had contacted *Pakan* of his own volition and told him "to come at once to join his band, and if he didn't, better get a fast horse and leave the country."[26]

The argument that Big Bear had not joined in the fighting at French-man's Butte was rejected by Scott, who said that everyone knew the young men did the fighting while the old men counselled them. And, in conclusion, he said that "it was the intention of the prisoner and his band to work their way down from that place to Duck Lake," showing that Big Bear wanted to join forces with Riel. Rather than the chief being powerless and opposed to the actions of Wandering Spirit and *Imasees,* Scott submitted, "the evidence shows conclusively that he was acting with them throughout."[27]

Judge Richardson then delivered his charge to the jury, stating that the accused should be considered guilty if he had willingly remained in the rebel camp; only if he feared for his own life by trying to leave could he be considered free of guilt. Robertson protested that this interpretation left no room to consider that Big Bear had not willingly participated in any illegal actions.

Reluctantly, Judge Richardson brought the jury back and, somewhat incoherently, restated the defence attorney's remarks, adding, "you should consider whether he was there compulsorily — I think I have got that right now to suit Mr. Robertson — or whether he was there against

his will, and acting solely in the interests of peace." When the defence
still persisted, the judge said, "And if he was there against his will
and giving no assistance whatever, then he would be entitled to an
acquittal."[28]

However, the judge could not resist giving the last interpretation. "I
cannot, however, drop my remarks without declaring to them the law
on that subject, and it is this: If a number of men band themselves
together for an unlawful purpose, and in pursuit of their object commit
murder, it is right that the court should pointedly refuse to accept the
proposition that a full share of responsibility for their acts does not
extend to the surgeon who accompanied them to dress their wounds, to
the clergyman who attends to offer spiritual consolation, or to the
reporter who volunteers to record their achievements; the presence of
anyone in any character aiding and abetting or encouraging the prosecution of those unlawful designs must involve a share of the common
guilt."[29]

The jury took only fifteen minutes to decide on a verdict of guilty,
with a recommendation for mercy.

Two weeks later, on 25 September, Big Bear appeared for sentencing,
and a Winnipeg newspaperman reported the proceedings:

"Big Bear," said Judge Richardson, "what have you to say why sentence
should not be passed upon you."

"I believe," replied the prisoner, "I should have something to say about
the occurrences which brought me here in chains." Then with an earnest-
ness, eloquence, and pathos, not without its appreciative weight on a curious audience, he went on excusing and exculpating himself from the seri-
ousness of his crime. He knew little or nothing of the Frog Lake massacre
beyond hearing shots fired. When any wrong was brooding he always did
his utmost to nip it in the bud. The more bloodthirsty spirits of his band
had gone beyond control and they shed the blood of those he would shelter.
and protect.

He was off his reserve during winter hunting and fishing, and the rebellion had started before he got back. When the white population was weak
and sparse, Big Bear extended the right of protection and good fellowship,
and he was sorry there was no one in court to relate his innumerable deeds
of humanity.

No one could come forward and say that he ordered the killing of a priest
or agent. People thought he had fostered the rebellion, but it was quite the
contrary. He felt sorry for what had taken place, but the truth was when
the result of the Duck Lake fight was known, his people ignored their
chief's authority and despised him. He never stole a white man's horse, and
his reason for befriending and cultivating the friendship of the whites was

that he himself would be assisted by the more civilized and wealthy palefaces. His motto had always been, Do all the good you can, and it will
return you "muzzhi" and blankets a hundredfold.

He looked around the court and saw it crowded with handsome faces —
far handsomer than his own. (Laughter.) He had ruled his country a long
time. Now he was chained and would be sent to prison; but he had no doubt
the fine countenances he admired in court would be competent to govern the
North-West. (Laughter.) At present he was as dead to his people. Many of his
band were hiding in the woods paralyzed with terror. Could not that court
send them an amnesty? Perhaps his own children were hungry and outcast
too, and afraid to appear in broad daylight. If the government did not come
forward with assistance before the winter set in, his band would inevitably
perish, but he had too much confidence in the Great Grandmother to fear the
worst should be allowed to overtake his tribe.

The time would come when the Indians of the North-West would prove
of signal service to the Great Grandmother, and he appealed again to the
court for pity and help to the remainder of his tribe. In conclusion, he
would say that whenever he spoke stiff to the Indian agents, he did so in
order to get his rights. The North-West belonged to him, but he, perhaps,
would never live to see it again. He asked the court to publish his speech
broadcast. He was old and ugly, but he had tried to be good. In conclusion
he made a powerful appeal for the children and helpless of his tribe.[30]

Judge Richardson told Big Bear that he had been given a fair trial by
an honest and patient jury and been given more favours than a white
man would have received. He said he had the power to shut him away
from daylight forever but would be lenient and sentence him to three
years in Stony Mountain Penitentiary.

As Big Bear shuffled from the courtroom, dragging his chains, a
group of Indians and half-breeds, also in irons, waited for their turn at
the dock. By the time the day was over, nineteen more prisoners had
been sentenced and were ready for shipment to Manitoba.

Big Bear's speech was never widely circulated; in fact many newspapers did not even report his sentence. So no one in Battleford or at Fort
Pitt heard of his appeal on behalf of the hungry and ragged refugees who
were huddled in tents, waiting for winter. He had fought the government with words and lost; his followers had fought them with bullets
and lost; now there was no one to protect them, no one to speak for
them. They were at the mercy of the government, just as Big Bear was
now at the mercy of his jailers.

The Final Years

Gracious Mother, hear our cry!
Save your red, unhappy children,
By bad laws condemned to die![1]

A HUGE GALLOWS, capable of hanging eight people simultaneously, was built in the barracks square at Battleford, and Robert Hodson, one of the captives from Fort Pitt, volunteered to be the executioner. On 27 November 1885, just eleven days after Riel had been hanged in Regina, the six convicted Crees from Frog Lake — Wandering Spirit, Round the Sky, Bad Arrow, Miserable Man, Iron Body and Little Bear — together with two Assiniboines, *Ikteh* and Man Without Blood — were led from their cells. They marched in single file, flanked by police, and mounted the scaffold; while Hodson adjusted the ropes and head coverings, they sang their death songs. At 8:28 A. M. the platform dropped, and the eight rebels were dead. Later in the day they were buried in a single grave below the barracks.

This was the last major act in the aftermath of the Riel Rebellion. The soldiers had gone home; the Indians were back on their reserves under surveillance; some of the convicted rebels were dead, and others were in prison. There were still some loose ends, of course. A few wanted men were still at large, claims were being made for rebellion losses, and the Conservatives were beginning to realize they had handled Riel and the North-West situation so badly that it would haunt them for years to come. Quebec had been alienated by Riel's execution, and the Liberals were demanding to know why a few more dollars and a little more honesty had not been invested in the West earlier, rather than a fortune spent and lives lost to put down a rebellion.

Many years later, Joe Dion, a grandnephew of Big Bear, summed up the effect of that tragic year on the Crees. "The rebellion of 1885 ended up absolutely nothing gained by anybody," he said, "only a deep rooted

feeling of distrust on both sides was the unfortunate result of the clash.
Throughout the years this feeling of distrust has diminished but very
little and may never be completely lived down. True, we were at fault.
We broke our treaty with the whites, but only after we learned that
honesty with them was as thin as the paper on which our X had been
drawn for us."[2]

The day before Big Bear was admitted to Stony Mountain Penitentiary, he and the other convicts disembarked from the train at Winnipeg,
where hundreds of people crowded the depot to get a glimpse of the
desperadoes. The Indians came out of a coach chained together and
shuffled over to waiting wagons. "A more lawless looking set can
hardly be imagined," commented a reporter. "They were clothed in all
the habiliments of the Indian, the ever-prominent blanket being drawn
closely about the body, leaving the head bare. Big Bear is not a very
prepossessing fellow, but on the other hand is a miserable looking
Indian."[3] After spending the night in the local jail, they were taken on
the half-day journey northward to the bleak penitentiary, which stood
on the slope of a small promontory on the vast plains of Manitoba.

The jail had been built to hold a hundred men, but since almost fifty
Indians and half-breeds had received penitentiary terms because of the
rebellion, a new wing was being constructed. When Big Bear was
admitted, he became Inmate No. 103 and was issued a prison uniform,
as well as the basic furnishings for his cell: a mattress, blanket, coverlet,
a small brown-coloured table, brown stool, washbowl, saltshaker, ink-
stand and a Bible.

Big Bear was put to work in the carpentry shop, Poundmaker became
a gardener and One Arrow, from Carlton, worked in the shoemaker's
shop. They were able to visit each other during their free periods and
sometimes went to see the warden's private zoo. It offered irrefutable
evidence to the Indians that the white man had conquered the West, for
among the warden's four-legged prisoners were a herd of tame buffalo
and two bears. If the white man could make the buffalo as docile as milk
cows, what hope was there for the Indians?

Big Bear liked to be with the animals, and after several months was
transferred to the barns. There, his main task was to look after the pigs,
a dirty job he did not enjoy, but which was better than being cooped up
inside. Also, it gave him a chance to see the bears more often. He was
their namesake; they were the ones who had given him his supernatural
powers when he was still a boy. "I got chummy with these bears," he
told a friend. "They were captives like me."[4]

But those were merely brief respites from the deadly, hateful life in
prison. Big Bear was a lonely, broken man: he had failed in his mission
to save his people and had been rejected by his family, his band and by

society itself. He did not look upon himself as being guilty and believed he had been betrayed by the white man when he was sent to jail after it was proven he had done his best to stop the uprising and save lives. He saw no future for the Indians, for they were a beaten race, outnumbered and driven to the sanctuary of their reserves. Now they had no voice, no power and no reason for hope.

After the hysteria of the rebellion died away, some of the harsh sentences meted out during the trials were reviewed. Popular opinion in Ontario was in sympathy with Poundmaker, whose classical features and humble pride captivated the imagination of the press and public. When visitors came to Stony Mountain, he was the person they wanted to see; the homely and aged Big Bear was ignored. James Trow, a member of parliament from Ontario, expressed sympathy only for Poundmaker, as did a group of French journalists who had their picture taken with him. Petitions were sent to Ottawa, and in the spring of 1886, after serving just six months of his three-year sentence, Poundmaker was released.

In fact, between February and July of that year, following Prime Minister Macdonald's general amnesty, thirty-one of the forty-five rebels were pardoned, some of whom had received sentences of up to ten years. Little Runner, The Idol, Little Wolf and others were quietly released. Among the freed men was One Arrow, but he was so ill that he got only as far as St. Boniface, where he died. The rest, who continued their journey to the Eagle Hills, were "all sick and weak, one of them especially having had to be lifted in and out of the waggon in which he travelled."[5]

During the summer of 1886, Big Bear's health began to decline, and he begged to be set free.[6] "Big Bear is pleading for liberty," commented the *Saskatchewan Herald* sarcastically. "He wants to live at liberty and in peace. He begs to be released because he was deceived. . . . It was always his plea to 'wait' when he was wanted to move. He is now in a good place to be made to put his precept into practice."[7] The question of a parole was raised in Macdonald's cabinet in October, but there was enough opposition for the idea to be shelved.

On 9 January 1887, Big Bear began to have fainting spells and was admitted to the prison hospital. The doctor expressed great concern and said, "although not asked to report upon the condition of Convict No. 103, I desire to say that he is very sick and rapidly getting worse. He is weak and shows signs of great dibility [sic] by fainting spells which are growing more frequent. Undoubtedly, his further confinement here will aggravate this condition and possibly lead to a fatal termination. I would therefore urge most strongly that he be released as soon as possible."[8]

Spurred by the possible political embarrassment of having Big Bear die in jail, authorities looked for a face-saving way of releasing him. This was accomplished by having Big Child and Star Blanket, the two loyal chiefs from Prince Albert who had just finished a tour of Ontario, sign a petition on his behalf. "Although we have no sympathy with the heinous crimes laid to his charge," stated the letter prepared for their signatures, "we humbly submit that it would be very gratifying to the Cree nation if her Majesty's Government would extend to this criminal the clemency shewn from time to time to the other prisoners, and grant his pardon for the unexpired term of his sentence."[9] On the basis of this letter and the medical report, the cabinet approved the release of Big Bear on 27 January. However, he was still bedridden at the time and was not fit to leave until a week later. He then travelled by train to Regina and waited there until a shipment of freight was being hauled north. He was placed on one of the wagons, and finally, more than a month after his release, he was unloaded at the Little Pine reserve.

He was a sick, tired and broken man. Thunder Child came to see him as soon as he arrived, but Big Bear just sat and looked at him, as though he were a stranger. Finally, the old man spoke. "Aaay, *nosesa*," he said feebly. "You must wonder why I don't speak. My heart is broken. All I can think of are my past deeds and the misfortunes which have happened to me more recently. I have had a hard time. My sons have gone to the States. I am alone."

"The jail was so different from the old times," he added. "I did the dirtiest work. One night I was put in a bad place, a dungeon; it was dark, and I felt something, a snake perhaps. I did not sleep at all that night. I hated it there, but I would not kill myself for I am not a coward. Now I will not last long. I am broken down."[10]

To make his humiliation complete, Big Bear learned that his wife had deserted him and was living with Heard Before He is Seen, an Ojibwa, on the Little Pine reserve. Big Bear tried to keep her at home during the ensuing weeks but without success, and pathetically, he would go out searching the reserve for her, begging her to come back.

His daughter Earth Woman made a place for him and nursed him for several months. He was alone most of the time, seldom having visitors and never attending dances or ceremonies. He was no longer a chief, for his medal had been taken away from him. He had no reserve, for it had not been surveyed. And his band had been broken up by a fearful government, so that it never would be a threat again. Some people were at Onion Lake, others at Frog Lake, some as far west as the Peace Hills and a few at Little Pine's and Poundmaker's. The rest were with *Imasees* in Montana, including most of his amily — King Bird, Earth Woman's family and the others. Big Bear knew he would never see them again.

He could remember the days when his children were small, learning to shoot with their blunt-ended arrows and riding their short-legged cayuses over the prairies. The land had belonged to the Indians then; the sky, the clouds, the hills, the rivers, all were part of the Great Spirit's domain, and it had been theirs for as long as anyone could remember. In winter they had camped in the forests, hunting and trapping, and in summer had roamed over the limitless plains.

Now, he looked along the valley of the Battle River, and all he saw were tiny log cabins, ragged people trying to cultivate the land on the tiny reserves that shielded them from the alien white world that had engulfed them. No longer did the Great Spirit direct their lives; now, it was the Great Mother. The Indians were mendicants in a land they once had ruled. Years ago they had greeted the traders and explorers as friends; now, there was only hatred and suspicion between the two races.

In December, a hunter rode through the reserves with the exciting news that buffalo had been sighted near Manitou Lake. Somehow, four of the lumbering beasts had avoided hunters in the barren hills and were out on the plains, as though nothing had changed. Maybe there was hope after all; if a few buffalo could survive the white man's onslaught, the Indians could too. Big Bear remembered something that *Imasees* had once told him, back in the days when they were still father and son. They had been talking about death and the kind of world that awaited them. "One thing makes me said," *Imasees* had said. "There will be no buffalo in the other world, for they have all been killed and their bones scattered to the four corners of the land."[11] But he had been wrong there, too. The buffalo were not all gone, nor would they be missing from the green grass world on the other side. Big Bear, unshaken in his faith in the Great Spirit, knew this to be true.

In mid-January 1888, as life began to fade from the eyes of Big Bear, a savage blizzard swept through the Saskatchewan country, winds tearing at the barren trees and snow swirling about in a blinding fury. The storm came suddenly, without warning, as though the sky spirits were angry at the world below. It pounced upon the tiny log cabins along the Battle River, dancing around the outlying stables and viciously mauling helpless horses huddled together for protection. Big Bear had been bedridden for weeks now, and he knew the end was near. Outside, the snow cascaded down from the skies and was carried along by the raging storm, which transformed the fluffy flakes into millions of tiny projectiles that were trying to strike down everything in their path. The snow blew in under doors, filtered between logs and dashed against stone chimneys.

Big Bear could only lie and listen to the furious onslaught of nature. He could accept this kind of attack, because he knew with proper shelter and clothing, a person could weather the storm. Not like the uneven battle he had fought against the white man. For that one, there had been no protection, no warm cabin or protective robe.

The storm devastated the country from Edmonton to Battleford and swept far out onto the plains past the Red Deer River. As the old chief grew weaker, the storm grew in intensity, attacking the land that once had been his and venting its wrath upon the places where he used to winter. The temperature plummeted to thirty below zero. Then, exhausted by its struggle, the storm eased, then died. And on 17 January 1888, in the calm after the storm, Big Bear passed away peacefully in his sleep. He was buried on a nearby hill on the Poundmaker Reserve, and shortly thereafter, Earth Woman left to join her family in Montana.

Epilogue

I*MASEES* WANTED TO BE CHIEF, but Big Bear would not step aside, so he had been forced to wrest the position from his father. By then, however, they were at war, and Wandering Spirit was in command. Not until he and Wandering Spirit separated near Loon Lake did *Imasees* at last become the ruler of his people. He led them out of the calamity he had helped to create and took them all the way to Montana. He had never forgotten that the Americans had once offered his father a reservation, so he went there to settle down.

But his actions, which had created a tragedy for his father's leadership, made his own chieftainship a continuing ordeal. Instead of being welcomed in Montana, *Imasees* and his followers were reviled and rejected, forced to wander from the garbage dumps of Helena to the unfriendly confines of the Blackfeet Reservation, any place where they could eke out a living. *Imasees* used his other name of Little Bear and constantly emphasized that his people were as much American as they were Canadian, but few people would listen. They were rounded up and sent back to Canada in 1896, but most of them were soon back in Montana. During that exodus, *Imasees* and Lucky Man were arrested by the Mounted Police for their part in the Frog Lake affair but were released for lack of evidence to convict them. *Imasees* then stayed in Canada for a couple of years but eventually felt obliged to return to Montana to lead his destitute band, who still were homeless wanderers. Finally, the concerns of such men as artist Charles M. Russell and naturalist Frank Bird Linderman were aroused, and with the help of the Great Falls press, *Imasees* and his followers finally were given the Rocky Boy Reservation in eastern Montana in 1916 after more than thirty years of wandering. *Imasees* was sixty-four when this happened — older than his father when he had deposed him. He died five years later.

Except for Horse Child, who changed his name to Joe Peemee, Big Bear did not see any of his sons again after the 1885 troubles. Even Twin

Wolverine failed to return; there was a rumour that he had died at Buffalo Lake. And after Big Bear's death, the family remained divided, with some of the girls living near Onion Lake, and the rest staying in Montana.

Big Bear's son-in-law Lone Man served his jail sentence, and disgusted by his own people's treatment of Big Bear, turned his back on the entire clan and on Indians generally. He changed his name to Sam Johnson and moved to the Crowsnest Pass, where he spent the rest of his life among the whites and half-breeds in that area. Two of his boys died in the Frank Slide of 1903, and a daughter married George Gladstone, an uncle of the author's wife.

Little Poplar was a wild warrior to the last; only two years after fleeing to Montana, he got into a drunken argument with a half-breed named Ward and was shot to death. Some say his skull was sent to a museum in Washington.

Big Bear's band in Canada was scattered and had no reserve of its own. Young Sweet Grass, who had left the Fort Pitt area in 1877 when his father Sweet Grass died, realized that many of Big Bear's followers had once belonged to his father's band, so he considered trying to unite the band. By this time he already was chief of Strike Him on the Back's band, and when their reserve was being surveyed near Battleford, he thought it would be a good place to combine the groups. However, Strike Him on the Back's followers were not enthusiastic about the idea and complained to the Indian agent, who then called to see the young chief.

"It was explained to him that the reserve now being surveyed was for the people of Strike Him on the Back," said historian Alphonse Little Poplar, "and not for his father's people. Young Sweet Grass, who was a very easygoing man, when told this, was disheartened. For a moment he said nothing, then looked at the agent and said, 'What about my father's people who are now stragglers? Are they to continue roaming the prairie like homeless dogs? I know they are destitute and in dire need of food and clothing. When my father signed the treaty, he was told that the heart of the Great White Mother was kind and would look after her red children, give them food and clothing when in need. The time is now. The longer the servants of the Queen wait, the longer the people will suffer.' "[1]

The Indian agent explained that the only way to reunite the band was for Young Sweet Grass to resign his current chieftainship and to get himself elected by his father's former followers. If this was done, they could have a reserve. Young Sweet Grass was pleased and enthusiastic; he marked an area six miles wide and twelve miles long (9.5 km by 19 km) adjacent to the west side of Strike Him on the Back's reserve and said this would be theirs. However, he already was in an advanced stage of tuberculosis and died before the plan could be fulfilled. So Big Bear's people remained scattered and never again became a cohesive unit: the destruction of the band was complete.

★ ★ ★

The question might be asked: In view of Big Bear's failure to achieve better conditions for his people, why has he emerged as a Canadian hero?

The fact is, Big Bear was right in almost everything he claimed and everything he tried to do. From 1876 until the rebellion, he was unyielding in his attempts to wrest from the government a better deal for his people. The fact that he failed did not reflect badly on his own greatness, but on the government's inflexibility and insensitivity to the needs of a people from a different culture.

Interestingly, the government had good intentions when it negotiated the treaties and regarded with some smugness the peacefulness of its settlements, compared with those of the American West. The land was needed so that the railroad could be built (huge land grants went to the railway corporation), but at the same time, there was pride in the knowledge that they were acting in the name of the Queen and British justice. The Royal Proclamation of 1763, which prohibited the Indians from being dispossessed without a settlement, was recognized and honoured. But the negotiators saw the land as simply real estate to be acquired and approached the treaties with the attitude that they were dealing with chiefs who were fully conversant with the white man's laws, business practices and values. They could not, or would not, understand that the Indian had few of these concepts. Therefore, the government offered the most minimal of terms and was pleased when the majority of Indians accepted without a murmur. The government did not realize that most Indians did not have any idea what the commissioners were talking about, that they signed simply because they thought they were getting food and presents.

Big Bear was different. At first, he saw the treaty as a trap, as a means of making the Indian give up his freedom. Later, when reservation life became inevitable, he wanted government help for as long as it would take for his people to become self-sufficient.

If the government had been more open-minded about the treaties, it might have altered some of the terms that were niggardly or misunderstood. The fact that it did so with Treaty One and Treaty Two was well known to the Indians, so with the precedent, even minimal changes would have been an act of faith.

Better implementation of the terms of the treaty was a more complex matter. Prime Minister Sir John A. Macdonald, for example, read the terms very carefully and concluded the government was doing more than it had promised to do. The problem was that no matter how many times the document was interpreted to them at treaty, the Indians left with the belief that it promised more than it really contained. It was an example of cultural noncommunication, but the government simply thought the Indians were being unreasonable.

The bottom line of the whole dispute was hunger. With the destruction of the buffalo in Canada by 1879, the Indians were thrown into a state of abject poverty. Rations fluctuated wildly from a pound of flour and a pound of meat per day, all the way down to one and a half pounds of flour and half a pound of bacon twice a week. The Indians believed they were being deliberately starved, so that the government could exterminate them. The government, on the other hand, went into Treaty Six with the naive belief that the Indians could become self-supporting in only two years. Beyond that, officials seemed to be in mortal terror of letting rations become a habit.

If they had listened to Big Bear, the government would have begun its agricultural program earlier; it would have staffed it with competent men, and it would have transformed many Indians into farmers before their spirit was broken and their hostility aroused. The transition still would have been difficult, and many would have fallen by the wayside, but Big Bear's way would have been better than Macdonald's or Dewdney's — and cheaper, too, for there would have been no expensive rebellion to fight. There would not have been nine graves in the cemetery at Frog Lake or eight Indians buried under a concrete slab at Battleford. Big Bear had tried to sow the seeds of communication and cooperation between Indians and whites, but the seeds had fallen on barren ground.

Notes

CHAPTER 1
BEGINNINGS

1. The name of Big Bear's father was provided by Four Souls in an interview by author. Further documentation came from the Hudson's Bay Company Archives and Paul Kane (see Harper, *Paul Kane's Frontier,* 81, 144).
2. Edmonton House Journals, 7 February 1827, B.60/a/24, HBC Archives. All references from the HBC Archives are published by permission of the Hudson's Bay Company.
3. Ibid., 3 March 1827, B.60/a/24, HBC Archives.
4. Carlton House Journals, 14 July 1827, B.27/a/16, HBC Archives.
5. Ibid., 12 May 1833, B.27/a/19, HBC Archives.
6. John Rowand to George Simpson, 25 December 1837, Edmonton House Correspondence, B.60/b/1, HBC Archives.
7. Ibid.
8. *Toronto Mail,* 25 July 1885.
9. Harper, *Paul Kane's Frontier,* 81.
10. John Sokwapance, interview by author, 17 August 1982.
11. *Toronto Mail,* 25 July 1885.
12. The terms half-breed, Métis, bois brûlés, etc., all have been used to describe people of mixed Indian–white ancestry in western Canada. In this book, the nineteenth-century term half-breed is used (in addition to Métis), since Maria Campbell's epic work *Halfbreed* (Toronto: McClelland and Stewart, 1973) has again legitimized its use.
13. Mandelbaum, *Plains Cree,* 244.
14. Alphonse Little Poplar to author, 26 February 1983, regarding his meeting with Mrs. Annie White Calf.
15. Ibid.
16. Rev. Stanley Cuthand, interview by author, 16 August 1982.
17. Dusenberry, *Montana Cree,* 80.
18. Adapted from Fine Day, *My Cree People,* 61.
19. Ibid.
20. Ibid., 60.

21. Alphonse Little Poplar to author, 26 February 1983. He was given the story by Eli Pooyak, who heard it from his grandfather, Gopher Shooter, and his uncle, *Mimiquas.*

22. Harper, *Paul Kane's Frontier,* 148.

23. Four Souls, interview by author, 10 August 1974.

24. Charles A. Messiter, in *Sport and Adventure Among the North-American Indians,* claimed he met Big Bear in 1860, as chief of a large camp of Crees near Moose Woods on the South Saskatchewan. He then related (p. 25) the torture and killing of a Sioux in the camp. At that time, however, Big Bear was only thirty-five and not yet a chief, and Moose Woods was far east of his hunting grounds and wintering area. Because of the fame or notoriety gained by Big Bear in 1885, Messiter may have inadvertently used his name for that of another Indian.

25. Edmonton House Journals, 28 March 1861. B.60/a/31, HBC Archives.

26. Edmonton *Bulletin,* 2 May 1885.

27. John Sokwapance, interview by author, 17 August 1982.

28. Ibid.

29. Identified by some informants as a Gros Ventre Indian.

30. Bloomfield, *Plains Cree Texts,* 37.

31. Ibid.

32. Ibid., 39.

33. Ibid.

34. Ibid.

CHAPTER 2
THE CYCLE OF LIFE

1. *Toronto Mail,* 25 July 1885.

2. McDougall, *George Millward McDougall,* 141–42. Significantly, this prediction was recorded and published by George McDougall in 1869, just three years after the incident and before the calamities began.

3. *The Nor'Wester,* 30 June 1863.

CHAPTER 3
PESTILENCE, WAR AND STARVATION

1. McDougall, *George Millward McDougall,* 151.

2. Cowie, *Company of Adventurers,* 401.

3. McDougall, *Red River Rebellion,* 116.

4. Dion, *My Tribe the Crees,* 67.

5. Cowie, *Company of Adventurers,* 405.

6. This figure (Johnston, *The Battle at Belly River,* 8) was provided by the Blackfoot and may be exaggerated. *The Manitoban,* 4 March 1871, estimated seventy killed.

7. Cowie, *Company of Adventurers,* 405.

8. Ibid., 171–72.

9. Letter from George McDougall, 9 January 1870, in *Wesleyan Missionary Notices* 7 (May 1870): 103.
10. Ibid., 18 June 1870, in *Wesleyan Missionary Notices* 8 (August 1870): 126.
11. W. J. Christie to Government House, Fort Garry, 24 April 1871, Archibald Papers, MG12/A1, PAM.
12. Only the name of Big Bear's first wife was remembered by even the oldest informants.
13. McDougall, *George Millward McDougall,* 204–5.
14. Robert Hamilton to W. Urquhart, 10 December 1877, Morris Papers, MG12/B1/575, PAM.
15. Letter from George McDougall, 25 April 1873, in *Wesleyan Missionary Notices* 10 (August 1873): 311.
16. Dion, *My Tribe the Crees,* 73–74.
17. Ibid., 70.
18. Thunder Child, interview by Rev. Edward Ahenakew, Writer's Book, 179, Ahenakew Papers, SAB.
19. Ibid., 185.
20. William McKay to Richard Hardisty, 6 April 1873, Hardisty Papers, A.H264c/f.68, GA.
21. Kerr, *John Kerr,* 240.
22. Ibid., 154–55.
23. Ibid., 155.
24. Ibid., 160.

CHAPTER 4
PRELUDE TO TREATY

1. Montreal *Gazette,* 18 April 1885.
2. Letter from W. M. Simpson, 27 September 1872, Indian Department Records, RG10/v.3576/f.378, PAC.
3. Memorandum by Charles Napier Bell, 23 March 1874, Morris Papers, MG12/B1/677, PAM.
4. Robert Bell to A. Morris, 19 October 1873, Indian Department Records, RG10/v.3604/f.2593, PAC.
5. Ibid.
6. A. Morris to the minister of the interior, 25 April 1874, North-West Mounted Police Records, RG18/v.1/f.63–74, PAC.
7. Memorandum by Charles Napier Bell, 23 March 1874, Morris Papers, MG12/B1/677, PAM.
8. Hughes, *Father Lacombe,* 189.
9. John Christian Schultz in the Montreal *Gazette,* 18 April 1885.
10. William McKay to Richard Hardisty, 28 August 1874, Hardisty Papers, A/H264c/f.96, GA.
11. Ibid.
12. A. Morris to chiefs of the Cree, 13 July 1875, Morris Papers, MG12/B1/267, PAM.
13. Ronaghan, "Three Scouts," 13–14.

14. George McDougall to A. Morris, 23 October 1875, Morris Papers, MG12/B1/1136, PAM.
15. *Toronto Mail*, 25 July 1885.
16. George McDougall to A. Morris, 23 October 1875, Morris Papers, MG12/B1/1136, PAM.
17. Ibid.
18. Ibid.
19. Montreal *Gazette*, 18 April 1885.
20. Hon. Sir Alex Campbell in the Montreal *Gazette*, 18 April 1885.
21. L. N. F. Crozier to the minister of the interior, 17 February 1876, Indian Department Records, RG10/v.36241/f/5152, PAC.
22. Morris, *Treaties of Canada*, 256.
23. Ibid.
24. Ibid.
25. William McKay to Richard Hardisty, 2 January 1876, Hardisty Papers, A/H264c/f.96, GA.
26. L. N. F. Crozier to the minister of the interior, 17 February 1876, Indian Department Records, RG10/v.36241/f.5152, PAC.
27. John Sinclair to Richard Hardisty, 7 January 1876, Hardisty Papers, A/H264c/f.96, GA.
28. James McKay to A. Morris, 28 March 1877, Indian Department Records, RG10/v.3636/f.6694-2, PAC.
29. Dempsey, *William Parker*, 23.
30. John McKay to Church Missionary Society, 25 August 1876, CMS Correspondence, microfilm reel A-102, GA, PAM and other archives.
31. Erasmus, *Buffalo Days*, 244.
32. Morris, *Treaties of Canada*, 223.
33. *Manitoba Free Press*, 3 October 1876.
34. Morris, *Treaties of Canada*, 354.
35. James McKay to A. Morris, 28 March 1877, Indian Department Records, RG10/v.3636/f.6694-2, PAC.
36. Morris, *Treaties of Canada*, 224.
37. Ibid.
38. Ibid., 228.
39. Ibid., 183.
40. Erasmus, *Buffalo Days*, 258.
41. Ibid., 259.
42. Morris, *Treaties of Canada*, 233.
43. McDougall, *Opening the Great West*, 59.
44. Morris, *Treaties of Canada*, 236–37.
45. James McKay to A. Morris, 28 March 1877, Indian Department Records, RG10/v.3636/f.6694-2, PAC.
46. English translation of "Notes et Souvenirs de Mgr. Grandin," M-253, Oblate Papers, B-II-102c, PAA.
47. Morris, *Treaties of Canada*, 238.
48. Ibid., 239.
49. Ibid., 239–40.

50. Ibid., 240.
51. Erasmus, *Buffalo Days*, 241.
52. *Saskatchewan Herald*, 22 June 1885.
53. Dempsey, *Crowfoot*, 102.
54. Stanley, *Birth of Western Canada*, 290.
55. Joe Kennedy, interview by author, 17 August 1982.
56. Morris, *Treaties of Canada*, 233.
57. Ibid., 240.
58. Ibid.
59. Ibid.
60. Ibid., 241.
61. Ibid.
62. Ibid.
63. Ibid.
64. Ibid., 242.
65. Montreal *Gazette*, 18 April 1885.

CHAPTER 5
FOUR YEARS TO WAIT

1. Little Bear, "My Own Story."
2. Ibid.
3. A. Morris to the minister of the interior, 2 March 1877, Morris Papers, MG12/B2/236, PAM.
4. *Toronto Mail*, 2 January 1879.
5. This ordinance was introduced too late to be effective and was repealed a year later.
6. M. G. Dickieson to David Laird, 14 September 1877, Indian Department Records, RG10/v.3656/f.9092, PAC.
7. *Manitoba Free Press*, 6 October 1877.
8. M. G. Dickieson to David Laird, 14 September 1877, Indian Department Records, RG10/v.3656/f.9092, PAC.
9. David Laird to the minister of the interior, 9 May 1878. Indian Department Records, RG10/v.3655/f.9000, PAC.
10. Ibid.
11. Port Arthur *Weekly Sentinel*, 8 May 1885. Report by Walpole Roland.
12. Ibid.
13. Rev. J. A. McKay to Church Missionary Society, 15 April 1878, CMS Correspondence, microfilm reel A-103, GA, PAM and other archives.
14. *Benton Weekly Record*, 12 April 1878.
15. John A. Macdonald to M. G. Dickieson, 24 February 1879, Indian Department Records, RG10/v.3670/f.10771, PAC.
16. Annual Report of Supt. James Walsh, 19 December 1879, in *North-West Mounted Police Force Annual Report for 1879*, 23.
17. *Winnipeg Daily Times*, 26 June 1885.
18. David Laird to the minister of the interior, 12 November 1878, Indian Department Records, RG10/v.3670/f.10771, PAC.

19. *Winnipeg Daily Times,* 26 June 1885.
20. McGregor, *Edmonton Trader,* 95–96.
21. Cameron, *Blood Red the Sun,* 36. Cameron indicates this incident happened in the United States, but it would explain Big Bear's decision here rather than any event that occurred in Montana.
22. *Saskatchewan Herald,* 5 August 1882.
23. David Laird to the minister of the interior, 12 November 1878, Indian Department Records, RG10/v.3670/f.10771, PAC.
24. Report by Hon. Edgar Dewdney, 2 January 1880, in *Annual Report of the Department of Indian Affairs for the Year 1879,* 96.
25. David Laird to the minister of the interior, 12 November 1878, Indian Department Records, RG10/v.3670/f.10771, PAC.
26. Dewdney, Diary, 19 August 1879. Dewdney Papers, GA. Paraphrased.
27. Letter from P. Breland, 28 February 1879, Indian Department Records, RG10/v.3670/f.10771, PAC.
28. Report by A. P. Patrick, 12 January 1880, in *Annual Report of the Surveyor-General,* 45.
29. *Lethbridge Herald,* 7 January 1909.
30. Report by A. P. Patrick, 12 January 1880, in *Annual Report of the Surveyor-General,* 45.
31. *Toronto Mail,* 2 January 1879.
32. *Saskatchewan Herald,* 18 November 1878.
33. Steele, *Forty Years in Canada,* 136.
34. *Saskatchewan Herald,* 9 February 1879.
35. Ibid., 24 March 1879.
36. Report by Hon. Edgar Dewdney, 2 January 1880, in *Annual Report of the Department of Indian Affairs for the Year 1879,* 77.
37. Ibid.
38. Four Souls, interview by author, 10 August 1974.
39. E. Dewdney to L. Vankoughnet, 4 July 1879, Indian Department Records, RG10/v.3636/f.6694-2, PAC.
40. *Saskatchewan Herald,* 8 September 1879.
41. Little Bear, "My Own Story."
42. Dempsey, *Crowfoot,* 120.
43. *Toronto Mail,* 27 February 1886.
44. Four Souls, interview by author, 10 August 1974.
45. *Benton Weekly Record,* 7 May 1880.
46. Report by Hon. Edgar Dewdney, 31 December 1880, in *Annual Report of the Department of Indian Affairs for the Year 1880,* 92.
47. Toronto *Globe,* 6 October 1879.
48. Ibid.
49. *Saskatchewan Herald,* 2 August 1880.
50. *Benton Weekly Record,* 12 March 1880.
51. Toronto *Globe,* 6 July 1885.
52. *Saskatchewan Herald,* 5 August 1882. Paraphrased.
53. Schultz, *My Life as an Indian,* 188.
54. Four Souls, interview by author, 10 August 1974.

55. Thunder Child, interview by Rev. Edward Ahenakew, Writer's Book, 156, Ahenakew Papers, SAB.
56. Note in Riel Papers, undated, MG3.D1/566, PAM.
57. Letter from J. M. Rae, 28 March 1881, Indian Department Records, RG10/v.3741/f.28856, PAC.
58. *Saskatchewan Herald,* 23 May 1881.
59. E. T. Galt to L. Vankoughnet, 13 July 1881, Indian Department Records, RG10/v.3744/f.29506-1, PAC.
60. W. H. Metzler, Diary, 9 August 1881, A/M546, GA.
61. *Benton River Press,* 4 May 1881.
62. Ibid., 17 August 1881.
63. Thunder Child, interview by Rev. Edward Ahenakew, Writer's Book, 156, Ahenakew Papers, SAB. Thunder Child, who was present when this happened, told the entire story, complete with dialogue.
64. *Helena Weekly Independent,* 21 October 1881.
65. Report by Hon. Edgar Dewdney, 1 January 1882, in *Annual Report of the Department of Indian Affairs for 1881,* 39.
66. Four Souls, interview by author, 10 August 1974 and 6 October 1981.
67. L. S. S. West to the Marquess of Lorne, 8 March 1882, Indian Department Records, RG10/v.3744/f.29506, PAC.
68. *Benton Weekly Record,* 30 March 1882.
69. Ibid.
70. Cameron, *Blood Red the Sun,* 34.
71. *Benton Weekly Record,* 4 May 1882.

CHAPTER 6
NO MORE CHOICES

1. *Winnipeg Daily Sun,* 22 February 1883.
2. *Toronto Mail,* 24 April 1885.
3. Report by Hon. Edgar Dewdney, in *Annual Report of the Department of Indian Affairs for 1881,* 54.
4. *Saskatchewan Herald,* 5 August 1882.
5. Dr. A. Jukes to Fred White, 7 October 1882, Indian Department Records, RG10/v.3744/f.29506-2, PAC.
6. E. Dewdney to J. A. Macdonald, 31 October 1882, Indian Department Records, RG10/v.3744/f.29506-2, PAC.
7. A. McDonald to E. Dewdney, 9 December 1882, Indian Department Records, RG10/v.3744/f.29506-2, PAC.
8. Frank Norman to E. Dewdney, 18 January 1883, Indian Department Records, RG10/v.3744/f.29506-3, PAC.
9. H. Reed to E. Dewdney, 28 December 1883, Indian Department Records, RG10/v.3668/f.10644, PAC.
10. *Benton Weekly Record,* 26 May 1883.
11. H. H. Adams to Lt. R. G. Bates, 30 May 1883, Indian Department Records, RG10/v.3740/f.28748-1, PAC
12. Little Bear, "My Own Story."

13. *Saskatchewan Herald,* 9 June 1883.
14. Port Arthur *Weekly Sentinel,* 8 May 1885. From the diary of Walpole Roland.
15. Ibid.
16. Ibid.
17. Ibid.
18. Ibid.
19. Ibid.
20. Ibid.
21. *Stratford Beacon,* 26 June 1885.
22. H. Reed to E. Dewdney, 13 June 1881, Indian Department Records, RG10/v.3755/f.30973, PAC.
23. *Calgary Weekly Herald,* 11 April 1907. Article by G. G. Grogan.
24. Toronto *Globe,* 13 April 1885.
25. *Stratford Beacon,* 26 June 1885.
26. Ibid.
27. Ibid.
28. Report by T. P. Wadsworth, 9 October 1883, in *Annual Report of the Department of Indian Affairs for 1883,* 123.

CHAPTER 7
THE STRUGGLE CONTINUES

1. Samuel Macdonald to E. Dewdney, 5 September 1883, Indian Department Records, RG10/v.3744/f.29506-3, PAC.
2. Hayter Reed to E. Dewdney, 28 December 1883, Indian Department Records, RG10/v.3668/f.10644, PAC.
3. Report by Com. A. G. Irvine, in *Annual Report of the North-West Mounted Police Force for the Year 1884,* 8.
4. J. Chambers to Hon. Alexander Campbell, 7 April 1885, Indian Department Records, RG10/v.3709/f.19550-1, PAC.
5. Little Bear, "My Own Story."
6. *Saskatchewan Herald,* 23 February 1884.
7. Ibid., 8 March 1884.
8. Jefferson, *Fifty Years,* 107.
9. J. M. Rae to E. Dewdney, 28 June 1884, Indian Department Records, RG10/v.3576/f.309-B, PAC.
10. L. Vankoughnet to E. Dewdney, 12 May 1884 and 24 July 1884, Indian Department Records, RG10/v.3576/f.309-A, PAC.
11. Cochin, *Louis Cochin,* 26.
12. Jefferson, *Fifty Years,* 109.
13. Jefferson in Innes, *Cree Rebellion,* 25–26.
14. Fine Day in Innes, *Cree Rebellion,* 14–15.
15. Jefferson in Innes, *Cree Rebellion,* 28.
16. Fine Day in Innes, *Cree Rebellion,* 16.
17. McKay in Innes, *Cree Rebellion,* 41.
18. Ibid.

19. L. N. F. Crozier to A. G. Irvine, 25 June 1884, North-West Mounted Police Records, RG18/v.1015/f.1462, PAC.
20. McKay in Innes, *Cree Rebellion,* 42–43.
21. Fine Day in Innes, *Cree Rebellion,* 16–17.
22. *Saskatchewan Herald,* 12 July 1884. Paraphrased.
23. L. Vankoughnet to E. Dewdney, 7 July 1884, Indian Department Records, RG10/v.3580/f.730, PAC.
24. Jefferson in Innes, *Cree Rebellion,* 24.
25. *Saskatchewan Herald,* 12 July 1884.

CHAPTER 8
THUNDER BEFORE THE STORM

1. J. M. Rae to E. Dewdney, 29 July 1884, Indian Department Records, RG10/v.3576/f.309-A, PAC.
2. *Saskatchewan Herald,* 8 August 1884.
3. L. N. F. Crozier to A. G. Irvine, 27 July 1884, North-West Mounted Police Records, RG18/v.1015/f.1647, PAC.
4. J. M. Rae to E. Dewdney, 29 July 1884, Indian Department Records, RG10/v.3576/f.309-A, PAC.
5. J. A. Macrae to E. Dewdney, 25 August 1884, Indian Department Records, RG10/v.3697/f.15423, PAC. Paraphrased.
6. Cited in Stanley, *Birth of Western Canada,* 290.
7. *Saskatchewan Herald,* 9 August 1884.
8. J. A. Macrae to E. Dewdney, 25 August 1884, Indian Department Records, RG10/v.3576/f.15423, PAC.
9. Ibid.
10. Stanley, *Birth of Western Canada,* 302.
11. *Prince Albert Times,* 22 August 1884.
12. Stanley, *Birth of Western Canada,* 303.
13. Montreal *Gazette,* 25 September 1886. This statement by Charles Quinney, the Anglican minister, must be approached with caution. He appeared to have little patience with the political aspirations of the Crees, which he saw only as impediments to the goals of Christianizing and educating them and transforming them into productive farmers.
14. *Toronto Mail,* 29 January 1886. Statement by Charles Quinney.
15. Ibid.
16. Stanley, *Birth of Western Canada,* 303.
17. *Saskatchewan Herald,* 6 September 1884.
18. H. Reed to T. Quinn, 23 August 1884, Indian Department Records, RG10/v.3580/f.730, PAC.
19. S. Ballendine to H. Reed, 10 October 1884, Indian Department Records, RG10/v.3582/f.949, PAC.
20. Little Bear, "My Own Story."
21. H. Reed to J. A. Macdonald, 23 January 1885, Indian Department Records, RG10/v.3697/f.15423, PAC.

22. J. A. Macdonald to E. Dewdney, 30 December 1884, Indian Department Records, RG10/v.3697/f.15423, PAC.
23. J. C. McIllree to A. G. Irvine, 16 September 1884, North-West Mounted Police Records, RG18/v.1018/f.1894-A, PAC. See also Cameron, *Blood Red the Sun*, 1–3, for a variation of the story.
24. Ibid.
25. *Toronto Mail*, 2 July 1885.
26. F. Dickens to L. N. F. Crozier, 9 November 1884, North-West Mounted Police Records, RG18/v.1818/f.2162, PAC.
27. Ibid.
28. *Toronto Mail*, 22 January 1886.
29. F. Dickens to L. N. F. Crozier, 15 February 1885, Attorney-General "G" Papers, file 168L, SA.
30. Little Bear should not be confused with *Imasees*, whose other name was Little Bear. Duplication of names was common among the Plains Indians.
31. Dion, *My Tribe the Crees*, 93.
32. Charette, *Vanishing Spaces*, 158.
33. Toronto *Globe*, 6 June 1885.
34. T. Quinn to E. Dewdney, 25 February 1885, Indian Department Records, RG10/v.3580/f.730, PAC.
35. T. Quinn to E. Dewdney, 13 March 1885, Indian Department Records, RG10/v.3715/f.21264, PAC.
36. Dion, *My Tribe the Crees*, 88.
37. Ibid.

CHAPTER 9
REBELLION!

1. Testimony of Henry Halpin, "Queen vs. Big Bear," *Sessional Papers*, 1886, 212.
2. F. Dickens to A. G. Irvine, 8 June 1885, North-West Mounted Police Records, RG18/v.1022/f.3094.
3. *Toronto Mail*, 6 January 1886. Immediately after the rebellion, W. B. Cameron provided interviews and written statements to the press. Wherever possible, these are used in preference to his books, *The War Trail of Big Bear* and *Blood Red the Sun*. By the time he wrote these, he had become a professional writer of adventure stories; as a result, they are less reliable than his earlier accounts.
4. Jimmy Chief, interview by author, 20 August 1982.
5. Testimony of John Pritchard, "Queen vs. Big Bear," *Sessional Papers*, 1886, 184.
6. Jimmy Chief, interview by author, 20 August 1982.
7. *Toronto Mail*, 10 June 1885.
8. Ibid.
9. Charette, *Vanishing Spaces*, 119.
10. Toronto *Globe*, 23 June 1885. This version by Mary Gowanlock and Theresa Delaney is used, rather than their book *Two Months in the Camp of Big Bear*, which obviously was done in collaboration with a journalist.

11. *Toronto Mail,* 10 June 1885.
12. Charette, *Vanishing Spaces,* 122.
13. *Toronto Mail,* 10 June 1885.
14. Charette, *Vanishing Spaces,* 123.
15. Toronto *Globe,* 23 June 1885.
16. Testimony of Catharine Simpson, "Queen vs. Big Bear," *Sessional Papers,* 1886, 203.
17. Ibid., 204.
18. *Toronto Mail,* 10 June 1885.
19. Little Bear, "My Own Story."
20. Jimmy Chief, interview by author, 20 August 1982.
21. Toronto *Globe,* 23 June 1885.
22. Ibid.
23. Testimony of John Pritchard, "Queen vs. Big Bear," *Sessional Papers,* 1886, 177.
24. Toronto *Globe,* 23 June 1885.
25. Testimony of *Sah-way-oo* in Rebellion trials, *Saskatchewan Herald,* 5 October 1885.
26. Stanley, "Frog Lake Massacre," 25.
27. Because of the speed with which the uprising occurred and the shock of the killings, there are a number of inconsistencies in the testimonies of various witnesses and in Indian traditions. This version attempts to follow the most authoritative accounts and the most logical unfolding of events. There also is considerable confusion as to who actually killed the nine people, so the account presented here is based primarily upon court testimony, supplemented with oral accounts. The earliest list of suspects appeared (in the *Winnipeg Daily Times,* 12 May 1885) before the Cree released their white prisoners, and is attributed to a Frog Lake Indian. He said Wandering Spirit killed Quinn, Little Bear killed three people, Bare Neck killed one priest, and chief Man Who Wins's youngest son killed the other priest. When Cameron was freed from the Indian camp, he claimed (*Toronto Mail,* 10 June 1885) Wandering Spirit shot Quinn and Marchand, Bad Arrow (mistranslated as The Worm) shot Gouin and Gowanlock, Little Bear killed Williscraft and Gilchrist, Man Who Speaks Our Language shot Dill, and Delaney and Fafard were wounded by Bare Neck and killed by Man Who Wins. However, in his book, he switched to those identified in the court testimony. Louis Goulet (in Charette, *Vanishing Spaces,* 124) said that Quinn was shot by Wandering Spirit and finished off by Carcajou. He identified only a couple more of the killers and these agreed with the court records. Mrs. Delaney and Mrs. Gowanlock did not identify any of the killers. An undated list of Indians "arrested Fort Pitt & now here waiting trial before Judge Rouleau" has Wandering Spirit killing Quinn and Gouin, and Little Bear killing Dill and Gilchrist. On the same page is a list of persons "arrested per Mr. Rae," according to which Wandering Spirit killed one priest, *Ohsawanasioux* killed the other priest, and Thunder, Big Bear's adopted son, killed a "Brother" (Mann Papers, A/M281, GA). In Indian oral accounts, Isabella Little Bear identified only Wandering Spirit; neither Mary Dion (Dion, *My Tribe the Crees*) nor George Stanley (*An Account of the Frog Lake Massacre*)

mentioned individuals. Jimmy Chief admitted that his grandfather had shot at Dill but stated that the actual killing was done by "this young fellow who shot from behind my grandfather and hit the man at the back of his neck." Little Bear made a similar claim in court.

28. *Toronto Mail,* 4 June 1885.
29. Testimony of James Simpson, "Queen vs. Big Bear," *Sessional Papers,* 1886, 192, 188–89.
30. Ahenakew, *Voices of the Plains Cree,* 108.

CHAPTER 10
ATTACK ON FORT PITT

1. Stanley, "Frog Lake Massacre," 27.
2. Charette, *Vanishing Spaces,* 129.
3. *Toronto Mail,* 25 July 1885.
4. Ibid.
5. *Toronto Mail* 9 July 1885.
6. *Pakan* to E. Dewdney, 16 April 1885, Indian Department Records, RG10/ v.3585/f.1130-2, PAC.
7. Testimony of John Pritchard, "Queen vs. Big Bear," *Sessional Papers,* 1886, 179.
8. Testimony of William Cameron, "Queen vs. Big Bear," *Sessional Papers,* 1886, 218.
9. McLean MS, "Reminiscences of the Tragic Event," 5, HBC Archives.
10. Testimony of John Pritchard, "Queen vs. Big Bear," *Sessional Papers,* 1886, 187.
11. Ibid., 11.
12. Ibid.
13. *Toronto Evening News,* 15 May 1885.
14. Cited in Hougham Papers, M539, GA.
15. W. McLean to his wife, 15 April 1885, quoted in full in *Saskatchewan Herald,* 23 April 1885.
16. *Saskatchewan Herald,* 4 May 1885.

CHAPTER 11
BATTLE OF FRENCHMAN'S BUTTE

1. If everyone is to be believed, the nine victims at Frog Lake must have been buried more often than a dog's favourite bone. On the day of the killings, Louis Goulet, André Nault, William Gladu and an Indian went to the village and placed the bodies of Fafard, Marchand, Gowanlock and Delaney in the basement of the church, at the request of the two widows. "We wanted to take Charles Gouin's body, lying on Johnny Pritchard's stoop," said Goulet, "and Tom Quinn who was stretched out beside a puddle just a few feet in front of Pritchard's house, but some young Indians warned us we'd better leave them be if we didn't want somebody else to have to come and fetch

our own corpses. We wanted to gather up the remains of George Dill, Johnny Williscraft and Gilchrist but the Indians were against it and we had to leave them there. I heard later from André Nault that he picked them up the next day with Dolphus Nolin." (Charette, *Vanishing Spaces,* 127–28.)

Then on 20 April some of William McLean's men went to the village and "did the best they could to inter the bodies of the massacred people, which were lying exposed to the weather where they fell." (McLean MS, "Reminiscences of the Tragic Events," 13.) He thought the bodies in the church had been placed there by Indians but said they had become exposed when the church was burned.

On 24 May an advance party of Steele's Scouts arrived at the scene, and the four charred bodies were seen in the ruins of the church and "the bodies of two men, whom we took to be those of Williscraft and Gilchrist, were found on the ground near the chapel." (Toronto *Globe,* 26 June 1885.) Graves were dug for the victims, and they were interred while Anglican missionary John McKay read the service.

The next day, the Winnipeg Light Infantry arrived and "for reasons best known to themselves, dug up the bodies in the cemetery and reburied them." (*Toronto Mail,* 8 August 1885.)

Then on 4 June, according to correspondent George Ham, a detachment of militia en route to Cold Lake stopped at the village where they found "the ruins of burned buildings, the graves of the butchered dead, and the mutilated bodies of poor Quinn, Gilchrist, Williscraft and Diel [Delaney] are before us. . . . The corpses were hurriedly interred, and Frog Lake, with its unhappy reminiscences, is left behind." (*Winnipeg Daily Times,* 29 June 1885.)

2. *Toronto Mail,* 27 June 1885.
3. McLean MS, "Reminiscences of the Tragic Events," 19–20, HBC Archives.
4. Ibid., 20. 5. Ibid., 26–27.
6. McLean, "The Siege of Fort Pitt," in *The Beaver* (June 1947): 15.
7. Jimmy Chief, interview by author, 20 August 1982. Although newspapers gave prominence to the savagery of the Indians, describing in detail the mutilation of Cowan's remains and the abandonment of the bodies at Frog Lake, no mention was made of *Maymenook* after Steele's Scouts finished with him. As trader Angus McKay stated, "I rode down with a friend to view his remains and found his body on the top of the hill where he evidently had been dragged by the scout. His body was stripped of all clothing with the rope (cut short to about one yard in length) still around his neck, which had cut into his jaw. . . . The Scout who had captured his mount (a swift-footed black stallion belonging to the H. B. Co.) had galloped around the prairie with the rope attached to his saddle pommel, trailing the body in the grass in circles, the trails of which were still visible. He had thus been exposed for days before being buried; and his body, from the intense heat, was huge in size when I saw him. I requested the authorities to have him buried." ("Reminiscences of Angus McKay," Hougham Papers, 16, GA.)
8. *Winnipeg Daily Times,* 20 June 1885.
9. *Toronto Mail,* 25 June 1885.

10. Jimmy Chief, interview by author, 20 August 1982.
11. *Montreal Daily Star,* 14 July 1885. Paraphrased from G. G. Mann interview.
12. McLean MS, "Reminiscences of the Tragic Events," 46, HBC Archives.
13. According to historian Hans J. Peterson, the separation was not a harmoni-
ous one. "John Burke related to the author that people in the Onion Lake
Fort Pitt area mention that Imasees commandeered (for his escape) the best
horses and many needed supplies and left his tribal kinsmen as a traitor
might leave his comrades." He added that the *Imasees* group "left behind
disgust and ill will among those who wanted to join the exodus but were
deserted by Imasees. Such ill will is said to manifest itself to this day at the
odd pow-wow when visiting Montana Cree get into fist-fights with Cree
from Cut Knife and Battleford 'by a word said, by some nasty comment
about somebody's forefather.' " (Peterson, "Imasees and His Band," 21–37.)
14. *Saskatchewan Herald,* 13 July 1885.

CHAPTER 12
ON TRIAL

1. Toronto *Globe,* 22 July 1885.
2. Little Poplar to author, 26 February 1983.
3. Jimmy Chief, interview by author, 20 August 1982.
4. *The Manitoban,* 6 August 1885.
5. "Queen vs. Big Bear," *Sessional Papers,* 1886, 173.
6. F. W. Spicer in Hawkes, *Story of Saskatchewan,* I:143.
7. "Queen vs. Big Bear," *Sessional Papers,* 1886, 182.
8. Ibid., 206.
9. Ibid., 217.
10. Ibid., 220.
11. Ibid., 197.
12. Ibid., 195.
13. Ibid., 201.
14. Ibid., 196.
15. Ibid., 217–18.
16. John R. Bunn to Celia A. Reynolds, 15 May 1935. Aurora Historical Society
Archives, Ontario.
17. Charette, *Vanishing Spaces,* 152, 153.
18. *Toronto Mail,* 5 October 1885.
19. "Queen vs. Big Bear," *Sessional Papers,* 1886, 221.
20. Ibid., 223.
21. Ibid., 224.
22. Ibid., 225.
23. Ibid., 226.
24. Ibid., 227.
25. Ibid., 228.
26. Ibid., 228–29.
27. Ibid., 229.
28. Ibid., 233.

29. Ibid.
30. Quoted in *Toronto Mail*, 5 October 1885.

CHAPTER 13
THE FINAL YEARS

1. Toronto *Globe*, 23 November 1885. Final verse from "The Petition of the Condemned Indians."
2. Dion, *My Tribe the Crees*, 113.
3. *Prince Albert Times*, 9 October 1885.
4. Thunder Child, interview by Rev. Edward Ahenakew, Writer's Book, 152, Ahenakew Papers, SAB.
5. *Saskatchewan Herald*, 17 May 1886.
6. Archbishop A. A. Taché claimed he tried to convert Big Bear in jail in the spring of 1886 and that the chief had finally been baptized by Father Clouthier in August. However, there is no evidence that Big Bear ever abandoned his own religion.
7. *Saskatchewan Herald*, 30 August 1866.
8. Dr. W. R. D. Sutherland to Warden Sam Bedson, 22 January 1887, Surgeon's Letter-Book, C-I-vii, 41, Admittance and Medical Records, Stony Mountain Penitentiary archives.
9. Petition from *Mistowasis* (Big Child), *Attakukoop* (Star Blanket), *Twatt* and John Smith to the Indian commissioner, 15 January 1887, Indian Department Records, RG10/v.3774/f.36846, PAC.
10. Thunder Child, interview by Rev. Edward Ahenakew, Writer's Book, 152, Ahenakew Papers, SAB. Paraphrased.
11. Cited in Gray, "History of the Cree Indians," 7.

EPILOGUE

1. Alphonse Little Poplar to author, 4 February 1983.

Bibliography

UNPUBLISHED SOURCES

Ahenakew, Rev. Edward. Papers and Writer's Book. Saskatchewan Archives Board, Regina.

Archibald, A. G. Lieutenant-Governor's Papers, 1870–73. MG12/A1, Provincial Archives of Manitoba, Winnipeg.

Attorney-General "G" Papers. Saskatchewan archives, Saskatoon.

Carlton House Journals and Correspondence, 1825–27. Hudson's Bay Company Archives, Provincial Archives of Manitoba, Winnipeg.

Church Missionary Society, Anglican Church. Correspondence. Microfilm copy, Glenbow archives, Calgary; Provincial Archives of Manitoba, Winnipeg, and other archives.

Cuthand, Rev. Stanley. Interview by author. Winnipeg, Manitoba, 1982.

Dewdney, Edgar. Papers, 1879–85. Glenbow archives, Calgary.

Dion, Joseph F. Papers, 1923–60. M331, Glenbow archives, Calgary.

Edmonton House Journals, 1827–65. Hudson's Bay Company Archives, Provincial Archives of Manitoba, Winnipeg.

Four Souls. Interviews by author. Rocky Boy Reservation, Montana, 1974–82.

Gray, Raymond. "History of the Cree Indians." WPA Writers' Project in Montana, 1941–42. Microfilm copy, Glenbow archives, Calgary.

Hardisty, Richard. Papers. A/H264c, Glenbow Museum archives, Calgary.

Hougham, R. H. Papers relating to Fort Pitt. M539, Glenbow archives, Calgary.

Indian Department Records. RG10 series, 1872–1887. Public Archives of Canada, Ottawa.

Jimmy Chief. Interview by author. Onion Lake Reserve, Saskatchewan, 1982.

Kennedy, Joe. Interview by author. Little Pine Reserve, Saskatchewan, 1982.

Little Poplar, Alphonse. Correspondence with author, 1982–83.

McLean, William J. "Reminiscences of the Tragic Events at Frog Lake and in Fort Pitt District with Some of the Experiences of the Writer and his Family during the North West Rebellion of 1885." MS. 372(5707), Hudson's Bay Company Archives, Provincial Archives of Manitoba, Winnipeg.

Mann, George Gwynne. Papers. A/M281, Glenbow archives, Calgary.

Metzler, William H. Diary, 1880–81. A/M546, Glenbow archives, Calgary.

Morris, Alexander. Lieutenant-Governor's Papers, 1872–77. MG12/B1, Provincial Archives of Manitoba, Winnipeg.

North-West Mounted Police Records. RG18 series, 1874–86, Public Archives of Canada, Ottawa.

Oblate Papers, B-II-102c, "Notes et souvenirs de Mgr. Grandin." M-253, Provincial Archives of Alberta, Edmonton.

Riel, Louis. Papers. MG-3.D-1, Provincial Archives of Manitoba, Winnipeg.

Sokwapance, John. Interview by author, Joe Kennedy, interpreter. Little Pine Reserve, Saskatchewan, 1982.

Stony Mountain Penitentiary. Admittance and Medical Records, 1885–87. Stony Mountain Penitentiary archives, Manitoba.

PUBLISHED SOURCES

Ahenakew, Edward. *Voices of the Plains Cree.* Toronto: McClelland and Stewart, 1973.

Allen, R. S. "Big Bear." *Saskatchewan History* 25 (Winter 1972): 1–17.

Bloomfield, Leonard. *Plains Cree Texts.* Publication of the American Ethnological Society. New York: G. E. Stechert & Co., 1934.

Cameron, William Bleasdell. *Blood Red the Sun.* Calgary: Kenways, 1950. Reprint, with introduction by Hugh A. Dempsey. Edmonton: Hurtig, 1977.

————. *The War Trail of Big Bear.* Toronto: Ryerson, 1926.

Canada. *Annual Report of the Department of Indian Affairs for the Year 1879,* Ottawa, 1880.

————. *Annual Report of the Surveyor-General for the Year 1879.* Ottawa, 1880.

————. *Annual Report of the Department of Indian Affairs for the Year 1880.* Ottawa, 1881.

————. *Annual Report of the Department of Indian Affairs for the Year 1881.* Ottawa, 1882.

————. *Annual Report of the Department of Indian Affairs for 1883.* Ottawa, 1884.

————. *North-West Mounted Police Force Annual Report for 1879.* Ottawa, 1880.

————. *Sessional Papers,* 1886, 48–91, 19:13. "Queen vs. Big Bear," 172–233.

Charette, Guillaume. *Vanishing Spaces: Memoirs of Louis Goulet.* Winnipeg: Editions Bois-Brulés, 1976.

Cochin, Louis. *The Reminiscences of Louis Cochin, OMI.* Battleford: Canadian North-West Historical Society, 1927.

Cowie, Isaac. *The Company of Adventurers.* Toronto: William Briggs, 1913.

Dempsey, Hugh A. *Crowfoot, Chief of the Blackfeet.* Norman: University of Oklahoma Press, 1972.

————. *William Parker, Mounted Policeman.* Edmonton: Hurtig, 1973.

Dion, Joseph F. *My Tribe the Crees.* Calgary: Glenbow Museum, 1979.

Dusenberry, Vern. *The Montana Cree: A Study in Religious Persistence.* Stockholm: Almquist and Wiksell, 1962.

Erasmus, Peter. *Buffalo Days and Nights.* Calgary: Glenbow Museum, 1976.

Fine Day. *My Cree People.* Invermere, B. C.: Good Medicine Books, 1973.

Fraser, William B. "Big Bear, Indian Patriot." *Alberta Historical Review* 14 (Spring 1960): 1–13.

Gowanlock, Mary, and Theresa Delaney. *Two Months in the Camp of Big Bear.* Parkdale: The Times, 1885.

Harper, J. Russell. *Paul Kane's Frontier.* Toronto: University of Toronto Press, 1971.

Hawkes, John. *The Story of Saskatchewan and Its People.* Chicago: S. J. Clark Co., 1924.

Howard, Joseph Kinsey. *Strange Empire: The Story of Louis Riel.* Toronto: Swan Publishing Co., 1965.

Hughes, Katherine. *Father Lacombe: The Black-Robe Voyageur.* Toronto: William Briggs, 1911.

Innes, Campbell, ed. *The Cree Rebellion of 1884.* Battleford: Saskatchewan Herald, 1926.

Jefferson, Robert, *Fifty Years on the Saskatchewan.* Battleford: Canadian North-West Historical Society, 1929.

Johnston, Alex, ed. *The Battle at Belly River.* Lethbridge: Historical Society of Alberta, 1966.

Kerr, Constance Sissons. *John Kerr.* Toronto: Oxford University Press, 1946.

Little Bear, Isabella. "My Own Story." *Bonnyville Tribune,* 18 and 25 April, 2 May 1958.

McDougall, John. *George Millward McDougall, the Pioneer, Patriot and Missionary.* Toronto: William Briggs, 1902.

———. *In the Days of the Red River Rebellion.* Toronto: William Briggs, 1903.

———. *Opening the Great West.* Calgary: Glenbow Museum, 1970.

McGregor, James G. *Edmonton Trader.* Toronto: McClelland and Stewart, 1963.

McKay, George. *Fighting Parson.* Kamloops, B. C.: privately published, 1968.

McLean, Elizabeth A. "The Siege of Fort Pitt." *The Beaver* (December 1946): 22–25, (June 1947): 14–17, (September 1947): 38–42.

Mandelbaum, David. *The Plains Cree.* Anthropological Papers of the American Museum of Natural History, vol. 37, pt.2, 1940.

Messiter, Charles A. *Sport and Adventure Among the North-American Indians.* London: R. H. Porter, 1890.

Moberley, Henry John. *When Fur Was King.* New York: E. P. Dutton, 1929.

Morris, Alexander. *The Treaties of Canada with the Indians of Manitoba, the North-West Territories, and Kee-Wa-Tin.* Toronto: Willing and Williamson, 1880.

Mountain Horse, Mike. *My People the Bloods.* Calgary: Glenbow Museum, 1979.

Paget, Amelia M. *People of the Plains.* Toronto: Ryerson Press, 1909.

Peterson, Hans. J. "Imasees and His Band: Canadian Refugees After the North-West Rebellion." *The Western Canadian Journal of Anthropology* 7 (1978): 21–37.

Ronaghan, Allen. "Three Scouts and the Cart Train." *Alberta History* 25 (Winter 1977): 12–14.

Schultz, James Willard. *My Life as an Indian.* New York: Fawcett Publications, 1956.

Stanley, George (*Mesunekwepan*). "An Account of the Frog Lake Massacre." *Alberta Historical Review* 4 (Winter 1956): 23–27.

Stanley, George F. G. *The Birth of Western Canada: A History of the Riel Rebellions.* Toronto: University of Toronto Press, 1960.

Steele, Samuel Benfield. *Forty Years in Canada: Reminiscences of the Great North-West with some Account of his Service in South Africa.* Winnipeg: Russell Lang & Co., 1915.

NEWSPAPER SOURCES

Edmonton *Bulletin*, 1885.

Benton River Press (Fort Benton), 1881–83.

Benton Weekly Record (Fort Benton), 1878–83.

Calgary Weekly Herald, 1907.

Helena Weekly Independent, 1881.

Lethbridge Herald, 1909.

Manitoba Free Press (Winnipeg), 1876–85.

Manitoban, The (Winnipeg), 1871–85.

Montreal Daily Star, 1885.

Montreal *Gazette*, 1885–86.

Nor'Wester, The (Red River), 1863.

Port Arthur *Weekly Sentinel*, 1885.

Prince Albert Times, 1884–85.

Saskatchewan Herald (Battleford), 1878–1887.

Stratford Beacon, 1885.

Toronto Evening News, 1885.

Toronto *Globe*, 1879–85.

Toronto Mail, 1879–86.

Wesleyan Missionary Notices, 1870–73.

Winnipeg Daily Sun, 1883.

Winnipeg Daily Times, 1884–85.

Index